Twain and Freud
on the Human Race

Twain and Freud on the Human Race

Parallels on Personality, Politics and Religion

ABRAHAM KUPERSMITH

McFarland & Company, Inc., Publishers
Jefferson, North Carolina, and London

LIBRARY OF CONGRESS CATALOGUING-IN-PUBLICATION DATA

Kupersmith, Abraham, 1940–
    Twain and Freud on the human race : parallels on personality, politics and religion / Abraham Kupersmith.
      p.   cm.
    Includes bibliographical references and index.

    ISBN 978-0-7864-3306-3
    softcover : 50# alkaline paper ∞

    1. Twain, Mark, 1835–1910—Knowledge—Psychology. 2. Freud, Sigmund, 1856–1939—Criticism and interpretation. 3. Twain, Mark, 1835–1910—Political and social views. 4. Psychological fiction, American—History and criticism. 5. Literature and society—United States—History—19th century. 6. Psychology in literature. 7. Self in literature. 8. Social problems in literature. I. Title.
PS1342.P74K87   2009
818'.409—dc22
                                                                                            2008044487

British Library cataloguing data are available

©2009 Abraham Kupersmith. All rights reserved

No part of this book may be reproduced or transmitted in any form or by any means, electronic or mechanical, including photocopying or recording, or by any information storage and retrieval system, without permission in writing from the publisher.

Cover photograph ©2008 Shutterstock

Manufactured in the United States of America

McFarland & Company, Inc., Publishers
   Box 611, Jefferson, North Carolina 28640
      www.mcfarlandpub.com

This book is for my wife, Edith,
whose help and love were necessary for its completion,
and for the memory of my daughter, Lydia

Acknowledgments

I wish to express my deep appreciation to a number of people whose help was invaluable to the completion of this book. First, I thank my wife, Edith Frank, for her love, inspiration, and editorial skills. Next, I will always be grateful to the late Carey Wilson McWilliams and The Mark Twain Society for their confidence in this project. I also wish to recognize the encouragement and editorial guidance of my good friend, Robert Ghiradella; the advice and support of my niece, Davy Rosenzweig; and the editorial suggestions of my colleague, Gabriella Oldham.

Table of Contents

Preface   1
Introduction   3

I   Two Models of Human Nature   9
"What Is Man?" and Freud's Structural Model of Personality

II   The Creation of Character   25
The Role of Circumstance in "The Turning Point of My Life"

III   Civilization and Group Psychology   32
Herd Behavior in "The United States of Lyncherdom" and The Adventures of Huckleberry Finn

IV   Character and Civilization   41
The Five Worlds of The Adventures of Huckleberry Finn

V   The Relationship Between Temperament and Training   58
Social Ideology in "The Man Who Corrupted Hadleyburg"

VI   Race and Temperament   73
Personality and the Ideology of Race in Pudd'nhead Wilson

VII   Religion and Civilization   88
The Democratic Demagogue in Christian Science

VIII   History and Character   100
Temperament and Training in Two Historical Periods: A Connecticut Yankee at King Arthur's Court

IX   Politics, Patriotism, and Leadership   117
The Democratic Leader in Personal Recollections of Joan of Arc

X   Leadership, Ideology, and the Church   126
Temperament and Religion in the Eseldorf Version of "The Mysterious Stranger"

Conclusion	137
Afterword	143
Appendix: "What Is Man?"	145
Notes	191
Bibliography	199
Index	203

Preface

Karl Dalmetsch's exciting study of the time Mark Twain spent in late nineteenth century Vienna, *Our Famous Guest*,[1] is a revelation, pointing the way to a little examined area of Twain studies. In his book, Professor Dalmetsch argues that, while in Vienna, Mark Twain was exposed to the same rich soil of psychological thought that fed the thinking of Sigmund Freud. Dalmetsch argues that Twain's stay there influenced the writing of "What Is Man?,"[2] Twain's important but often underestimated essay on human psychology.

In his book *The Death of Sigmund Freud*,[3] Mark Edmundson points out that there was a strong intellectual bond between Freud and Twain. Freud had read a number of works by Twain and used parts of them to illustrate his own ideas about the human psyche, "...for he [Freud] clearly loved Twain's work and even went to see him in Vienna once."[4] Edmundson goes on to explain why he believes it was Twain who influenced Freud more than the reverse: "Twain, in fact, spent a few years in Vienna when he was at the height of his fame and Freud was a relative unknown."[5]

My study begins from this point. Although Twain's reputation was established by the time of his visit to Vienna, I contend that he, indeed, had been influenced by European psychological thought. However, characteristic of Twain, he transformed the influences on his thinking into an original creation. Earlier than Freud, Twain developed a model of human nature and, like Freud, he evolved a theory of the relationships between individual psychology and social behavior. Twain used his model as a basis for his depiction of character and American society in his novels and political writing.

Scholars have noted the parallels between the psychological thought of Twain and that of Freud. R. W. Irwin published an article, "Mark Twain and Sigmund Freud on the Discontents of Civilization."[6] Irwin believes that these two intellectual giants shared much in their view of how human beings respond to the demands of civilization. In "Be It What It Will, I'll Go to It Laughing,"[7] Raymond Sousa argues that Twain's theory anticipated Freud's. In another work of scholarship, "Mark Twain, Isabel Lyon and the Talking Cure,"[8] Jennifer Zancora contends that Twain's use of free association as a route to the unconscious paralleled Freud's development of psychoanalysis. In her book *Dark Twins: Imposture and Identity in Mark Twain's America*, Professor Susan Gillman recognizes Twain's development of a three-part theory of personality: "In part, then, because hypnosis suggests the possibility of multiple levels of communication within the self, Twain's notebook entry postulates a triadic theory of personality."[9]

In addition to the parallels noted above, Freud made several references to Twain's work in his own writing. In a footnote in Chapter VII of *Civilization and Its Discontents*,[10] Freud uses a Twain story about stealing a watermelon to illustrate a point. The point is that an individual may become more conscious of his guilt in committing a crime if the outcome of that crime is not pleasant. In his story, Twain recalled that the first watermelon he had stolen was unripe; then he questioned whether it had actually been the first. The clear implication is that there had been others, but they had not been memorable to his conscience because they were ripe. It was only the frustration of the unripe melon which activated his feelings of guilt.

An even better example of Twain's awareness of the role of conscience acting much like Freud's concept of the superego appears in his story "The Facts Concerning the Recent Carnival of Crime in Connecticut."[11] In it, the narrator personifies his own conscience: "Well, I am your conscience ... I am not your friend, I am your enemy. I am not your equal, I am your master."[12] His conscience goes on to say, "I so enjoyed the anguish which certain pet sins of yours afflicted you with that I kept pelting at you...."[13] It is only because the narrator succeeds in murdering his personified conscience that he is then able to go on a guilt-free crime spree.

Beyond some of the parallels in their psychological thinking, Twain and Freud shared an interest in understanding many of the same aspects of human mental activity. Although their conclusions in certain areas differed, both thought and wrote about topics such as mental telepathy, humor, dreams, daydreams, and the role of conscious and unconscious processes in human psychology. Thus, it is no accident that Freud, when questioned about his favorite writers, included Mark Twain among them.

A number of dots point to the parallels between Twain's and Freud's psychological thought, and it is time for one study to connect these dots into a systematic argument. This is the task that I have undertaken in *Twain and Freud on the Human Race: Parallels on Personality, Politics and Religion*.

Introduction

When most critics comment on the psychological writing of Mark Twain, they tend to find it derivative of the commonplace deterministic theories of his day. However, if one connects the dots in Twain's psychological thought with the insights and vocabulary developed by Sigmund Freud, one can see that Twain's psychological thought is at once innovative and systematic.

One researcher has seen that some of Twain's psychological thought corresponds to Freud's. In his highly respected study of Twain's writing, *The Fate of Humor*, James Cox notes a parallel between the psychological thought of Freud and that of Twain: "Freud's psychoanalytic theory was itself a culmination of nineteenth century thought and sensibility, of which Mark Twain was so conspicuous a part."[1] Although Cox identifies this parallel between the psychological facet of Twain's writing and Freud's systematic exploration of human psychology, he does not identify a correspondence between Twain's systematic overview of and approach to the human psyche and Freud's exploration of the psychological order in human nature. However, a close reading of Twain's "What Is Man?" reveals that Twain developed a model of human nature before Freud, a system that integrated inborn personality traits, the social conditioning of these traits into internalized training and problem-solving (reason). Twain continued to refine his model in his political essays and works of fiction. Instead of exploring his theory of personality in clinical case studies, Twain developed it through the invention of characters in his fiction and the analysis of historical figures in his nonfiction.

As Twain continued to clarify the working of his psychological model, he discovered certain psychological mechanisms that Freud was later to identify as well, mechanisms such as internalization and identification with the aggressor. Twain's application of these psychological processes involved in the formation of personality allowed him to build a bridge between the psyche of the individual and the social psychology of the group. Through insights into the relationship between the individual and the group, Twain was able to evolve a theory of civilization.

Twain's view of civilization has been explored to some extent by scholars of his work, but that exploration has not recognized the contributions of Twain's theory of personality. When that theory is used as a lens through which to examine Twain's view of civilization, one discovers new meanings for common psychological terms such as "civilization," "conscience," "training," "temperament," and "reason."

Twain, like Freud, believes the human psyche consists of three components. Freud's well-known model is made up of id, superego, and ego, while Twain's less familiar model divides the human psyche into temperament, training, and reason. Freud's id and Twain's temperament share one important similarity. Each is defined as containing the inherited emotional predisposition of the individual. However, they also differ in one critical way. According to Freud, each person's id consists of the same sexual and aggressive instincts. Thus, all people share a consistent aspect of human nature, the aggressive selfish side of the id. By contrast, in Twain's view, each individual inherits a unique temperamental pattern of emotional predispositions. All people have the potential for individuality, based on the inheritance of their own unique temperaments.

Freud conceived of the ego as the structure of personality associated with the human capacity for perceiving and responding adaptively to the constraints of the interpersonal and impersonal environment. The ego includes the capacity for reason and operates according to the reality principle in contrast to the pleasure principle of the id. Its primary function is the survival of the individual. It is capable of implementing unconscious defense mechanisms to inhibit or channel the excessively risky impulses of the id.

Freud's idea of the superego grew from his concept of the ego. The superego stores the internalized rules of civilization that act as a moral and civilizing force on the aggressive id. Consequently, the individual's personality is formed through the interaction of the various components of the mind. Twain also views personality or character as resulting from the interaction of mental components. In his formulation, temperament and internalized training are the most significant of these, with reason playing a negligible role. Despite the value of Twain's work in this area, he has never been recognized for contributing a systematic approach to a theory of the human psyche in the development of American psychology.

The shared similarities between Twain's and Freud's systems of mind do not stop at the structural level. Each model allowed its creator to derive a theory of personality formation for individuals and a theory of civilization for society. Each writer used his theory of personality to link the social reality of society with the psychological reality of the individual. In my study, I discuss the similarities between the psychological systems of Twain and Freud, and how Twain's system underlies his development of key characters and depictions of society in such novels as *The Adventures of Huckleberry Finn*, *Pudd'nhead Wilson*, and *A Connecticut Yankee at King Arthur's Court*. To complement the long works, I also examine a number of Twain's short stories and essays that further clarify these aspects of his thought. Together, this selected body of work will demonstrate that Twain used his psychological system in defining the relationship between the characters in his novels and their society.

In Chapter I, Two Models of Human Nature, I offer a new interpretation of Twain's long essay on human psychology, "What Is Man?," and argue that in it, Twain anticipates the dynamic structural theory of personality discovered by Freud. I compare and contrast the components of psyche proposed by each thinker, showing how each derived his own theory of group psychology and civilization from his model of personality. I demonstrate how each writer evolved theories of free association, the relationship between wit and the unconscious, and identification and internalization from his respective model of human nature.

In Chapter II, The Creation of Character, I analyze Twain's autobiographical work, "The Turning Point of My Life," to identify how Twain went beyond his theory of personality to include the influence of random circumstance on psychological development. For Twain, random circumstance creates the moving element in the narration of any individual life. When added to the components of his model of personality—temperament, social training, and reason—Twain had a method to create character in both his autobiographical writing and fiction. In different works, Twain uses different aspects of his model of human nature, sometimes emphasizing temperamental influences, at other times the impact of culture or random circumstance on the formation of personality and personal destiny. In the autobiographical work, "The Turning Point of My Life," Twain weaves all these aspects into an explanation of how he became a writer. "The Turning Point of My Life" stands as one of the clearest examples of how Twain uses his psychological theory of personality to explain the development of aspects of his own character.

In Chapter III, Civilization and Group Psychology, I begin to explore Twain's theory of personality as a bridge between individual and group psychology, and as a dynamic element governing the function of social systems. Twain developed this idea in such essays as "The United States of Lyncherdom" and such novels as *The Adventures of Huckleberry Finn*. Freud also addresses these issues in several works including *Group Psychology and the Analysis of the Ego*. In my analysis, I show the similarities and differences between Twain's and Freud's concepts of group psychology. In addition, I discuss how each of these writers built a theory of civilization from his ideas about the dynamics of group psychology.

Chapter IV, Character and Civilization, continues the analysis of Twain's idea of the formation of group psychology by highlighting an additional element of it, the rebellious individual. Both Twain and Freud demonstrated the power of the individual's rebellion against the repressive forces of the society. To clarify Twain's theory further, I trace the journey of Huck and the slave Jim through the five different political worlds depicted in *The Adventures of Huckleberry Finn*. Huck reacts differently to the demands of each political world, depending on the harmony—or lack thereof—between his temperamental traits, training, and the current political structure he encounters. It will become obvious that Twain's ideas of the clash between the individual and the political structure of society somewhat parallel Freud's ideas in *Civilization and Its Discontents*.

In Chapter V, The Relationship between Temperament and Training, I explain how "The Man Who Corrupted Hadleyburg" clarifies a question concerning Twain's theory of personality. In some of his work, Twain was not precise in defining the relationship between training and temperament. In my analysis of "Hadleyburg," I demonstrate how Twain understood the interaction between these two components. In it, he creates characters who fall into three different temperamental categories. He then illustrates how the individuals with each type of temperament translate their temperamental impulses through the medium of culture (training) in Hadleyburg. In this way, Twain demonstrates that temperament determines the individual's choices in reacting to cultural demands, particularly in shaping responses to ideologies such as the ideology of honesty that structures the society of Hadleyburg.

Chapter VI, Race and Temperament, centers on Twain's theme of racism as an ideology in *Pudd'nhead Wilson*. This chapter demonstrates how Twain may well have derived his theory of racial identity from his psychological model of human nature, to indicate that race is a construct of social training. For Twain, in any society, the real conflict exists between one's inherited temperament and one's training as created by that society. Thus, in this novel, the concept of race determines how society treats the individual, but does not determine how the individual responds to other people, since that is determined by inborn temperament. Twain uses individual fingerprints to symbolize the idea of individual inheritance of temperament, rather than racial inheritance of genetic psychological predisposition. He further illustrates in *Pudd'nhead Wilson* how race as a social category is created by political and racist ideology. Twain, in essence, satirizes the social concept of race as rooted in a group's biological inheritance, for such "racial" inheritance stands in direct contradiction to his concept of one's inheritance of unique temperament.

In Chapter VII, Religion and Civilization, I continue to examine Twain's idea that ideology forms mass psychology and permits an aggressive individual to control large groups of people. Twain's book *Christian Science* seems to best exemplify this theory through his attack on Mary Baker Eddy for using religion to political and economic ends. These ideas are similar to those expressed by Freud in *The Future of an Illusion*. Both writers proposed that the need for religion was rooted in a regressive need in human nature to identify with a strong leader who controls the common people by creating the illusion of having power over natural forms. In his analysis of Mary Baker Eddy's use of religion, Twain points out how religion can be manipulated for corrupt political purposes by converting individuals into groups who blindly follow religious leaders because of the leader's use of illusory magical power to dominate them. This potential to misuse religion allows those who have inherited domineering temperaments to rise to powerful positions by convincing the common people to surrender their wills and judgments to them.

In Chapter VIII, History and Character, I explain how Twain further elaborates this concept of domineering leaders in *A Connecticut Yankee at King Arthur's Court*, in which Twain presents a "historical laboratory" for his psychological model of human nature. Through the American Hank Morgan, a character with a forceful, domineering temperament, Twain demonstrates the impact of one set of historical forces rooted in late nineteenth-century American culture on that temperament. Twain then transports Morgan through time travel to sixth-century Arthurian England, exposing him to a different set of historical forces. Moving one character through two different historical periods allows Twain to test his theory. Can different historical periods produce different personalities in the same person or only, as Twain contended, modify inherited temperament? One needs to read *A Connecticut Yankee* through the lens of Twain's model of human nature. On one level, the novel treats the conflict between Morgan's temperament and his democratic values. On another level, the novel demonstrates how Morgan's temperamental drive to dominate employs problem-solving reason as an instrument to facilitate his drive for power. While reason, for Twain, cannot have a major impact on temperament through insight into self, it can be employed to solve problems in the physical environment in the service of controlling the world technologically. Morgan uses his reason to create the technological means to promote his aggressive temperament, but he cannot use it to understand his temperament itself. Thus, the novel ends with great and inevitable destruction.

In Chapter IX, Politics, Patriotism, and Leadership, I show how Twain applies his theory of personality to illustrate the role of leaders' temperaments in determining the nature of patriotism. As he did through Hank Morgan's attempt to create a democratic revolution in the Arthurian English society of

A Connecticut Yankee, in *Personal Recollections of Joan of Arc*, Twain introduces Joan's democratic leadership to a medieval French society which is not yet ready for it. Although Hank Morgan is a flawed character, Twain depicts Joan of Arc as a leader with a genuine democratic temperament, who does not have long-term political ambitions, but emerges only in relation to a specific political problem, the occupation of France by English troops. Her eventual demise, for Twain, seems inevitable because of the masses' relative inexperience with democratic leadership and their basic vulnerability to manipulation by selfish leaders who fear democracy because of their own political ambitions.

In the final chapter of the book, Leadership, Ideology, and the Church, I demonstrate how Twain's late story, "The Mysterious Stranger," brings together almost all the components of his theory of human nature. Through his descriptions of the relationship between a few strong characters, the majority of the townspeople, and the cultural climate of Eseldorf, Twain illustrates the operation of individual temperament, internalized training, reason, group psychology, and identification with the aggressor.

In the Conclusion, I summarize the themes presented in the preceding chapters by offering an overview of similarities and differences in the psychological systems of both Twain and Freud, and presenting the six essential character types that Twain created for his fiction from his system. With this spectrum of human types, I conclude with an acknowledgment of the major impact that Twain's writing—and through it, his psychological system—has had on modern American fiction.

Because of the centrality of Twain's thinking in "What Is Man?" to the thesis of my book, I have included this Twain essay as an appendix. Although it is not one of his widely-read works, the scholar Linda Wagner-Martin recognizes that "In fact, one can read Mark Twain's fiction backward from the perspective of the issues in *What Is Man?* and discern a consistency that the sage of Hartford would have found unsurprising."[2]

CHAPTER I

Two Models of Human Nature

*"What Is Man?" and
Freud's Structural Model of Personality*

In 1898, and for the only time in their lives, Mark Twain and Sigmund Freud met in Vienna. No one knows what they said to each other, but certainly these two cigar-smoking geniuses had much to discuss. In fact, they shared similar beliefs and values, an identification with the underdog, a commitment to fairness, and a passion for truth. Perhaps as a result of these shared interests, Freud years later identified Twain as one of his favorite writers.

Anyone familiar with the writings of both men can identify a crucial linking thread: their interest in human nature and the deterministic forces that shape an individual's psyche. Twain and Freud both attempted an illusion-less view of man, as free from grandiose fantasies as possible. Despite their similar visions not only of human psychology but also of politics and other social institutions, no one has formally compared Twain's thoughts with those of Freud. Perhaps too many think of Twain only as a humorist or of Freud only as a scientist, thereby discouraging comparisons. Nevertheless, a certain basic resemblance of thought links these two great thinkers. In his essay "What Is Man?"[1] Twain developed a systematic model of human psychology which anticipates some ideas that Freud later, independently of Twain, evolved into the science of psychoanalysis. In this work, Twain unfolded a multi-part model of human psychology that could be considered a harbinger of Freud's three-part structural model of personality.

Although their models differ in some important ways, Twain and Freud were pioneers in developing the idea that the human mind can be depicted as an interactive mental structure. Each model can be used to derive ideas about its writer's insights into cultural institutions such as politics and religion. This does not suggest that Twain directly influenced Freud's creation of psychoanalysis, only that each man in his own way held some similar views.

Twain believed that his "What Is Man?" significantly contributed to understanding the human mind, codifying his view of human psychology. Referring to this work as his "book on psychology,"[2] Twain rewrote it from 1881 to 1906, when it was finally published. Twenty-five years after he first presented its basic ideas as a talk before the "Monday Evening Club" in Hartford, Connecticut, Twain withheld his name as author of the publication. He later explained that he published the book anonymously because he feared public reaction to his provocative ideas.

As usual, Twain was a good forecaster of public opinion. Even his own wife Livy "loathed the book."[3] Like Freud, Twain tried to strip away the illusions associated with a self-important, egocentric view of human nature, and demonstrate that human behavior is determined by factors outside of human awareness and control. Until recently, most critics have rejected Twain's view of deterministic psychology, arguing that he added nothing new to an old philosophical issue, free will vs. determinism. In some ways, Twain's unclear terminology and concepts contributed to the negative reaction to his book. Still, something of value has been missed. In "What Is Man?" Twain provided a map of the human mind that attempts to explain the process through which external forces determine human consciousness and form personality.

I have encountered only a few critics who feel that Twain's "What Is Man?" is related to Freudian theory. In his introduction to the Oxford edition of "What Is Man?," one such critic, Charles Johnson, points out that Freudian terms can be used to describe some of Twain's psychological ideas. According to Johnson, Twain "casts men as slaves shaped by their social conditioning, specifically by a superego, to use a Freudian term Twain did not know."[4] While this insight is worth exploring in depth, Johnson does not plumb further. In addition, the parallels between Twain's and Freud's psychological thought transcend the use of a somewhat similar structural schema: they indicate some shared views of human psychology.

In "What Is Man?" and other works, Twain anticipates Freud's interactive three-part model of human personality: id, supergo, and ego. Although his vocabulary differs from Freud's psychological terms, Twain develops psychological concepts that resemble many of Freud's pioneering insights: defense mechanisms; identification and internalization; and free association, dreams, and wit as manifestations of the unconscious.

Most important, Twain anticipates Freud's modeling of mind, although the mechanics of Twain's model differ somewhat. However, both thinkers believe that one can model the human psyche to track the influences of deterministic forces on human behavior and personality formation. Twain develops his model of mind for the first time in "What Is Man?" by structuring a Socratic dialogue between an old man (representing Twain's point of view on human psychology) and a young man (whose view is based on the sentimental individualism of the genteel tradition). Perhaps Twain particularly crafted the young man's arguments and questions by anticipating the critical reactions of his contemporaries.

The old man in the dialogue introduces an overview of Twain's three-part model of human psychology. "To me, man is a machine made up of many mechanisms; the moral and mental ones acting automatically in accordance with the impulses of an interior master who is built out of born temperament and an accumulation of multitudinous outside influences and trainings."[5] Through the old man, Twain has structured an interactive psychological model in which "the moral" or internalized training loosely corresponds to Freud's superego, "mental" to ego, and "temperament" to id. In Twain's paradigm, internalized training involves the storage of moral ideas that the individual, consciously and unconsciously, takes from the society. Both internalized training and superego account for how moral ideas and performance standards are imparted through a process of identification with external authority figures.

Twain's mental component of mind parallels Freud's idea of the ego. Here, the mental element involves the reality principle, but Twain limits it mostly to problem-solving in external reality. Freud similarly defines ego as regulating the relationship between individual and environment. Thus, both Twain and Freud attribute scientific problem-solving to this component of mind. However, unlike Freud, Twain did not consider humans to be capable of applying rational problem-solving to emotional problems. Freud, in contrast, believed that the ego also has a role in regulating relationships among the components in his mental system. In addition, through psychoanalysis, the ego can be used for insights into emotional conflicts in a way that can ultimately free the individual from such conflicts.

Despite their similarities, Twain's idea of temperament also differs from Freud's concept of id. Both temperament and id are regarded as an individual's biological inheritances that are to be shaped by other elements of the mental system. However, for Freud, the id consists of primitive drives of hunger, sex, and aggression; for Twain, temperament is composed of inherited emotional predispositions that affect an individual's ability to either measure up or fail to measure up to social expectations. In other words, temperament is an inborn emotional predisposition determining an individual's responses to social stimuli. While it can be modified, it cannot be completely changed.

At first appearance, the significant differences between the inherited components of the two mental models seem to outweigh the similarities; however, one must keep the central point in mind. Twain and Freud each believed he could account for the formation of individual personality through an interaction of elements of mind, as represented by a mental model. Each writer believed that his respective model permitted an analysis of forces that determine behavior, thus subjecting the psychological make-up of any individual to rational analysis. Freud translated his model into the practice of psychoanalysis while Twain used his to create characters and situations for his fiction even before its formal explication in "What Is Man?"

In fact, as Twain's young man complains about the system, the similarities between Twain's and Freud's systems become more evident. "You keep me confused and perplexed with your elusive terminology. Sometimes you divide a man up into two or three authorities, jurisdictions and responsibilities of its own."[6] The young man's inability to understand the old man's (Twain's) mental model of mind places him squarely within nineteenth-century psychological thought, which could not comprehend the modeling approaches to the problem of human personality formation. The young man's complaint propels the old man to describe the separate components of Twain's mental system and demonstrate how they interact to form only one psychological authority, one personality.

To facilitate understanding his three-part system, Twain (as would Freud in later years) explains his system by first breaking it into separate components, then demonstrating how the different aspects collaborate to form personality. In identifying the separate components, both Twain and Freud began with the most basic, biologically inherited component of mind (Twain's temperament, Freud's id), an individual's collection of drives and feelings. However, Twain's idea of the relationship between temperament and social training differs from Freud's concept of the interaction between superego and id. For Twain, temperament is based on man's inherited emotional predisposition to act in response to social demands. Thus, an individual's temperament can help that person meet social obligations or prevent him from doing so. In contrast, Freud believes that the id is composed only of primitive drives (sex, aggression, and hunger); therefore, the individual must be socialized to adopt society's rules and ideas in order to shape and civilize the id. Thus, while Twain's temperament either fits a society or not, Freud's id needs to be shaped by any society's rules for the individual to be civilized.

According to Twain, an individual's temperament will determine whether and how that person can live up to the moral standards of a given society, and whether that individual's inherited impulses will permit bravery or honesty, for example, in response to society's demands for those traits. Twain believes that each individual inherits a slightly different pattern of emotional predispositions; thus, temperament appears close to the idea of individuality, a kind of personality template.

In contrast to Twain's idea of temperament as individually inherited, Freud sees the id as the same for all people, but differentiated into character through social experience. Born with the same instinctual drives, each person's unique character emerges as it is modified by social experience. However, for Twain, each person's individually inherited temperament is then modified into a more socially recognizable identity by social experience. Thus, in Freud's definition of id, individuality is a result of social experience, whereas in Twain's definition of temperament, individuality is inherited before social experience.

Both temperament and id are shaped by social experience, represented in Twain's model of mind by social training and in Freud's mental model by the superego. Freud believes the superego's restraint of the id is predominantly good, for it harnesses primitive drives and translates them into social forms. For Twain, the shaping of temperament by social experience can be positive or negative: positive if it shapes or modifies the individual's emotional predisposition in moral ways, and negative if it shapes the temperament in immoral directions.

In either case, Twain defines personality as the modification of temperament by social training: "It is his make and training. He has to content the spirit that is in him."[7] Here, Twain, like Freud, sees that personality is determined from the interaction of the different components of his mental model. Much like Freud's idea of id, Twain's concept of temperament is as a source of energy; it is a series of inborn emotional and physical traits that spring to action. In contrast, internalized training defines an individual's ideals as well as his moral and political ideas, and these concepts can agree or disagree with the content of temperament. Thus, temperament and internalized training can work together or conflict with each other to shape behavior.

In most cases, character is formed, according to Twain, by the blending of temperament and internalized training: "his born disposition and the character which has been built around it by training and the environment."[8] Temperament then is the emotional make-up that is shaped into character or styled by social interaction and random circumstance. In this sense, the interaction between temperament and internalized training is like Freud's interaction between id and superego. Social expectations shape the inherited material into Twain's character of social style and ideals or Freud's character of personality. Temperament ultimately determines whether an action will be carried out. As the old man says, "You know that a born character's make and temperament would be an absolute and insurmountable bar to his [a man's] essaying such a thing [a brave act]."[9] Still, one's ideals gained from social interaction can create conflict by making that person think he should be brave. This demand for bravery resulting from socialization can modify one's degree of cowardice but not eliminate it.

Twain's challenge is to demonstrate how temperament is influenced by social ideals. Using the example of heroism, which he calls a social ideal, Twain shows its derivation from inborn temperament. Social ideals are indeed more complex than individual temperamental traits: "There are seven elemental colors, they are all in the rainbow; out of them we manufacture and name fifty shades of them."[10] The elemental colors correspond to temperamental traits; the derived shades correspond to social ideals imposed on those basic traits. For example, heroism (a social ideal) is composed of "courage and magnanimity"[11] (inborn traits). If an individual experiences a demand for heroism but lacks the corresponding inborn traits, he will not be able to choose that path. His action will be determined by his temperament, even though his perception of the act will be shaped by social conditioning.

When speaking of temperament as emotional predisposition, Twain suggests that this predisposition is translated into consciousness in a way that determines an individual's choices. "The temperament is master of the man ... he is its fettered and helpless slave and must in all things do as it commands. A man's temperament is born to him and no circumstances can ever change it."[12] By changing it, Twain means eradicating it. However, he clearly says elsewhere that temperament can be modified by ideals drawn from social training and the human need for social approval.

Like Freud's idea of id, Twain's concept of temperament is that it is inborn and cannot be eradicated: "Beliefs are acquirements, temperaments are born."[13] Still, Twain acknowledges society's role in modifying temperament: "You will never get rid of it [temperament] but by watching it, you can keep it down [a temperamental bad temper]; nearly all the time its presence is your limit."[14] Twain's point is that each individual inherits a unique set of predispositions that determine behavior; however, those predispositions can be shaped to a degree through the importation of social ideals. Thus, Twain sees personality formation as a result of the interaction of elements of mind.

Freud also considered the presence of this interaction of superego, id, and ego to determine individual behavior. The id is shaped and repressed by the superego (social ideas and moral ideals) and the ego (reality principle). The interaction of the superego and id is deterministic since the individual has unconsciously absorbed the social ideas of authority figures and the society in general. One is thus determined by these influences, often without being aware of their origin in the superego. Similarly, Twain views social training as unconsciously shaping temperament and influencing behavior. To fully understand this process, one needs a clear sense of Twain's definition of social training and Freud's concept of superego.

Twain considered social training as the sum of external influences that shape the individual temperament. Thus, this concept is more inclusive than

Freud's concept of the superego. According to Twain, social training is broad: "I mean all outside influences ... during all his waking hours, the human being is under training."[15] However, Twain particularly emphasizes the role of training in imparting moral systems and political ideologies to the individual. "It is [one's] human environment which influences his mind and his feeling, furnishing him his ideals and sets him on his road and keeps him on it."[16] For Twain, society shapes individual consciousness by providing external models of behavior such as authority figures, moral ideas, and ideologies, all models that the individual consciously and, more likely unconsciously, absorbs.

Through this process of identification, Twain envisions a kind of social programming that points the individual's temperament in a specific direction. The training focuses the temperament, except when the temperament conflicts with it. At that point, the individual experiences inner conflict. However, in Twain's model, while temperament is stronger than belief systems, those belief systems that are imported from society shape and organize the temperament. They provide the social demands to which temperament responds, thus calling for decisions.

In the mental models of both Twain and Freud, a process of identification leading to internalized training in the one case and the superego in the other gives the individual social ideals and "moral ideas." For both, civilization involves the importation of these ideals and moral concepts in the form of systems of ideas and values. In Twain's system of social or moral training, the individual forms an identification with an authority figure or ideological system of moral or political ideas, as far as his temperament will allow. For Twain, the wish to please is the driving force in this identification process. "If he [the individual] leave that road, he will find himself shunned by the people whom he loves and esteems and whose approval he most values."[17] This creates an unconscious desire to obey the rules and ideas of the society.

Twain stresses the importance of social training and other circumstances in shaping the foundation of consciousness in an individual's psyche. Through identification, a person comes to accept a code of ideas from the society in which he resides. Only his temperament determines the extent to which he will go in carrying out those ideas. "He [man] is a chameleon; by the laws of his nature he takes the color of the place of resort. The influences about him create his preferences, his aversions, his politics; his tastes, his morals, his religion."[18] With this design, Twain has thus created a two-part structure of the psyche. Consciousness is shaped by the ideas imported from the society by the individual. However, those ideas are either expressed and followed successfully or not through the often-unconscious agency of temperament.

The shaping of temperament by social training can be morally positive or negative for Twain. When the influence is positive, Twain calls the process "moral development." When social ideas weaken a positive trait of temperament, Twain calls that "training downward," leading to a loss of self and possibly alienation from the community. In contrast to "training downward," Twain defines moral development as the individual's identification with actions or ideas that profit not only the self but also the society. "Diligently train your ideals upward and still upward toward a summit where you will find your chiefest pleasure in conduct which, while contenting you, will be sure to confer benefits upon your neighbor and the community."[19] Thus, Twain's concept of moral development involves acting in one's own self-interest in a way that also benefits others.

Twain's system of social training parallels Freud's idea of superego in its focus on processes of identification and internalization. However, for Freud, the impetus for these processes in developing the superego stems from his theory of psychosexual development. The sexual drives of the id place the individual in potential conflict with the culture's authority figures—in particular with the parents who maintain a socially-sanctioned, exclusive sexual bond. As a result, an individual who expresses his or her drives risks incurring parental wrath and punishment. To avoid this, the individual's sexual drives are transformed into an identification with the parental/authority figure, thereby internalizing that figure's values and behavior.

Both Freud and Twain find a key to the development of individual pathology in problems that may occur during the socialization process (training for Twain, superego development for Freud). Pathological development for Twain takes place when the individual absorbs negative ideas from the society that conflict with the positive traits of his or her temperament or when an individual's negative traits prevent him or her from adapting to positive cultural norms. In those cases, the individual can suffer alienation from the society or from his own temperament. Twain refers to this alienation from temperament as "petrified thought," which not only separates the individual from his temperament, but blocks moral development and the constructive, loving, and spontaneous elements of temperament. Twain describes a subsequent problem: "Petrified thought; solidified and made inanimate by habit; thought which was alive and awake, but is become unconscious—walks in its sleep, so to speak."[20] Thus, for Twain, social ideals and ideologies can interact with elements of the individual's temperament in such a way as to impede access to it. Although these elements of temperament have been driven underground, they still exist in the individual's psyche—an obvious parallel with Freud's idea of neurosis.

Twain links "petrified thinking" with being driven by unconscious forces internalized from the society as well as with submerged elements of temperament being driven underground by social ideas. When "petrified thought" takes over in such cases to deaden positive, constructive impulses of temperament, the individual loses part of his moral spontaneity and relies on social training, often amounting to ideological programming, for direction. In this sense, the individual finds it more difficult to be an individual because social programming damages the decision-making ability that is rooted in one's temperament.

This concept of pathology is similar to Freud's concept of neurosis, with some important differences. For Freud, neurosis is clearly related to the theme of psychosexual development, from the oral to the anal and genital stages. Without full development, the individual becomes fixed at one of the less mature stages because of inner conflicts generated between aspects of mind, for example, id and superego. Freud's sense of neurosis concerns excessive cultural repression of instinctual drives so that healthy psychosexual development does not take place.

Twain similarly sees neurosis developing from inner conflict. If the individual's temperamental traits do not match the social demands placed on him, he will feel inadequate and alienated from society and/or himself. However, that conflict is not focused on psychosexual development, but, rather, on individual variations in temperament and cultural differences among societies. Nonetheless, the experienced consequences—the symptoms of neurosis—are similar in both models. Both Twain and Freud attribute a sense of inadequacy, shame, and guilt to the conflict generated by aspects of each mental model. In both cases, the neurotic individual feels unaccepted by the society.

Twain's stated goal in writing "What Is Man?" was to demonstrate that man is determined by "his make and the influences which wrought upon it from the outside." Thus, the old man tries to explain to the younger man that free will is an illusion. He is, in fact, responding to the young man's trying to prove how a particular individual makes a free choice. The young man describes a time when a person has willingly given all of his money to another, and that, he claims, is an example of free choice and free will. However, the old man responds:

> Yet we clearly saw that in that man's case he really had no free will; his temperament, his training and the daily influences which had molded him and made him what he was, compelled him to rescue the old women and thus save himself from spiritual pain ... he did not make the choice, it was made for him by forces which he could not control. Free will has always existed in words [illusions] but it stops there.[21]

Twain believes that the individual has an illusion of freedom, but the choice is really determined by psychological forces that come together unconsciously to fix behavior through the formation of an inner sense of personality.

Twain directly states this in his reference to the machine or model of the psyche that controls an individual's behavior. "That authority [free will] is in other hands ... in the machine [tripartite model of mind] which stands for him."[22] In this sense, the integrated machine or mental structure represents personality formation, much of which occurs on an unconscious level. The interaction of temperament and training forms personality, and they, in the form of conscience, determine choice. "His temperament and training will decide what he shall do and he will do it."[23] Here, and throughout "What Is Man?," Twain uses the term "conscience" in a specific, idiosyncratic way—as the dynamic process or "inner compulsion" that determines individual behavior, which may or may not reflect conventional moral standards. Whether or not the latter are reflected in an individual's "conscience" is a function of the natures, relative strengths of, and consistency between that person's temperament and internalized training.

Twain views personality as the inner voice that translates the demands of conscience into action. It is the program of behavior produced by the impulses of temperament that is shaped by social exposure, mainly the political, social, and religious ideologies absorbed by the individual. Twain calls this sense of determined "personality" the inner monarch, the element in man which he tries to please for the pleasure that pleasing it brings. "The impulses of an interior master who is built out of born-temperament and the accumulation of multitudinous outside influences and trainings. A machine whose one function is to receive the spiritual contentment of the master ... a machine whose will is absolute and must be obeyed."[24] For Twain, this inner monarch is a metaphor for the developed personality formed through the process of determinism.

Twain's model for personality formation draws primarily on the interaction of two elements: temperament and internalized training. It is unlike Freud's model of mind that draws on three: id, superego, and ego. Twain sees little room for the "mental" (corresponding to Freud's ego) in the process of personality formation. The "mental" exists mainly in the arena of abstract reasoning, e.g., mathematics and science. In contrast, Freud's ego, the encompassing reason, is a broader concept with a larger role in personality development. Moreover, Freud is more hopeful about the role of reason and the reality principle in facilitating self-awareness and insight. Psychoanalysis can teach the individual to use reason and the reality principle to regulate the workings of the three parts of the mind, thereby granting some freedom of choice for those who have been analyzed.

For Twain, reason in humans works primarily in relation to solving problems in external reality.

Does the human being reason? No, he thinks, muses, reflects but does not reason. Thinks about things; rehearses its statistics and its parts and applies to them what other people on his side of the question have said about them, but he does not compare the parts himself and is not capable of doing it. That is, in the two things which are the particular domain of the heart—not the mind—politics and religion.[25]

Twain believes that man cannot be objective when he identifies emotionally with individuals or ideologies. This identification process of necessity involves subjective attachment that blinds him to rational analysis in these areas. The attachment is based on unconscious identification and association with authority figures or ideologies that replace the authority figures. Twain sees these attachments leading to individual defenses against reason and the truth.

> I told you that there are none but temporary truth-seekers; that a permanent one is a human impossibility; that as soon as the seeker finds what he is thoroughly convinced is the truth, he seeks no further, but gives the rest of his days to hunting junk to patch it and caulk it and prop it with, and make it weather-proof, and keep it from caving in on him.[26]

While Twain's view is strongly metaphoric, one can still see his belief that subjective emotional attachment blinds the individual to an objective view of the subject with which he identifies, particularly in the areas of politics and religion. Once the identification with a position is established, the very bond to the position blinds the individual to a truth that contradicts his position.

Twain provides an example of how this process works once identification is formed. "If religions were got by reasoning, we should have the extraordinary spectacle of an American family with a Presbyterian in it and a Baptist, a Methodist, a Catholic, a Mohammedan, a Buddhist, and a Mormon. A Presbyterian family does not produce Catholic families or other religious brands; it produces its own kind; and not by intellectual processes, but by association."[27] The term "laws of his constitution" refers to Twain's view that the parts of mind unconsciously determine human behavior and personality formation. The interaction of social training and temperament in Twain's system determines the individual's perception of the truth and thus makes objectivity impossible.

In contrast to Twain's highly deterministic model of mental structure, Freud's model allows for the ego to rationally regulate the id and superego, providing reason and the reality principle as guides. For Freud, the use of the ego to regulate the mental structure of mind is facilitated through the process of psychoanalysis. However, both Freud's and Twain's systems are mostly deterministic. The unconscious aspects of Freud's mental model block off deterministic forces from the individual's consciousness. The instinctual drives in the id are unconscious, as are many parts of the superego. Each individual is determined by the identifications that have led to his moral codes and ideals. Even the ego has its unconscious elements—ego defenses—that repress information when reality becomes too difficult. Thus, in Freud's structure of mind, such determination by forces remains outside of human consciousness.

Both Twain and Freud believe that the unconscious is a major source of deterministic elements that shape human behavior without individual awareness. In both systems, the unconscious has various functions. The primary one is as a storehouse of information not available to the conscious mind; it houses memories and other experiences that shape behavior without personal awareness of the stored information. In addition, Twain and Freud believe that the unconscious is a source of creative activity, of which the individual is not aware until it is expressed.

Unlike Twain's view of the unconscious, however, Freud explains its existence through a theory of repression. The unconscious exists to store information and experience which the conscious elements of the psyche cannot tolerate, repressing that information and moving it to the unconscious. In contrast, Twain describes aspects of the unconscious processes, but does not offer a reason for their existence. He uses the unconscious to note that the individual is acted on by forces of which he is unaware, and the effects of such interactions remain unconsciously stored by the individual.

The most important role in Twain's view of the unconscious is its influence on internalized training and temperament. That is, the individual is often not aware that he holds certain beliefs as a result of identification with authority figures. Instead, the person justifies his belief systems because of the alleged truth of the held position. In addition to its function in social training, the unconscious operates in relation to temperament. The individual is frequently unaware of the composition of temperamental influences until they are expressed in behavior. Even then, awareness is not automatic because it requires a certain degree of reflection.

Clearly, both writers present evidence of the unconscious. Freud and Twain use a lack of awareness of psychological invention—dreams, wit, and free association in thought—as proof of the existence of the unconscious. For Twain, one of the most obvious manifestations of the unconscious process is the internalization of social rules, moral ideas, and ideologies beyond individual awareness. This lack of awareness leads the person to identify beliefs taken from others as his own. In "What Is Man?," the old man himself explains that his own belief system is "gathered from a thousand unknown sources mainly unconsciously gathered."[28] Given this reality, Twain concentrates on the power of being shaped by unconscious material.

Twain illustrates this principle of unconscious determination of behavior by telling the story of a young lay preacher who leaves a happy life among his friends and family to become a missionary on the Lower East Side of New York. There, he is mocked and scorned, but initially feels proud that he is doing "the right thing." Twain analyzes the reality of his action to show that his identification with the suffering figure of Christ and the internalization of that ethic have caused him and his family harm, but the preacher "counts it happiness to make this sacrifice for the glory of God and for the cause of Christ."[29] Twain then shows that the religious mission of the man is driven by illusions taken in from external sources. "Meanwhile, in sacrificing himself—not for the glory of God, primarily, as he imagined, but first to content that exacting and inflexible master within him."[30] Thus, for Twain, conscience becomes an internalized god made up of training and emotional predisposition. Man serves this master, according to Twain.

Twain's meaning is clear. The man is serving the internalized moral ideas to please himself. Twain continues to detail the damage this person does in the name of good. Those in the man's family do not receive support from him. "What a handsome job of self-sacrificing he did do. It seems to me that he sacrificed everybody except himself.... When a man's Interior Monarch requires a thing of its slave ... that command [will be] obeyed ... that man [the missionary] ruined his family to please and content his inner Monarch."[31] This individual has damaged his own family because of an unconscious desire to content and please his inner monarch, his sense of self produced by temperament and social training. In this case, the inner monarch is strongly shaped by the institution of religion, and this internalization of religious rules has led him to misconstruct reality. Thus, he does damage to those close to him without helping anyone. The individual's unconscious desire to please the internalized monarch creates illusions which lead him away from reality, preventing him from understanding the relationship between his unconscious motivation and the real harm he has wreaked upon his family. Moreover, he eventually abandons his missionary post only because his work is insufficiently appreciated by the other staff at the mission. Thus, it is his desire for recognition, his vanity—components of his inborn temperament—that is ultimately dissatisfied and leads him away.

Twain believes that prosocial behavior usually occurs when the individual's inner monarch or conscience has been sufficiently shaped by identification—often unconscious—with prosocial authority figures, creating prosocial internalized training. For such individuals, the unconscious wish to serve the inner monarch is a wish to please the internalized authority figure. As such, conscience in Twain's system is similar to Freud's views of the superego. However, for Twain, anti-social or amoral behavior may also result from the unconscious wish to please the inner monarch; this occurs in individuals with strong anti-social temperaments or identification with unsavory associates.

Twain also recognized the role of unconscious processes in determining other aspects of human thought and behavior. For example, the young man in "What Is Man?" recounts a train of free associational thought that is remarkable for what it reveals about the path of thought. He begins with a recent memory of a yellow cat and moves to a memory of a yellow cat in childhood to a scene in a church to a scene in Tierra del Fuego to a memory of a dream. The old man's point is that this course of associations is controlled by the unconscious:

> ... moved to this by the spectacle of a yellow cat picking its way carefully along the top of a garden wall. The color of the cat brought the bygone cat before me and I saw her walking along the sidestep of the pulpit. I saw her walking onto a large sheet of sticky flypaper, and get all her feet involved; saw her struggle and fall down, helpless and dissatisfied ... saw the silent congregation quivering like jelly and the tears running down their faces ... the sight of the tears whisked my mind to a far distant and a sadder scene—in Tierra del Fuego—and with Darwin's eyes I saw a naked great savage hurl his little boy against the rocks for a trifling fault; saw the poor mother gather up the dying child and hug it to her breast and weep, uttering no word. Did my mind stop to mourn with that nude black sister of mine? No—it was far away from that scene in an instant and was burying itself with an ever-recurring and disagreeable dream of mine. In this dream I always find myself, stripped to my shirt, cringing and dodging about in the midst of a great drawing room throng of finely dressed ladies and gentlemen and wondering how I got there. And so on and so on, picture after picture, incident after incident, a drifting panorama of ever changing, ever dissolving views manufactured by my mind.... Without any help from me.[32]

This lengthy passage clearly indicates Twain's precise awareness of how the mental force of unconscious thought can determine the path of conscious thought.

At this point, the old man suggests to the young man a way to identify a hidden pattern concealed in the seeming randomness of the associations. "A man's mind left free has no use for his help. But there is one way whereby he can get its help when he desires it."[33] He suggests a method for putting free association into focus, a method that is close to Freud's talking cure in psychoanalysis. "When your mind is moving from subject to subject and strikes an inspiring one, open your mouth and begin talking on the matter.... It will interest your mind and it will pursue the subject with satisfaction. It will take full charge and furnish the words itself."[34] Here, Twain seems to suggest that one can become conscious of unconscious thought simply by talking about the unconscious associations in detail.

Twain, like Freud, understands that experiences are gathered in the unconscious and influence behavior. In addition, Twain believes that speaking about such experiences can draw them up from the unconscious in a way that provides access to the material. However, Twain does not provide a well-developed methodology for calling up unconscious material as Freud does, nor does Twain have a theory about why the material was banished into the unconscious in the first place.

Also, like Freud, Twain considers wit and dreams as other paths to the unconscious. "Well, take a Flash of wit repartee. Flash is the right word. It is but instantly where there is a wit mechanism it is automatic in its action and needs no help."[35] However, lacking Freud's theory of repression, the most that Twain can make of wit is that it is, like free association, an automatic unconscious response, much like a dream. Similarly, because Twain does not have a theory of repression to account for dreams, he finds their causation elsewhere. He believes that dreams are expressions of unconscious, submerged material, which the unconscious integrates into dream stories. "Yes, asleep as well as awake, the mind is quite independent. It is master. It is so apart from you that it can conduct its own affairs, sing its songs, play its chess, weave its complex and ingeniously constructed dreams while you are asleep."[36] Twain argues that the deterministic patterns residing in the unconscious shape dreams without the help of consciousness. "Your dreaming mind originates the scheme and artistically develops it and carries the little drama creditably through, all without help or suggestion from you."[37] A further implication of Twain's description of the role of the unconscious in dream formation is the idea that all human creativity originates in the unconscious. In this respect as well, Twain's thinking is similar to Freud's.

For both Twain and Freud, the mental structures function automatically, involving many unconscious processes. For Twain, the most important element is the unconscious integration of internalized training and temperament to form personality, the inner monarch that rules behavioral choices. For Freud, the central element is the largely unconscious balancing process among conflicting elements of id, ego, and superego that determines thought and behavior. However, because of the ego's capacity for conscious understanding, an individual may become more aware of his unconscious processes through psychoanalysis. Moreover, by gaining this insight, Freud believed the individual would be able to more adaptively resolve the internal conflict.

Unlike Freud, Twain sees only a minor role for conscious reason in his model of personality. In examining the application of his model to his fiction and other writing, perhaps Twain's most interesting personality element is temperament. He suggests that each person is born with a unique nature and the role of society and civilization should be to develop the positive aspects of that nature. In contrast, the suppression of positive aspects of that nature by a repressive society and civilization can lead to inner conflict and, in some cases, pathological development. Twain's model of mind can be used to illuminate how he created fictional characters and their struggles with the societies that shape their temperaments. Unlike Freud who explored his mental model in his practice of psychoanalysis, Twain developed his view of human nature in his fiction.

The differences between the two models reflect some of the prejudices that come with place. Twain's idea of mental structure rests on inherent temperament, which then is shaped by society. Temperament as the driving force in Twain's system is a highly American view. Even though Twain's psychology is strongly deterministic, each person inherits a unique temperament and, thus, is an individual.

In Freud's system, each person inherits the same set of instinctual drives, which must be shaped by civilization in the form of culture. For Freud, then, civilization is more important than the individual, while for Twain, the individual temperament remains more important than the civilization that shapes it. Twain, the American, produced a psychology that placed the individual above social conformity. Freud, the European, created a society in which social control humanizes the individual and thus is more important.

Despite this influence of place in constructing a model of human behavior, Twain confirms that his model can be used to understand how forces determine personality. In this sense, Twain anticipated Freud's more complex and fully developed model. As the critic Sherwood Cummings sees it, Twain's "What Is Man?" deserves more credit than it has received for having compressed his view of character formation into a coherent view:

> Without connecting the movement of naturalism [identified with such contemporary American novelists as Stephen Crane and Theodore Dreiser], Mark Twain expressed naturalistic ideas and emphases. Without studying two centuries of behavioral sciences, he apprehended its ideas in historical order.... In the matter of "What Is Man?" he was a stubborn literary critic of one, depending on a few seminal books read years before, on private thoughts and on an exquisite sensitiveness to ideas in the air.[38]

Thus, Cummings clearly acknowledges Twain's contribution to the study of human nature and his use of his own psychological theory to create his fictional characters.

CHAPTER II

The Creation of Character

*The Role of Circumstance in
"The Turning Point of My Life"*

The preceding chapter focused on Mark Twain's theory of personality and its impact on the development of individual character and social dynamics in his fiction. In "The Turning Point of My Life," Twain emphasizes the central role of yet another factor—circumstance—in shaping character and personal destiny.

When *Harper's Bazaar* magazine asked Mark Twain to identify the turning point of his life, he responded by writing an essay which indicated his becoming a writer as such a point. Nevertheless, Twain argued that no life has clear turning points, only a series of circumstance-driven events which interact with an individual's temperament. Each case then is composed of temperamental and circumstantial elements beyond the control of the individual. This essay, aptly called "The Turning Point of My Life,"[1] was published in 1910, the year of Twain's death.

In this essay, Twain argued that he could describe the flow of events, the steps leading to his literary career, as the results of the unconscious interaction of environmental forces and his temperament. In this way, he used his model of personality development to partially account for this direction in his life, but with an added feature: the role of the stream of external historical events interacting with one's personality to shape an individual's destiny.

With the addition of this historical dimension, as illustrated by his use of the narrative flow of events, Twain demonstrated the influence of random circumstances in shaping part of his own personal destiny, becoming a writer. By doing so, Twain also highlighted and added a new component to his theory of personality development, one which allowed him to trace the influence of chance circumstance on a character's destiny. Thus, when he traced his own development as a writer, he was able to transcend the influence of training and temperament, and tell a story resulting from the interaction of temperament, training, and circumstance.

Twain's understanding of the role of circumstance as a driving force in the narrative of any person's life must have helped him utilize his theory of personality development in constructing characters for his novels, for the novel is a form that develops the interplay of circumstances with the character's personality. Twain underscores his notion that anyone's destiny is shaped by events:

> [Any turning point] is only the last link in a very long chain of turning points commissioned to produce the weighty result; it is not any more important than the humblest of its ten thousand predecessors. Each of the ten thousand did its appointed share, on its appointed date, in forwarding the scheme and brought about some other result.[2]

He applies this event-driven idea of destiny to explain how he became a writer: "I know how I came to be literary and I will tell the steps that led up to it and brought it about."[3]

Twain begins with a major event in his chain of destiny: the death of his father and an epidemic of measles. At the age of twelve in 1847, he explains his fear of not knowing if he would survive the epidemic. This anxiety drove Twain to play with a friend who had the disease in order to catch it, as a way of confronting his fears. After taking this risk, Twain did contract the disease. He notes in the essay that for him, this illness was a historical event, a turning point in a long series of turning points leading to his becoming a writer. He considered the result of the event as very significant. "For when I got well my mother closed my school career and apprenticed me to a printer.... I became a printer and began to add one link after another to the chain which was to lead me into the literary profession."[4]

Twain then identifies the role of circumstance in such an event-driven determination of destiny. "Necessity is a circumstance; circumstance is man's master, he must obey."[5] In a sense, in telling the story, Twain is turning himself into a character like one of those in his novels. He uses circumstance to move the plot and carry the character closer to his destiny. Twain describes how his experience as a printer led to his traveling through the country, which, in turn, led to gathering information that triggered his desire to travel to the Amazon in South America. Twain had discovered a traveler's account of how one could become rich in the Amazon by raising coca. As a result of reading this account, Twain felt drawn to plan a trip to the Amazon. In recalling how one event led to another, Twain forms a chain of narrative that resembles an outline for a novel.

II. The Creation of Character

The circumstances create a flow of events in his narrative. Twain attributes his ability to begin his journey to circumstance. "A person may plan as much as he wants to, but nothing of consequence is likely to come of it until the magician circumstance steps in and takes the matter off his hands."[6] As a writer who has constructed flows of events through which his characters move, Twain understands how circumstance can drive a narrative. Now he follows this narrative pattern to explain how he became a writer. "At last circumstance came to my help. It was in this way, circumstance, to help or hurt another man, made him lose a fifty dollar bill in the street; and to help or hurt me find it. I advertised the find and left for the Amazon the same day. This was another turning point, another link."[7]

Perhaps because Twain was an experienced writer by the time he wrote "The Turning Point," he understood that in a narrative, there is a role for personality as well as circumstance in determining events. "Circumstance is powerful but it cannot work alone, it has to have a partner. Its partner is man's temperament."[8] Twain knows that a character in reality or in a novel cannot be purely circumstance-driven since it would be too mechanistic. Instead, Twain indicates the character's temperament itself—in many cases, already shaped by the environment—determines how he will react to circumstances. For example, a man with a brave temperament will respond to a challenge; when and how he responds are determined by cultural training.

In this way, Twain uses his model of psychology to create fictitious characters and their motives for actions. Twain devised a formula for personality development and applied it to the actions of fictional characters. For Twain, what a fictional character does or does not do results from his temperament modified by training as he encounters different circumstances. Thus, the path building the narrative of his life is determined by the role played by accidental circumstance, detail or events beyond an individual's control, events that move a life in one direction or another.

In his life story, Twain assumes that his own character has been largely formed by his interaction with the life circumstances he encountered; therefore, he talks of circumstance uniquely shaping the destiny of any character. "A circumstance that will coerce one man will have no effect upon a man of a different temperament."[9] Here, Twain assumes that temperament has been modified by culture and therefore reacts or not to a given circumstance.

Twain views circumstance as a narrative device. For example, after he found the fifty dollar note, his character propelled him to set out for the Amazon. Another person with a different temperament would have spent more than a day looking for the owner of the note. In either case, the circumstance of finding the note shapes the story as it interacts with character. "If circumstance had thrown the bank note in Caesar's way, his temperament would not have made him head for the Amazon."[10] Twain concentrates on the interaction of circumstance and temperament because he senses that these two elements have the power to determine the direction of narrative.

Twain does not forget about the interaction of training and temperament as factors also determining personality development. As a novelist, he understands the difference between plot development and personality development. When he wants to develop a picture of character, he uses the interaction of culture and temperament. "Sometimes a temperament is an ass. When that is the case, the owner of it is an ass, too, and is going to remain one. Training, experience and association can temporarily so elevate him that people will think that he is a mule for the time being but at bottom, he is an ass."[11] In his novels, when Twain wants to develop character, he uses the interaction of temperament and training. When he wishes to advance the plot, he employs the interaction of circumstance and character.

Twain is clear about how character-driven behavior interacts with chance circumstance. "Very well circumstance furnishes the capital and my temperament told me what to do with it."[12] In this instance, he is using temperament to represent developed personality. Circumstance presents the material which moves the story by giving temperament (character) material with which to work.

In "The Turning Point," Twain uses temperament to mean already developed personality or character. When he refers to his own temperament, he says, "By temperament, I was the kind of person that does things. Does them and reflects afterwards."[13] This reference is to more than his temperament; it is to a temperament conditioned by training into personality. Twain uses this sense of personality to explain his impulsiveness in deciding to travel to the Amazon once circumstance had given him the money to make the trip.

Good storyteller that he is, Twain intuitively knows that character provides a predictable reaction to external events, but chance circumstance is responsible for creating the variety of events.

> Then circumstance arrived, with another turning point in my life—a new link. On my way down [the Mississippi en route to the Amazon] I made the acquaintance of a pilot; I begged him to teach me the river and he consented. I became a pilot. By and by circumstance arrived again, introducing the Civil War, this time to push me ahead a stage or two towards the literary profession.[14]

Twain here is very clear about his narrative strategy. Destiny, represented by the literary profession, is arrived at through an unconscious process. The formed personality is an agent which reacts unconsciously to the direction of external events determined by circumstance. This is indeed the storyteller's art.

Twain utilizes his model of personality formation to render the interaction between formed personality, character, and circumstance. In this sense, Twain is able to use his model as a novelist's tool. As a novelist, Twain understood the need for action (narrative development to reveal personality); in "The Turning Point," action is provided, not by dramatic art but by autobiographical outline.

Thus, Twain traces his turning point's origin from the time he was twelve and facing a measles epidemic. He then shows that the consequence of his rash temperament led him to confront the disease as a way of facing his fears of contracting it, but then getting it and surviving. As a result, his mother ends his school career and apprentices him to a printer. In acquiring the printing trade, Twain established another step towards explaining his evolution as a writer. Using circumstance, he explains his interest in going to the Amazon, although this direction was interrupted by other circumstances. He meets a riverboat captain from whom he learns to become a pilot. Once again, this new direction of his destiny is interrupted by the Civil War.

The only constant in this unconscious process is Twain's rash character, formed long before the story began by the interaction of training and temperament. Twain's rash character provides the one consistent element in his unconscious march towards his destiny. He rashly contracts the measles, he impulsively moves around the country, he yearns to travel to the Amazon and ends up learning a new trade. This combination of character and circumstance could easily form the outline for a novel. It certainly demonstrates how Twain's application of his psychological model could lead to the creation of fictional characters.

In explaining how he became a writer, Twain concludes and demonstrates that his destiny resulted from the interactions of training, temperament, and circumstance. Circumstance determines the end of his career as a riverboat pilot since the Civil War made travel on the Mississippi impossible. After the outbreak of the war, Twain describes how circumstance created a new direction for him. "Circumstance came to the rescue with a new turning point and a fresh link. My brother was appointed Secretary to the new territory of Nevada and he invited me to go with him and help him in his office. I accepted."[15] Thus, Twain describes an additional circumstance moving him towards becoming a writer.

Once Twain's new circumstance takes the narrative to Nevada, he then uses temperament to show how his interest was suddenly directed toward becoming a writer. Twain describes his own temperamental interest in writing. "For amusement I scribbled things for the *Virginia City Enterprise*."[16]

Twain next shows how his developed personality interacts with circumstance, but he also does not forget that cultural forces can further develop personality. For example, Twain describes how his training developed his interest in literature. "One isn't a printer ten years without setting up acres of good and bad literature and learning unconsciously at first, consciously later—to discriminate the two, within his mental limitation and meanwhile he is unconsciously acquiring what is called a 'style.'"[17] Twain draws on the process of personality development, in addition to circumstance and character-driven action, to explain his becoming a writer. However, for the most part, he drives the narrative through circumstance, as he explains: "Now what interests me, as regards these details [circumstance], is not the details themselves, but the fact that none was foreseen by me. None was planned by me. I was the author of none of them."[18] According to Twain, the individual's direction, the narrative flow in one's life, is unconsciously determined by the interaction of circumstance and temperament. "Circumstances do the planning for us all, no doubt by the help of our temperament."[19] Twain then identifies the two circumstantial events that best defined his direction in becoming a writer. The *Sacramento Union*, a newspaper, sent him to the Sandwich Islands, and then he was asked to write *Innocents Abroad*, the book that launched his literary career.

At times, Twain makes his journey to becoming a literary figure seem totally event-driven. However, at the end of the essay, he returns to personality formation, temperament, and training as other determining elements. Twain clarifies this with a reference to the Garden of Eden: "Necessarily the scene of the real turning point of my life (and of yours) was the Garden of Eden. It was there that the first link was forged.... Adam's temperament was the first command the Deity ever issued to a human being.... it said 'Be weak, be water, ... be cheaply persuadable.'"[20] Thus, Twain sees the whole of human drama greatly affected by temperament.

As a result of Adam's personality formation, Twain reasons, "The later command, to let the fruit alone, was certainly to be disobeyed."[21] The later command becomes a circumstance which determines Adam's narrative fate, the plot, and the expulsion from the Garden, but it is Adam's personality that determines his action, "For the temperament is the man."[22] Twain then speculates on the outcome of the story of Eden had its characters been different. "What I cannot help wishing is that Adam and Eve had been postponed, and Martin Luther and Joan of Arc put in their place—that splendid pair equipped with temperament not made of butter, but of ashes too. By neither sugary persuasions nor by hell fire could Satan have beguiled them to eat the Apple."[23]

Twain here does what he would do in many of his novels. He applies his psychology of personality to literature by adding the narrative force of circumstance to it. It is no accident that he substitutes Joan of Arc for Eve. In his novel about Joan of Arc, *Personal Recollections of Joan of Arc*, Twain demonstrates that her personality results from temperament, and her existence takes narrative shape through the uncontrollable force of circumstance. In like manner, some of his other novels such as *Pudd'nhead Wilson*, *The Adventures of Huckleberry Finn*, *The Prince and the Pauper*, and *A Connecticut Yankee at King Arthur's Court*, share one common element: the application of Twain's psychology of personality to the formation of literary characters, and the interaction of the narrative flow of circumstance with these personalities, to create the novel's structure.

For each novel in which Twain's creation of character is influenced by his own psychic model and theory of circumstance, I will trace that influence on the construction of the character's psychology. No novel of Twain's fits this framework more clearly than *The Adventures of Huckleberry Finn*. In it, Twain moves Huck through five different political environments, each of which shapes his given temperament in slightly different ways. Applying Twain's own psychological theory to his characters begins to illuminate previously unexplored dimensions of their personalities.

In the following chapter focusing on "The United States of Lyncherdom" and *The Adventures of Huckleberry Finn*, I will identify how Twain establishes a link between the process of individual character formation and the surrender of individual judgment. In these works and others, Twain illustrates a process of group character formation, once again with certain parallels to Freud's subsequent writing in this area, that involves the imposition of a strong leader's will onto temperamentally weak individuals.

CHAPTER III

Civilization and Group Psychology

Herd Behavior in "The United States of Lyncherdom" and The Adventures of Huckleberry Finn

Sigmund Freud enjoyed reading the work of Mark Twain, referring to him as one of the world's great writers.[1] In fact, both Freud and Twain were fascinated by human behavior, and each writer paid close and unique attention to the causes of its dark and destructive side. However, unknown to either man, each had arrived at an amazingly similar view of group psychology as one of those causes. Freud approached the psychology of groups from a psychoanalytic perspective, upon which he particularly expounded in *Group Psychology and the Analysis of Ego*.[2] Twain illustrated his point of view in essays and novels, most explicitly in "The United States of Lyncherdom"[3] and *The Adventures of Huckleberry Finn.*[4]

Twain's literary descriptions of group psychology foreshadowed Freud's more technical approach. In retrospect, then, Freud's work sheds light on Twain's genius and intuitive recognition of the causes of group psychology. Consequently, understanding Freud's work on groups permits a clearer recognition of the nature of Twain's satiric indictment of "civilization" in *Huckleberry Finn* and its development, specifically in the mob scenes.

In attempting to explain group behavior, Twain, like Freud, created a model that explained why so-called civilized men commit uncivilized acts in the name of civilization. Twain begins with the idea that a group is composed of followers held together by the strength of a leader or by an ideology replacing the leader's influence. For Twain, the need to accept the leader's direction is rooted in human nature as a herd instinct—the need to follow and relinquish to a strong leader any capacity for individual reasoning and action. "The human race is made up of sheep. It is governed by minorities, seldom or never by majorities. It suppresses its feelings and its beliefs...."[5] Both Twain and Freud understood that a group needs to follow a leader, and also recognized that good can sometimes come from group behavior. However, in most cases, Twain saw that the herd instinct inhibits individual judgment and makes it difficult, if not impossible, to maintain personal points of view. An acceptance of the herd instinct conflicts with all forms of individualism, particularly one's search for truth and moral decision-making.

Twain attacked those who submitted to the herd instinct as living a sheeplike existence. "To create man was a fine and original idea, but to add the sheep was a tautology."[6] Elsewhere, he adds, "now my idea of instinct is, that it is merely petrified thought; solidified and made inanimate by habit; thought which was once alive and awake but is become unconscious—walks in its sleep, so to speak."[7] Twain believed that the "sleeping" state of the herd instinct is activated by the group leader or ideology. This interaction between leader and masses forms the centerpiece of Twain's group psychology.

> We teach [our boys] to take their patriotism at second hand; to shout with the largest crowd without examining into the right or wrong of the matter—exactly as boys under monarchies are taught. We teach them to regard as traitors and hold in aversion and contempt, such as do not shout with the crowd, and so here in our own democracy we are cheering a thing which of all things is most foreign to it and out of place—the delivery of our political conscience into somebody else's keeping.[8]

Twain's view of patriotism also indicts group-dominated thought. He saw a danger in following a leader or ideology because doing so robbed the individual of "political conscience" or the chance to employ individual judgment based on personal experience. Therefore, the very nature of group psychology, according to Twain, makes the democratic experience impossible.

In addition, Twain recognized another element of group psychology: the group process produces the "outsider," one who differs from the group. Twain had, in fact, isolated five separate elements that work together to form the psychology of group dynamics: the leader; the followers' herd instinct; the leader's hypnotic control inducing the followers into accepting a view without critical examination; the release of primitive instincts by following a leader or an ideology; and an outsider who is the victim of the group's primitive instincts which are unleashed by the leader.

For Twain, the lynch mob was a perfect example of these group dynamics at work. In "The United States of Lyncherdom," Twain illustrates how these dynamics operate: the lynch mob has its leader who hypnotizes the followers and triggers the unleashing of primitive, unconscious instincts. Realistic judgments are lost, resulting in a victim or scapegoat. Twain believed that lynchings grew out of

> ... a law of our communities ... a much talked of lynching will infallibly produce other lynchings. ... the increase comes of the inborn human instinct to imitate—that and man's ... aversion to being ... shunned.[9]

The herd instinct triumphs over individualism because most individuals are governed by the need to conform, what Twain called chameleon-like behavior. "We are chameleons and our partialities and prejudices change places with an easy and blessed facility, and we are soon wonted to the change and happy in it."[10]

Twain feels the only way to resist this natural instinct is to realistically and frequently test the world in one's search for the truth. Finding a truth requires strength of character to maintain that truth against social pressures. For Twain, this strength often results from a sense of loving others which, paradoxically, fortifies one to confront social convention and social conscience. Twain believes that once the social conscience is not operative, people can begin to identify with each other instead of internalizing the social ideology, thereby connecting self-love with the love of others. Thus, Twain believes the enactment of the "Golden Rule" can lead to acts of moral courage, stemming from an identification with all people upon extending oneself and treating others as one would want to be treated. This seems impossible, though, when one identifies with a leader and follows a herd instinct, which leads others to be treated according to the "rule" of the leader or ideology. The rules further the interests of the leader who is often driven by a need for power, obliterating any chance for individuality and democratic functioning.

Twain sees that the group members identify with the leader and understands that they thus mirror the leader's ideas and feelings. Clearly, groups or mobs derive their emotional courage from the leader; when faced with a brave man, a mob without a true leader will panic. "A [s]avonarola can quell a mob of lynchers with a mere glance of his eye."[11] Twain understands that the mob's sense of reality is based primarily on internalizing the leader's ideas and feelings, without which the mob loses its cohesion.

Within groups of leaders and followers, only the leaders can render independent judgments leading to action. In contrast, for Twain, courage is an individual act; "courage observes, reflects, calculates, surveys the whole situation; counts the cost, estimates the odds, makes up the mind; then goes at the enterprise resolute to win or punish."[12] Group members cannot perform this individual act since their social conscience has internalized the leader's own ideology or order. "Conscience is the mysterious aristocrat, lodged in a man, which compels the man to content its desires. It may be called the master passion—the hunger for self-approval."[13] In groups, there is no chance for individual thought (or what Twain calls "live thought"), except for the leader. Only through individuation from the group can one exercise moral courage, and that separation comes as a result of one's strength to test experience against the ideology's or leader's version of reality. For Twain, self-approval in groups comes from obeying the leader's internalized voice, but this obedience leads to the loss of temperamental strengths. Twain's formulation of group psychology stems from his view of humans as falling into two categories: those capable of moral courage and freedom, and those controlled by the unconscious forces of social pressure and the herd instinct. Twain believes that perhaps only one out of ten thousand is capable of seeing reality without a group filter, thus attaining the individual sense of truth that is required for truly moral judgment.

Although living in a completely different world from Twain's, Freud arrived at the same conclusions about the psychology of groups. His book *Group Psychology and the Analysis of the Ego*, published eleven years after Twain's death, provides psychoanalytic support for Twain's insights into group psychology. Like the American author, Freud searched for the causes of group psychology in the individual's psyche. Freud wanted to pave "a way from the analysis of the individual to the understanding of society,"[14] hoping to explain the relationship between individual psychology and group behavior as the basis of his theory. Freud began by identifying groups in society. "Group psychology is therefore concerned with the individual man as a member of a race, of a nation, of a caste, of a profession, of an institution or as a component part of a crowd of people who have been organized into a group at some particular time for some definite purpose."[15]

In investigating groups, Freud found the same five elements in group psychology, mentioned earlier, that Twain had discovered. Freud's investigation of these elements begins with a summary of the ideas of Le Bon, a French social psychologist, which Freud called a "brilliantly executed picture of the group mind."[16] These echo many of Twain's recognized elements:

> A group is an obedient herd, which could never live without a master. It has such a thirst for obedience that it submits instinctively to anyone who appoints himself its master.... He must himself be held in fascination by a strong faith (in an idea) in order to awaken the group's faith, he must possess a strong and imposing will which the group, which has no will of its own, can accept from him.[17]

Freud was concerned that Le Bon provided no theoretical exploration of why a group would submit to a leader's rule. The issue for Freud lay in explaining the cause of the group's collective inhibition of intellectual functioning. He initially phrased the issue as a question: "Why, therefore, do we invariably give way to their contagion when we are in a group?"[18] Freud sought to understand how the group process can lead to the loss of individual ego and reality-based judgment. He did so by using the concept of libido. For Freud, the need for the leader's love and energy holds any group together.

Freud also observed that group members identify with and internalize the leader's views, just as males in primal families identify with the father. He believed this identification to be part of a social instinct rooted in human genetics, a phenomenon he calls "the horde or herd instinct." Accordingly, the process of internalization in modern groups is activated by the leader's hypnotic ability to captivate the group members so they will follow. The leader uses the group's herd instinct to produce unity of thought. To Freud, this leader clearly shapes the thoughts of the members. "The dwindling of the conscious individual personality, the focusing of thoughts and feelings into a common direction.... All this corresponds to a state of regression to a primitive mental activity, of just such a sort as we should be inclined to ascribe to the primal horde."[19] In short, Freud believes that social groups are modeled on the primal horde's love of the father-leader, and the leader can free the often-repressed primitive feelings in the unconscious to be directed at enemies. Freud notes that the group often directs these feelings against those who seemingly do not share the group identity. "Therefore a religion, even if it calls itself the religion of love, must be hard and unloving to those who do not belong to it."[20] The group's unconscious instincts are unreservedly unleashed against an outsider.

In addition to the outsider, another element is responsible for unifying the group. Freud was challenged in identifying the energy that apparently binds the group and prevents it from dissolving: "the leader of the group is still the dreaded primal father; the group still wishes to be governed by unrestricted force; it has an extreme passion for authority ... the primal father is the group ideal."[21] Group members are governed by the wishes of the leader and feel guilt when they do not act in agreement with them. "There is always a feeling of triumph when something in the ego coincides with the ego ideal [the leader's ideology]. And the sense of guilt can be understood as an expression of tension between the ego and the ego ideal."[22] Freud claims that the individual allows himself self-love when he follows the leader's wishes, but punishes himself through the conscience when he falls into disagreement with the leader or group's belief system.

Both Twain and Freud are very sensitive to how the group member internalizes the leader's voice. Twain identifies the voice of the ego ideal as social *conscience*, which, if followed, would lead to loss of individual experience and judgment. Twain attacks social conscience as the voice of the group that leads the individual away from himself. He believes that man surrenders freedom to gain self-approval—a seeming paradox. Twain's notion of self-approval echoes Freud's meaning exactly: the feelings of self-worth gained from following the leader, the ego ideal, and conformity with other group members.

Both Twain and Freud offer similar explanations for group dynamics. They both believe in the following process. In joining a group, the individual replaces individuality by identifying with a leader. Because of each person's genetically-inherited herd instinct, the acceptance of a leader is a natural experience, particularly under the leader's hypnotic influence that causes group members to view him in an idealized way. This identification leads to the release of inhibited primitive emotions that become directed to those beyond the group or those who challenge the leader or ideology from within. The major difference between the two writers is in the way each views rebellion against the leader.

For Freud, the hero is the individual who breaks the power of the leader's spell. "The hero myth, then, is the step by which the individual separates from the group psychology."[23] In this way, the hero begins the journey from the individual controlled by the group to individuation. However, Freud does not stop here, for if he does, his formulation of the hero closely resembles Twain's. Freud continues to state that once a hero has broken the spell of the leader, he can then replace the leader. This formulation of the hero suggests the model of the primal horde in which one of the sons overthrows the father's authority and replaces him. Thus, the heroic action of breaking the leader's hold becomes idealized by other group members who have a new leader to worship. Freud's idea of the hero myth is conservative. It suggests that breaking away from the leader's control is only part of the cycle of group psychology, a cycle rooted in the human need for a leader.

The views of the two writers also differ in the value they place on individuality and rebellion in society. Because Freud believes each person inherits primitive drives located in the id, the leader's rules reinforce the socialization of the followers' ids. For Freud, the individual who opposes order is asserting uncivilized, instinctual needs. Thus, for Freud, social order has inevitable benefits. Freud is characteristically European in championing social order over individual freedom. In contrast, Twain, the American, values the individual and his honest, reasoned perceptions more than the rules of the social order.

Unlike Freud, Twain views the rebel or outsider more individualistically, in a characteristically American way, suggesting the possibility of progressing beyond group psychology. The key for Twain is the democratic possibility created by the Golden Rule. While for Freud, the route to individuality was the hero myth which leads to a cycle of authoritarianism, for Twain, it was the simple democratic figure. This figure is the democratic picaro or outsider, the rogue trickster, personified in the character of Huck Finn. Although at times Huck is fooled by a leader's authority, Huck has the power to rebel against the voice of the herd, the internalized group conscience. As a wanderer, he is not fully conditioned by group customs, laws or ideology; because of this freedom of perception, the picaro is guided by his own sense of self. As a result, the picaro identifies with others as an extension of himself and treats them as he wants to be treated. In *The Adventures of Huckleberry Finn*, Twain pits the power of the traditional group leader against the democratic picaro. Both types of characters have freedom not available to other characters in the book.

The leaders in *Huckleberry Finn* use their power to dominate the members; the traveling rogue understands this reality and rebels against the undemocratic control of the leader or ideology. The first oppressive leader is Tom Sawyer, whose band of children exhibits the characteristics of group behavior identified by both Twain and Freud. Tom gathers a group of boys and compels them to swear allegiance to the gang—that is, to him as leader. The goal of Tom's gang is to rob Spanish merchants; in reality, the gang attacks a Sunday school picnic. However, once the gang accepts his distortion of reality, Tom can establish control and carry out his illusions. Only Huck challenges Tom's illusions with reality: "But there warn't no Spaniards, ... no elephants."[24] Huck, unlike the other members, is not really a town-boy with parents. He is not conditioned to accept illusion via middle-class convention and parental authority. He is an outsider. His lack of conditioned acceptance of authority leads him to directly test his own reality against Tom's version. As a result of his own understanding, Huck leaves the gang.

Based on Huck's early experiences and rejection of Tom's leadership, some readers have difficulty understanding why Huck allows Tom to dominate him when helping Jim escape from the Phelps Plantation. Before Huck follows Tom's lead, Tom has expressed his willingness to become a kind of abolitionist and risk his place in conventional society. Thus, Huck thinks of Tom as a hero—and is in effect blinded to Tom's deception. Huck perceives Tom not as a leader but as a partner in helping a victim with whom Huck identifies, and he erroneously assumes that Tom is acting out of an equal sense of identification with Jim. Because Tom disguises his plot in the form of democratic behavior, Huck becomes the unwitting follower of a group in one of the few episodes of this type in the novel. As a result of Tom's distortion of reality, a group of farmers gathers to kill "the abolitionists"—Tom and Huck. Only at the end of the novel does Huck realize he has been victimized by Tom's leadership. Tom knew Jim had been freed even before the attempted rescue.

In the Grangerford-Shepherdson feud episode, two families are driven into a murderous war against one another because of a meaningless ideology called a feud. In fact, the name Shepherdson might be Twain's way of symbolizing that both families are controlled by the herd instinct—acting like sheep. Huck learns that the feud is a meaningless act of conformity for both families because no one knows its origin. Each family is led by leaders who blindly follow an irrational code of honor: despite similarities and mutual respect, they are each driven to combat by this feud ideology. Huck observes that any marriage between members of the warring families creates even greater antagonism. The feuding families cannot permit the love of one couple to open any identification with each other. Instead, they must cling to the images of the other family as dangerous outsiders and marriage as a war-provoking violation. An intermarriage ignites terrible hostilities. As a result, Huck watches as his friend Buck Grangerford is cruelly murdered by a Shepherdson mob. Huck cannot forget the rage and useless destruction released by the ideology of the feud, by the need to follow leaders.

Episode after episode in *The Adventures of Huckleberry Finn* are organized by Twain's understanding of group psychology. In the Shellbourne-Boggs episode, Shellbourne murders Boggs because the former is blinded by the ideology of a code of honor. However, Shellbourne is able to disband a lynch mob that pursues him simply because he understands the nature of group psychology. Shellbourne delivers a long speech about the cowardice of mobs who lack a true leader. He intimidates the mob by indicating that while he is willing to fight and die, some of the mob will die as well. Not surprisingly, the mob panics and runs, like a routed army.

Twain presents countless other examples that portray people who follow mob mentality; in particular, the episode of a mob tar-and-feathering the Duke and the King illustrates Twain's vision of how one can resist the conformity imposed by group psychology. Huck can identify with the Duke and the King because of their suffering. Although Huck has every reason to hate them and identify with mob rage, he cannot. He applies the Christian "Golden Rule" and forgives them because of his identification with the victims. In another painful episode, Huck tries to explain to himself why he does not want murderers to suffer. While he does not want to free them, he wishes to spare them the needless agony of a painful death: "I begun to worry about the men ... I says to myself, there ain't no telling but I might come to be a murderer myself, yet and then how would I like it."[25] This is the creed of the democratic picaro, who employs his sense of realism to form his own connection to others. He then identifies not with the leader or the group ideology, but with all that is humane. He sees the potential for all human actions within his own humanity, allowing him to identify with the human condition. For Twain, the democratic picaro resists the pull of the herd instinct by maintaining his own individuality through a search for the truth and the experience of empathizing with those who need it. This permits, in turn, moral courage and the establishment of the individual's own political conscience. Together, these values construct the only barrier against the herd instinct and social conscience.

Twain's understanding of group psychology helped him create the character Huck Finn. Huck's search for truth and his desire to base his behavior on it leads him to reject the voice of the leader and the illusions that bind the mob or society to him. It is the truth-seeking individual, for Twain, who stands in opposition to the selfish, power-driven leader. Moreover, while even rarer than the rebel, Twain sees the possibility of a democratic hero who does not have to replace the authoritarian leader, but rather can opt to identify with the group by applying the Golden Rule: love another as one would love oneself. This identification with others as an extension of one's self creates democratic possibilities.

The democratic hero then can become a model for other group members who can also identify with the group and serve the good of the whole rather than the leader. Because he is a model, a kind of teacher, Twain's hero does not need group obedience to establish leadership. This leadership is moral and spiritual, and depends on love rather than power.

In contrast, for Freud, the suppression of the masses through the mechanisms of group psychology is a necessary step in the evolution of civilization. Because of the universality of the primitive, selfish id, Freud believes that the individual who rebels against the order of society threatens the process of civilization in the service of his own instinctual gratification. Twain and Freud agree on the psychological dynamics required for the formation of group psychology, but disagree about its effects on human nature.

Twain's handling of Huck's conflict between temperament and civilization will be addressed more fully in the following chapter "Character and Civilization." Twain's view of Huck's struggle to maintain his own temperamental traits against the forces of destructive aspects of group psychology provides a framework for the structure of the novel.

CHAPTER IV

Character and Civilization
The Five Worlds of The Adventures of Huckleberry Finn

In *The Adventures of Huckleberry Finn*,[1] Mark Twain examines the relationship between individual psychology and the political context that helps to shape that psychology into group psychology. Like Twain, Freud also posits a close relationship between individual psychology and group behavior. However, Freud understands group psychology—particularly mass behavior and the interaction between the masses and their leaders—as primarily a recapitulation of the dynamics of the nuclear family. Although Twain, too, acknowledges parallels to the child-parent relationship in the interaction between the masses and their leaders, another significant factor for him is the role of temperament in social leadership, which he views as pivotal in shaping the political and cultural climate of any society. As a political novel, *Huck Finn* is a complex allegory which intertwines political, social, and psychological ideas. It ranks with such masterpieces of political insight as Swift's *Gulliver's Travels* and Orwell's *1984*.

From this perspective, the novel *Huck Finn* is most like *Gulliver's Travels*. Like Gulliver, Huck and Jim travel from one world to another. However, in *Huck Finn*, their journey takes place along the Mississippi River, instead of among the series of clearly demarcated worlds of *Gulliver's Travels*. While Huck and Jim are on their journey, they visit five different political worlds: the corrupted republic in the antebellum South,[2] the tribal theocracy of Jackson Island,[3] the democratic republic of the raft on the river,[4] the aristocracy of the Grangerfords and the Shepherdsons,[5] and the tyranny of the Duke and the King on the raft.[6] Each of these worlds has its own social system which strongly influences the group psychology of the people who live in that world.

The social order in these various societies symbolizes different political relationships which, in turn, influence the perception and behavior of those who reside there. Thus, in *Huck Finn*, Twain stresses the influence of "training" in shaping the false perception of reality by the average individual.

In each of the five worlds, Twain illustrates how, in most cases, individual psychologies are woven into mass psychology by the politically ideological script of that world. As Huck and Jim discover a different political form in each world, they struggle to maintain their own temperamental traits when their temperaments conflict with the social ideology. However, in such cases, the behavior of both is influenced by the politics of place. When their temperaments are in harmony with a political form, they are most comfortable and "at home," for then the political form fits the psychology of each character.

While Huck and Jim try to remain in touch with their own temperamental drives in each world, most of the other people involved are alienated from their temperaments by the ideology they have internalized. Twain is careful to create a distinct ideological or dominant behavioral ethic[7] for each separate world. For example, the ethic of greed is designated for and drives the corrupted republic; a folkloric superego for the tribal theocracy; political virtue and empathy for the democratic republic; honor for the aristocracy; and violence and deception for the tyranny. Each political form has its own spirit or group psychology shaping its respective ethic. At times, the boundaries of these worlds are difficult to determine because they appear, disappear, and reappear in the novel. However, each world's belief system and its ethic as reflected in the majority of people in that world are often cues identifying a particular world.

Although *The Adventures of Huckleberry Finn* moves the protagonist through several different cultural worlds, it is not the only novel in which Twain uses the theme of characters from one world with a fixed set of values colliding with a character or characters from another. Critic Roger Salomon feels this clash of cultural values to be one of Twain's central themes:

> The central scenario or myth in Mark Twain's writing, the sharp confrontation of one society, one set of values ... with that which is markedly different. The innocent goes to Europe, the tenderfoot goes West ... Huck goes down the river ... the Duke and King board the raft.[8]

Salomon's analysis points to separate worlds in *Huck Finn*; however, he views general value differences rather than specific political structure as a basis of their separateness. Critic James Cox also notices a conflict of worlds in *Huck Finn*, but sees it as the antagonism between the social conscience of the slaveholding South and Huck's own conscience. Cox does come closer to the idea of the clash of political form and individual personality:

> The social conscience represented by the slave[-holding] South is easily seen and exposed. But what of the true conscience which the reader wants to project upon Huck? Although the book plays upon the notion that all conscience is finally social, it does not stand on that line.[9]

Cox points out the split between the social conscience of the slave-owning South and Huck's individual conscience at different times in the book. However, Cox does not consider that Huck travels through more than the world of the slave-holding South. He assumes that Huck's personal growth leads him to transcend the impact of the corrupted republic of the slave-holding South, but he fails to account for the other four worlds or their influence on Huck's political consciousness. In addition, Cox does not attribute the development of Huck's personality to his temperamental drives.

Twain, as Cox indicates, was a social determinist; he viewed personality as formed by the interaction of both "training" and an individual's inherited temperament. Thus, Twain believes that society in part shapes an individual's consciousness and behavior, and he uses social determinism to understand which forces shape human temperament in the political arena: "I wish I could learn to remember it is urgent and dishonorable to put blame upon the human race for any of its acts ... it is moved wholly by outside influence."[10] Twain considers both social and temperamental forces as outside the individual's control and totally responsible for human behavior. As he says, "Whatsoever a man is, is due to his make, and to the influences brought to bear upon him.... He is moved, directed, COMMANDED by exterior influences solely."[11] Twain's deterministic view can be traced back to his psychological model of human nature, in which the inherited drives of temperament and social training, together with reason, shape an individual's character. At the same time, Twain demonstrates that training can create mass psychology that alienates people without strong temperaments from their own temperamental drives. In this way, Twain's social determinism features a political side. He believes that many temperaments interact with changing environmental conditions to make a given society more receptive to one political form than another. Thus, Twain understands that group psychology can change as a function of inadvertent political or environmental change—that is, circumstance.

In *The Adventures of Huckleberry Finn*, each of the separate worlds shapes the events within it until temperamental traits or circumstances force Huck and Jim to leave that world. In their travels from world to world, Huck and Jim, accompanied by the reader, gain insight into the possible social and political relationships within each world. However, they do not remain detached, like political observers; rather, they are shaped by each of the societies they travel through, and at times their political thoughts and feelings change accordingly. Nevertheless, both characters struggle to remain in harmony with their own temperaments. Moreover, the bond between them grows because they share similar temperamental reactions to each world.

The first world Huck and Jim encounter is the world of the corrupted republic, with its dominant ethic of greed. Twain has loosely drawn the boundaries of this world, as he seems to associate the issue of slavery with the greed and corruption that underpin this world. Huck and Jim are in the corrupted republic in Saint Petersburg, as well as the other towns along the Mississippi, while the novel ends on the Phelps Plantation, another segment of the corrupted republic. In this world of slaves and masters, slavery is the clearest evidence of the shaping of mass psychology by greed. However, the group psychology in this corrupted republic affects individual behavior beyond the institution of slavery, as in the ferry boat captain's refusal to rescue people stranded on the *Walter Scott* without promise of payment and the slave hunters' desertion of Huck's invented family. People shaped by the group psychology in the corrupted republic have lost the ability to identify with others as human beings. Many do not see all people as belonging to a human community, entitled to rights as members of that community. Instead, they measure value only in terms of profit. For Twain, the corrupted republic symbolizes the loss of the truly democratic spirit, the empathic ability to identify one's self with the condition of another. This alienated political state encourages selfishness and allows the individual to compensate for the loss of human love, the loss of a sense of community, with a vision of personal wealth. This substitution of money for human relationship leads to an erosion of humanistic values and their eventual replacement by commercial ones.

Prior to writing *Huck Finn*, Twain, with the help of Charles Dudly Warner, developed the theme of the corrupted republic in *The Gilded Age*. In *Huck Finn*, he projected it backwards into the prewar South as an explanation of Southern acceptance of slavery. In the corrupted republic, Miss Watson sells her faithful servant Jim for a good price, although she does not need the money. When Huck's father reappears in Saint Petersburg, Huck has no illusions about Pap's motivation: Pap wants the six thousand dollars that belong to Huck. Understanding Pap's motivation, Huck gives away his money to Judge Thatcher, believing that his father will leave once he realizes Huck no longer has the money. Pap directly confirms Huck's belief by telling him, "I heard about it [Huck's wealth] ... that's why I came. You get me the money tomorrow."[12]

In addition to his own aggressive temperament, Pap has been blinded by the greed valued by his society. As a result, like other members of the corrupted society, he has lost his capacity for human attachment. He lives in a world that measures one's worth by material possessions, and by these standards, he knows he is worthless. Therefore, he destroys his relationship with Huck and replaces it with his wish for wealth.

By contrast, because of his own temperamental tendencies and social training, Huck is able to understand that citizens of the corrupted republic are shaped by its beliefs and values in the same way that Pap is. Whenever he and Jim are in trouble, Huck seems capable of understanding that greed and selfishness motivate people in this world of corruption. In turn, he uses that insight to manipulate the greedy to serve his own temperamental need to protect Jim. After an adventure on the stranded steamboat, the *Walter Scott*, Huck and Jim flee, leaving the thieves and murderers marooned on the boat. Because he knows they will die unless rescued, Huck appeals to a ferry boat captain, telling him that Huck's family is on the boat. While the captain would like to help, he is more concerned over "who in the dignation's going to pay for it? Do you reckon your Pap?"[13]

The behavior of the ferry boat captain is a perfect example of the erosion of community values in the corrupted republic. Understanding it, Huck informs the captain that the niece of the richest man in town is also on board. Only then does the captain attempt the rescue. The captain, like Pap and Miss Watson, places no value on human life, only on financial gain. Life is a commodity for the captain and others like him in the corrupted republic.

Huck's insight into the decadent behavior that characterizes the corrupted republic often involves the institution of slavery. When two slave traders approach Huck's skiff, they suspect runaway slaves are on the raft. To protect Jim, Huck says to them that his father is on the raft and "cons" them into thinking his father has smallpox. The slave traders protect themselves by telling Huck to keep heading down river. However, feeling guilty about their inability to help, they compensate him with forty dollars. Huck seems to deduce that self-interest dominates the thinking of people in the corrupted republic, particularly those who identify with that culture's slave ideology.

Although Huck understands how others are affected by the corrupted republic, he is not aware of how strongly his relationship to Jim is influenced by that society's group psychology and its dominant ethic. As a result, he too occasionally sees Jim as property rather than as a person. In this world, Huck and Tom do not hesitate to play a practical joke on Jim, making a fool out of him. They allow him to think he was given a five-cent piece by witches when, in fact, Tom provided the money. Jim innocently gains a sense of newfound importance because he believes he has communicated with supernatural beings. However, Huck feels that Jim is a fool for believing this and comments that his sense of personal importance has now ruined him as a slave: "Jim was most ruined for a servant, of having seen the devil and been rode by witches."[14]

After arriving at the Phelps Plantation in the corrupted republic, Huck tells Aunt Sally that he was late because of a steamboat accident. She asks if anyone was hurt and he answers, "No'm. Killed a nigger."[15] One might argue that Huck does not generalize what he has learned about Jim to other slaves; however, on the Phelps Plantation, Huck clearly is shown to revert to viewing Jim as property. Specifically, Huck justifies rescuing Jim simply because Jim is Huck's property: "When I start to steal a nigger, or a watermelon or a Sunday school book, I ain't no ways particular how it's done. What I want is my nigger or what I want is my watermelon or what I want is my Sunday school book."[16] Thus, influenced by the ideology of the corrupted republic, Huck is conscious of Jim as being property much like a watermelon or book. However, on an unconscious level—a temperamental level, he is driven to rebel against the ideology of the corrupted republic.

Because of his temperamental drives, his capacity to love and be fair, Huck wants to save Jim from slavery and help him escape from the corrupted republic. Huck demonstrates his ability to hold a relationship with Jim separate from the slave ideology that is part of his social conditioning. He uses reason to establish truths about Jim's character that explode the racist definitions imposed on Jim's behavior by the social training of the corrupted republic. At other times, Huck is overwhelmed by his own human need to be accepted by those who ascribe to the slave-owning ideology. Thus, Huck remains torn in the world of the corrupted republic.

Nevertheless, he attempts to free Jim because he is temperamentally able to love Jim as an extension of himself; Huck is able to appreciate Jim's need for freedom because he can temperamentally love his own freedom. Huck's split between conscious perception and unconscious motive must be translated through Twain's psychological model. For Twain, the temperament is more important than training. Huck may feel guilty about helping Jim remain free, but that is only his training. His temperament and problem-solving reason compel him to support Jim's escape.

Twain treats the split between Jim's training and temperament in much the same way. At the beginning of the novel, Jim rebels against the ideology of the corrupted republic by escaping slavery. When Miss Watson threatens Jim's temperamental love of his family by selling him "down the river," he reacts but never consciously abandons the ideology of the corrupted republic. When he dreams of freeing his family, he wants to buy their freedom with the money he has saved. In this case, Jim is still playing by the rules of the corrupted republic, defining his own family as property. Moreover, he never complains about the necessity of buying their freedom, which may imply that he too cannot see beyond the ideology of slavery that he has internalized. However, his temperamental drive to free his family is stronger than his training. In this, he shares much with Huck.

Both Huck and Jim rebel against the corrupted republic because of each man's unique temperamental drives. Huck's rebellion is best illustrated by his decision to leave the corrupted republic at different times throughout the novel. By the end of the novel, Huck is forced to realize that he cannot be happy in the world of the corrupted republic. "But I reckon I got to light out for the territory ahead of the rest, because Aunt Sally she's going to adopt me and civilize me and I can't stand it. I been there before."[17] With the help of Twain's psychological model of human nature, it is easier to examine the meaning of Huck's statement. His temperament has made it impossible for him to conform to the corrupted republic's concept of "civilization."

When Huck first escapes from Saint Petersburg at the beginning of the novel, he encounters Jim on Jackson Island, which has become a mutual haven; there, they discover the second world, the tribal theocracy. In this world, Jim is able to assert his temperamental strengths and his cultural African wisdom without any constraint from the White world. In this tribal theocracy, Jim is the tribal Priest-King who can base his authority on the accumulated folk wisdom of the Black slave culture. Thus, the behavioral ethic of this world is a "folkloric superego,"[18] a term created by Ernest Becker that means "a society whose culture is organized by a sense of taboo, a society that has established its taboos by observing nature and making associations between the performance of individual actions and the outcomes of natural events."[19] Becker explained the folkloric superego through an anthropological example:

> If two groups of hunters went on a hunt and one was successful while the other was not, a cause for the success of the one group would be sought in their behavior. Perhaps the one that was successful had abstained from sexual relations the night before the hunt. Then sexual abstinence would be identified as the cause of the success and it would become the social rule for the hunters before the hunt. This would be the formation of the "folkloric superego."[20]

In a state of nature on Jackson Island, the folkloric superego becomes a central organizing principle for a primitive society threatened by the constant challenges of nature. Twain was conscious of placing Huck and Jim in this state, for he toyed with the idea of having their actions parallel those of Robinson Crusoe and Friday on their island. For example, when Huck arrives on Jackson Island, he experiences a terrible sense of isolation. Like Crusoe, Huck proclaims himself master of the island, "Boss of it." Like Crusoe, Huck panics when he sees evidence of another human being. Like Crusoe who decides to rescue Friday, Huck decides to help Jim. However, here the parallels end. On Jackson Island, Jim, unlike Friday, asserts himself as an adult; unlike Robinson Crusoe and Friday, who reconstruct the social and political realities of England, Huck and Jim create a tribal society in which Jim is the Priest-King; the Black man is the leader and the White boy, the follower.

This can happen only on Jackson Island, since it is a world separated from the historical realities of the time. There, Jim's slave status is forgotten and Huck and Jim need to carve out a social world in nature. Faced with this task, Jim asserts his adult authority as Priest-King which rests on his accumulated folk wisdom: "The heritage of ... custom and belief about right and wrong, reality and illusion."[21] As Priest-King, Jim presents a totally different side of his temperament than he did in the corrupted republic. There, Huck recalled what Jim said about Tom and Huck: "He allowed we was white folks and knowed better than him."[22] According to this statement, Jim had internalized the slave owners' ideology. In a natural world, however, Jim can put forth his true temperamental traits.

As Priest-King, Jim repeatedly uses reason to interpret nature for Huck, and those interpretations become a blueprint for their social actions and survival. For example, upon seeing birds in flight, Jim explains this natural fact for Huck who wants to catch them. As he tells Huck, "[Jim's] father laid mighty sick once and some of them catched a bird and his old granny said his father would die and he did."[23] Thus, Jim informs Huck that catching the bird would mean death and Huck accepts Jim's admonition. Jim also tells Huck that the birds "was a sign it was going to rain"[24] and they must escape the predicted storm. Thus, Huck and Jim carry their gear to a cave on the island where, once safe inside, they build a fire and have dinner. Huck tells Jim, "I wouldn't want to be nowhere else but here."[25] This is Huck's way of acknowledging that he feels safe with Jim, who has become the leader of their society. Jim responds by continuing to assert his authority and pointing out to Huck that it was Jim's folk wisdom that led to their safety: "Well, you wouldn't a been here if it hadn't a been for Jim. You'd a been down dah in de woods without any dinner in getting mos drowned too; dat you would, hony."[26]

Jim has no doubt in his mind that their welfare rests on his personal ability to interpret nature on Jackson Island and he states that fact to Huck, who in turn recognizes Jim's folk wisdom is powerful. "Jim knowed all kinds of signs. He said he knew most everything. I said it looked to me like all the signs was about bad luck and so I asked him if there weren't any good luck signs. Jim answers, no."[27] Jim the Priest-King knows that their safety rests on not violating the taboos of the folkloric superego, the rules of their society's ideology.

Jim's understanding, however, surpasses his folk wisdom. His temperament also allows him to understand Huck's need for emotional protection. In one episode, for example, Huck wants to look at the face of a dead man in the floating house of death, a house dumped into the river by a storm that Jim predicted. Unfortunately, the dead man is Pap, and Jim knows Huck should not discover his father's death in this brutal way. Jim keeps Huck from entering the house until Pap's face has been covered. Later, Huck wants to

IV. Character and Civilization

talk about the dead man, but Jim invokes the folkloric superego to end the discussion: "He said it [talking about the dead man] would fetch bad luck ... he might come and ha'nt us. That sounded pretty reasonable, so I didn't say no more."[28]

At times, Huck certainly tests Jim's authority, but learns that Jim is the true leader and that his wisdom is powerful. Jim tells Huck that handling a snakeskin will bring bad luck, yet Huck points out that he already violated that taboo but they still had good luck. Later, Huck handles a snakeskin a second time, putting a dead rattlesnake into Jim's bed; soon after, the snake's mate appears and bites Jim. Through this experience, Huck finally concedes that Jim is right again, and his wisdom must be obeyed. "I made up my mind I wouldn't ever take ahalt of a snakeskin again ... now I see what had come of it. Jim said he reckoned I would believe him next time."[29] On Jackson Island, Huck has internalized the ideology of the folkloric superego, its pattern of training.

Huck's perception of Jim on Jackson Island is very different from his view of Jim in the corrupted republic. On Jackson Island, Huck sees Jim as Priest, King, Wiseman. He learns to obey Jim's authority. Only at the beginning of the Jackson Island chapters does Huck refer to Jim's slave status. After that, he accepts Jim's folkloric superego because this belief system does not conflict with Huck's temperament.

In the corrupted republic, Huck and Jim fled because of temperamental conflicts with the culture. In contrast, they leave Jackson Island because of circumstances beyond their control. Slave hunters are heading toward the island. By this time, Huck has identified with Jim and tells him, "Get up and hurry yourself, Jim, there ain't a moment to lose. They're after us!"[30] Huck feels a new connection to Jim that has emerged from their experience in the tribal world on Jackson Island, an experience which has allowed for the expression of Huck's temperamental need for love and freedom.

Both Huck and Jim have internalized a series of taboos that function as an ideology on Jackson Island. The taboos are constructed to create the illusion that nature can be controlled if the rules are followed. Nevertheless, both Huck and Jim are compelled by temperamental drives that make life in the political world of Jackson Island successful. They both experience a sense of harmony. Huck is able to love Jim for his humanity and Jim recognizes that Huck is a child who needs the direction of a caring parent. Jim has the capacity to love and Huck's nature allows him to accept Jim's authority. In short, each has the temperamental qualities to live in a happy family. As such, both characters leave Jackson Island because they must, not because they choose to do so.

Huck and Jim flee Jackson Island on their raft. On the river they discover the third and most democratic world, that of the democratic republic. Here, Huck and Jim learn to identify with each other as equals. Each identifies his personal well-being with the welfare of the symbolic community on the raft. In the process of living in a democratic world, they are able to empathize with each other and with other humans as well. Their temperamental drives for love are reinforced by the democratic ideology that governs life on the raft.

This world conforms to Twain's picture of democracy: "Strip the human race absolutely naked and they would be a real democracy."[31] Such is life on the raft. However, Twain also believed that the democratic state was fragile and short-lived. Thus, the world of the democratic republic on the raft lasts briefly. In this transient world, Huck and Jim comprise a small, virtuous, and poor society, one in which the dominant behavioral ethic is equality and empathy, an ethic which fits the temperaments of Huck and Jim.

This world of equality, or at least near-equality, between Huck and Jim on the raft resembles life in a small virtuous republic. Huck and Jim democratically discuss most of the decisions affecting life on the raft. A clear political structure prevails on the raft. Through empathy with each other and others, Huck and Jim confront their common problems in a cooperative way. The prevalent belief in this society is that the rights of all humans should be recognized and respected. Twain's view of democracy, as exemplified on the raft, is based on Christ's Golden Rule.

To illustrate this, at one point, Twain has Huck and Jim encounter murderers on the steamship, the *Walter Scott*. The ship begins to sink and Huck knows they will die if he does not get them help. However, he and Jim leave them stranded because they fear the murderers, if rescued, would jeopardize their own safety on the raft. In wondering why he is so interested in saving them, he tells the reader, "I begun to think how dreadful, even for murderers, to be in such a fix. I says to myself, there ain't no telling but I might come to be a murderer one day myself yet and how would I like it."[32] Huck's empathy reflects the dominant ethic of the democratic republic. Huck identifies himself with the condition of these killers. He understands the need to treat them as he would want to be treated. This is Huck in the democratic world, a person capable of understanding that humans are equal because each possesses a self, a being, a soul.

In another episode, however, Twain illustrates how Jim, as the adult, must at times remind Huck of the importance of mutual respect. On the river one night, Huck is separated from the raft because of a storm and fog; Jim worries and finally believes Huck has drowned. When Huck reappears on the raft, Jim tells him how happy Huck's return has made him. Huck replies that Jim's idea of what happened is not true and he is only dreaming. Jim uses his problem-solving reason and discovers evidence that the experience that night was real. As Huck's equal, he observes that Huck does not know how to treat a friend: "En all you waz thinking bout was how you could make a fool of ole Jim wid a lie. Dat trick is trash, en trash is what people is dat puts dirt on de head of dey friends 'n makes them ashamed."[33] Jim proclaims the dignity of the self and the necessity for mutual respect. This behavior illustrates the republican ethic. In his lecture to Huck, Jim extends the concept of empathy to include a principle of compensation. In essence, Jim is telling Huck that when one damages the other, one damages oneself. This is as well the democracy of Emerson and Whitman. Jim's thinking reflects the ability to see the one in the all and the all in the one.

Huck shows that he has learned this democratic lesson, affected as he is by Jim's assertion of the need for empathy in their world: "I didn't do him no more tricks and I wouldn't done that one if I'd knowed it would make him feel that way."[34] Huck's time in the democratic republic reinforces his inborn temperament. Jim supplies lessons to Huck which make sense to him and Huck in turn is able to treat others as he wants to be treated. Still, even in the world of democracy, Huck is plagued by the training that he received in the corrupted republic. Influences acquired in each of the worlds are carried forward by Huck and Jim into the next worlds they encounter. These influences manifest themselves in the form of internalized rules of conduct stored in each character's conscience. Thus, even in the world of democracy, Huck struggles with the rules of the slave-owning ideology which he has internalized. This "old morality" stored in his conscience at times causes him to continue viewing Jim as property; however, the more time he spends with Jim in the democratic republic, the more Huck can see Jim as a human extension of himself.

While in the democratic republic, Huck must struggle to fully accept Jim as his brother. However, because the world features little political machinery to repress the truth, Huck eventually understands Jim's motives and decency. When Jim tells Huck of his plans to free his wife and children, Huck at first feels threatened by Jim's assertion of his rights, to the point of thinking he should turn Jim over to the authorities: "I was sorry to hear Jim say that, it was such a lowering of him."[35] However, the dominant ethic of the democratic republic is allowed to reemerge as Jim communicates directly and honestly with Huck. He tells Huck, "You's de bes' fren' Jim's ever had, en you's de only fren' old Jim got now."[36]

At the end of the novel and once again on the raft, Jim provides a final example of empathy in the world of the democratic republic. Huck and Tom help Jim escape from slavery. They all run to the raft and momentarily revisit the world of the democratic republic. Tom has been wounded and Jim, rather than escape, decides to stay with Tom. He explains that because Tom would not leave him, so he will not leave Tom. This is a democratic, empathic Jim, who understands that he should treat people the way he wants to be treated. This is a man whose temperament allows him to accept that democracy is more than being free to assert one's own rights; it involves a bond to the community, to the welfare of the other.

Of all the worlds in the novel, the democratic republic on the raft seems the most fragile. At one point, this world is physically smashed to pieces by a steamship, forcing Huck and Jim to swim for their lives. They swim ashore to the fourth world, the world of aristocracy. The Grangerford family takes Huck into their home, and he is immediately impressed by the advantages of aristocratic status: "It was a mighty nice family, a mighty nice house, too."[37] As a newcomer in the world of aristocracy, Huck is most awed by its grandeur. "Col. Grangerford, he adds, was a gentleman, you see. He was a gentleman all over; and so was his family. He was well born, as the saying is, and that's worth as much in a man as it is in a horse, so the widow Douglas said, and nobody ever denied that she was of the first aristocracy in our town."[38]

At the outset, Huck is in awe of the aristocrats. He describes Colonel Grangerford as "tall and slim, the thinnest kind of nostrils and a high nose. His forehead was high; his hands were long and thin ... there weren't no forwardness about him." The sons, Huck tells us, "were tall beautiful men." Of the daughters, he says they were "proud and grand.... They were as high toned and well born and rich and grand, as the tribe of Grangerfords."[39]

Initially, Huck feels accepted by and part of the Grangerford family. He is given a slave and has a symbolic brother, Buck, the Grangerfords' youngest son. Huck and Buck become very close friends and, in general, Huck feels at home in this world, until he learns that this family is locked in a feud with another aristocratic family. When he asks Buck to explain the feud, Buck asks in return, "Where was you raised?" Huck tells Buck that he has "never heard of a feud before,"[40] admitting he is, in fact, a traveler from another world.

When Huck questions Buck about the Grangerford-Shepherdson feud, he discovers that Buck has no idea how or why it started. Unlike Huck, Buck is fully conditioned to accept the feud as a necessary fact of life. Buck describes the feud in such a way to show that it functions like an ideology that irrationally determines human behavior: "A man has a quarrel with another man and kills him, then that other man's brother kills him; then the other brothers, on both sides, goes for one another; then the cousins chip in—and by and by everybody's killed off, and there ain't no more feud."[41]

When Buck dies in the feud, Huck feels the destructiveness of the aristocratic code of honor, its blindness and irrationality, which leads to tragedy:

> When I got down out of the tree, I crept down the river bank a piece and found two bodies laying in the edge of the water and tugged at them till I got them ashore; then I covered up their faces and got away as quick as I could. I cried a little when I was covering up Buck's face, for he was mighty good to me.[42]

Huck's temperamental traits conflict with the ethic of the aristocracy. Its code of honor, Huck discovers, is nothing but a code of rules that add up to "frozen ideas" of the past, ideas that lead to war. Huck's capacity to love, learned to its fullest in the democratic republic, is challenged by the constant state of conflict created by the rules of aristocracy.

Huck's ultimate sense of tragedy triggers a reversal in his feeling about aristocracy. At first, Huck is attracted to the elegant and supportive culture of this aristocratic family. He observes that its members follow a code of honor, the dominant ethic of this world. He admires their adherence to the values that make up this code of honor: honesty, courage, and loyalty. However, the feud was also caused by the code of honor (as Buck explained), and needlessly destroys his young friend. Consequently, Huck realizes that a blind adherence to tradition renders individual judgment impossible. As Huck leaves the world of aristocracy, the reader understands, as did Mark Twain, that "Any kind of aristocracy, however pruned, is rightly an insult; but if you are born and brought up under that sort of arrangement you probably never find it out for yourself."[43] As a stranger to it, Huck is able to realize that he wishes to leave the world of aristocracy.

After Huck's grave loss and disillusionment in the Grangerford and Shepherdson world of aristocracy, he and Jim flee to the raft and there again briefly experience the brotherhood of the democratic republic. This temporary return to the democratic republic provides a background against which one can observe the Duke and the King's usurpation of the raft and the consequent fall of the democracy.

Huck and Jim are lulled into trusting the Duke and the King when they first arrive on the raft. The Duke and the King further lure Huck and Jim into accepting the new order by providing a false historical foundation for their usurpation of power; this use of manufactured history is a common characteristic of totalitarian or despotic regimes. Both the Duke and the King trace their roots to European royalty and use this fake background to justify the appropriation of the raft and the destruction of the democratic equality that existed before their arrival. Huck describes how the Duke manipulated both Jim and himself. According to the Duke, he was

> the rightful Duke of Bridgewater; and here I am forlorn, torn from my high estate.... Jim pitied him ever so much, and so did I.... He said we ought to bow, when we spoke to him and say "your grace" or "my Lord." ... Well, that

was all easy, so we done it. All through dinner Jim stood around and waited on him.[44]

Thus, a new order emerges on the raft, a dictatorship run by the Duke and the King, with its ruling ethic of fear and deception. Using this ethic, the Duke and the King create an order in which their will reigns supreme, a regime whose justification rests on a falsification of history using models of European authoritarian rule.

Once Huck realizes control of the raft has been taken away from Jim and himself, he understands that the Duke and the King are frauds:

> It didn't take me long to make up my mind that these liars warn't no Kings nor Dukes, at all, but just low-down humbugs and frauds. But I never said nothing, never let on kept it to myself.... If I never learnt nothing else out of Pap, I learnt that the best way to get along with his kind of people is to let them have their own way.[45]

Thus, Huck links the Duke and the King to Pap. He understands that Pap also attempted to rule him in tyrannical ways. Pap imposed his will with force and deception, without any concern for Huck's rights as a family member, and sought to take Huck's property as his own. However, Pap's drunkenness made him only a parody of a tyrant.

In contrast, the Duke and the King successfully create a world of tyranny, where they impose their wills on the masses. For example, they appropriate the raft, sell Jim, take money from the townspeople, and attempt to steal the entire inheritance from the Wilkes sisters. Like tyrants, they believe that no one else has the right to own anything for themselves. In each instance, the Duke and the King use physical force or deception to maintain their power over others. This becomes the dominant behavioral ethic of the world of tyranny on the raft and in some of the towns victimized by the Duke and the King. In these towns, the pair view the people as fools who deserve to be dominated. In addition, while Huck travels through the world of tyranny, he observes the townspeople behaving in undemocratic, herd-like ways. In the world of tyranny, democratic values and beliefs disappear.

The Duke and the King are eventually challenged by Dr. Robinson during the Wilkes episode, when they attempt to convince the town that they are the rightful heirs to a small fortune. As they discuss his threat to their con game, the King tells the Duke, "Hain't we got all the fools in town on our side? And ain't that a big enough majority in any town?"[46] The King expresses a highly anti-democratic ethic. Together, they demonstrate a traditional disregard of democracy characteristic of tyrants.

This theme of tyrannical disregard for democracy is continued in another scene witnessed by Huck. After a townsman, Shellbourne, murders an innocent man, Boggs, Huck watches Shellbourne face down a lynch mob and tell them, "Do I know you? I know you clear through, I was born and raised in the south, and I've lived in the north; so I know the average all around. The average man is a coward ... a mob without any man at the head of it is beneath pitifulness."[47] Shellbourne delivers his sermon standing on the roof of his house, looking down at the mob. He represents a kind of "overman" who, through an act of strength, reduces the mob to his will. He is the embodiment of a tyrannical spirit which attacks the capacity of the individual to govern himself.

In the novel, Twain presents tyranny as a form of corrupted aristocracy. The rulers, the Duke and the King, have no system of beliefs that limit their aggressive temperaments. Instead, they make up the rules to free their aggressive temperaments. Like Huck's father, they are, in essence, a parody of aristocrats who are driven by blind allegiance to a code.

Twain illustrates this difference between aristocrats and con men like the Duke and the King by having this pair rehearse the play *Romeo and Juliet*. They mangle the lines of the play and turn their imitation of aristocracy into an absurd farce in the same way that tyranny turns the already destructive form of aristocracy into an absurd expression of pure selfishness supported by violence.

While the Duke and the King rule the raft, Huck and Jim experience a sense of despair unknown in any of the other worlds of *Huck Finn*. At one point, Huck believes that he and Jim have escaped from the Duke and the King, and he feels the ecstasy of a person who has just escaped from jail:

> I had to skip around a bit and jump up and crack my heels a few times. I couldn't help it; but about the third crack, I noticed a sound that I knowed mighty well—and held my breath, and listened and waited—and sure enough, when the next flash busted over the water, here they come.... It was the King and Duke. So I wilted right down into the planks, then and give up and it was all I could do to keep from crying.[48]

The spirit of both Huck and Jim is crushed while they suffer under tyrannical rule. Any brotherhood they feel comes from sharing the same destiny as slaves of the tyranny.

The tyrannical world of the Duke and the King resembles actual tyrannies in another way. The Duke and the King produce nothing of value. Like parasites, they invade and take over the institutions of the corrupted republics in the towns or the democratic republic of the raft. They generate no real or lasting social institutions. This lack of real cultural energy implies that their world must end in ruin.

At last, when the Duke and the King fall, they, like many other tyrants, are caught and punished by the mob, which has finally seen through the illusions that formerly protected the tyrants. Huck describes their fall:

> Here comes a raging rush of people, with torches, and an awful whooping and yelling, and banging tin pans and blowing horns, and we jumped to one side to let them go by; and as they went by, I see that they had the King and the Duke astraddle of a rail, that is, I knowed it was the King and the Duke, though they was all over tar and feathers and didn't look like nothing in the world that was human—just looked like a couple of monstrous big soldier plumes.[49]

The fall of these tyrants marks the end of the world of tyranny, leaving the novel to conclude at the Phelps Plantation, within the corrupted republic where the action began. The issues of Jim's slavery resurface as the major problem of the novel. Leo Marx criticized this ending for not carrying through Huck's and Jim's downriver search for freedom. This critique grew from the view that *Huck Finn*'s plot was linear, that the purpose of the book was the search for Jim's freedom. However, if one accepts the thesis that Huck and Jim travel among different political worlds like Gulliver, then the return to the world from which they started makes sense. Like Gulliver, Huck and Jim come full circle, returning home only to realize they cannot be happy there. Huck is by temperament a seeker, a rare individual who must find a political world that matches his temperament. Although finally granted his freedom in the late Miss Watson's will, Jim, too, has ambitions that lead him away from the corrupted republic.

In the structure of *The Adventures of Huckleberry Finn*, two significant aspects of Twain's political and social thought can be identified: his belief in the fragility of the democratic-republican form of government and his belief in the rarity of the temperamentally strong, empathic individual who neither conforms to corrupted social norms nor manipulates others to gain personal power. While the republicanism of the larger society in the novel had been corrupted prior to the start of the story, the intrusion of the temperamentally aggressive Duke and King destroys the fragile democracy of the raft. In addition, the behavior of the citizenry in relation to the Duke and the King demonstrates how this imposition of will is accomplished by manipulating people into abandoning individual temperaments and problem-solving reason, reverting to the primitive herd instinct and blindly following ideological, authoritarian leaders.

Twain also indicates that Huck's rebellion against the conformity imposed by civilization cannot be the norm. Huck is the exception. According to Twain, the ordinary person in any world has an inborn temperamental need to conform. "It is our nature to conform; it is a force which not many can successfully resist."[50] Twain roots the need to conform in the herd instinct, located in the temperaments of most people. For Twain, this temperamental need to conform, a need of the average person, is stronger than the need to express traits of individuality.

As Huck travels through the five worlds in the novel, he feels the pull of the herd instinct, but remains an individual with an uncommon temperamental drive for love and community. Paradoxically, at times, he allows himself to arrive at conclusions that differ from those held by the leader-indoctrinated group. He can resist because he possesses the temperamental courage to stand up to mob opinion and register his own private judgments based on his personal perceptions of reality.

Twain sees Huck's rebellion against an exploitative social order as part of a necessary process, determined by his temperamental need to express the truth. In tracing this process of Huck's rebellions against certain political forms and even against Huck's own socially conditioned conscience, Twain creates a truly American character. Huck's goodness does not represent an American belief in the goodness of all human nature. Instead, Huck represents an ideal that the exceptional individual can provide a model—democratic empathy—worthy of imitation by those of lesser natures.

CHAPTER V

The Relationship Between Temperament and Training

Social Ideology in "The Man Who Corrupted Hadleyburg"

In "The Man Who Corrupted Hadleyburg,"[1] Mark Twain clarifies the answer to a question central to his model of personality formation. This question is created by Twain's lack of consistency. In some works, Twain is not clear on whether training or temperament is primary in character development. For example, at times in "What Is Man?," Twain identifies temperament as the most powerful force, but in other works, he gives pre-eminence to training. In writing "Hadleyburg," he presents a sophisticated resolution to this apparent contradiction.

In "Hadleyburg," Twain illustrates that temperament is the original source of impulses that are expressed through the medium of social training. Thus, for Twain, inherited temperament determines the choices made in reacting to cultural demands, particularly in the shaping of reactions to ideologies. To develop this idea, Twain creates the town of Hadleyburg with an ideology of honesty whose principles and rules are imposed on all its citizens. On one level, the story is about three distinct kinds of reactions to that ideology, reactions caused by different temperamental inheritances.

The town of Hadleyburg is made up of various temperamental types, but Twain focuses on three major ones. There are those who exhibit the outsider's temperament, men like Barclay Goodson, Jack Halliday, and the Reverend Burgess. These are people whose strongest temperamental trait is a powerful but reasonable will. As a result, they are men who render judgments independent of the mob or ideological influence. They try to be realistic and have a need to honestly report what they believe to be the truth. They identify the town's unrealities as illusions. This tendency to tell the truth causes most people in the town to resent their gadfly-like behavior. Thus, the town isolates them and they accept the outsider's status as a badge of honor, the price of their honesty. Goodson, in particular, is not afraid to incur the town's disapproval. He attacks the town's ideology of honesty as based on illusion. It is a narrow, moralistic, empty code. As a result, most people in the town dislike him. However, his criticism has a positive influence, keeping the town from becoming too authoritarian in its application of its code of honesty.

The second group of people in the town is driven by a temperamental need for social, political, and economic power. These are the leading citizens of the town, men like Harkness and Pinkerton. They are both strong-willed and temperamentally corrupt and dishonest. To achieve power, they use the town's ideology to manipulate the common people to accept their authority. The paradox of the story is that the outsiders who attack the town's ideology of honesty as false keep the town honest while the town's leaders use the ideology to corrupt.

Unlike the first two groups, the third is made up by the majority of people in the town. They are fearful people whose training leads them to internalize and conform to the town's ideology. They fear that breaking the rules will lead to disapproval from those with authority. These people live ordinary, controlled lives. They follow the lead of those in authority, although some sense, at times, that the outsiders are correct in their critiques of the power structure. Many like Edward Richards and his wife are such people, and the story of Hadleyburg is the story of their destruction. When circumstances offer economic temptation that leads them to violate the local code of honesty, they are conflicted, wanting to obey the local rules of honesty and simultaneously wanting to break those rules to acquire wealth. This is a conflict that ultimately disorganizes the personality of Edward Richards.

Most of the townspeople, like the Richardses, are motivated by a herd instinct in their temperaments. Those with authority activate this instinct in the majority by reinforcing their fear of social rejection. In his essay, "Cornpone Opinions,"[2] Twain explains how this herd instinct influences those of weak temperaments. Twain argues that the weak need to please public opinion, but the powerful control public opinion and utilize it to control the common people. Twain believes that most people possess the temperamental need to follow the herd, the commonly accepted fashions, "and ... that a ... thought-out and independent verdict ... is rare."[3] Thus, in Twain's view, the maverick is the exception.

For Twain, the majority internalize the rules of society without rationally analyzing them. They obey the rules because of fear, especially fear of the disapproval of those in authority. However, the average person, having internalized the town's rules, is not aware of his fear. Instead, he experiences it as a need for self-approval or conscience. By meeting authority's demands, that is, conforming to social rules, the individual experiences the sense of inner pleasure that comes from self-approval. Thus, as a result of the socialization process, Twain identifies a clear relationship in most people between social approval and self approval, "our self-approval has its source in but one place ... the approval of other people."[4]

For Twain, the need to conform is rooted in the temperament of the average person; that is, the majority have a temperamental need to please authority. In this sense, Twain sees the need to conform as a child-like need to please the parent and those who blindly obey social authority are like children who must please their parents before they can be satisfied with themselves.

Twain, like Freud, uses the family as a model of society. The powerful father imposes order and the children obey to gain his love. For Twain, self-approval can be attained only through the acceptance of the parent, and that acceptance is gained only by obeying the rules of the family or society. "A person of ... consequences can introduce any ... novelty ... and the world will adopt it—moved to do it, ... by the natural instinct to ... yield to authority."[5]

The world of Hadleyburg is one run by the town leaders whose authority is reinforced by public opinion. Only the outsiders understand the situation, but they lack the inclination to change the world. In a sense, the story of Hadleyburg is Twain's allegory of a corrupt civilization. Those who control it make the rules that they themselves do not follow. The masses, following the herd instinct, "sheepishly" obey, while the discontents stand at a distance, observing the truth of the unfair situation.

Twain's model of civilization as family shares some commonalties with that of Sigmund Freud. Freud also identified parallels between the child's relationship to the powerful father in socialization and the group member's relationship to the leader in civilization. For Freud, the exceptional, powerful people impose order and the common people follow that order, resulting in civilization. In the main, the process for Freud is constructive. Most of the rules of civilization, according to Freud, repress the instinctive drives of aggression and sex. The rules of civilization socialize the id.

Twain departs from Freud by suggesting that civilization is more destructive than helpful to man. In Hadleyburg, the strong impose the ideology of honesty on the poor, but they serve their own needs in doing it. The imposition of the rules of the ideology tends to create an authoritarian society in Hadleyburg, alienating people from their own temperaments or, in the case of a few, from society rather than themselves.

For Twain, the temperamental group that suffers the most is the com-

V. The Relationship Between Temperament and Training

mon people, plagued by the need to please authority, or what Twain called the herd instinct. In contrast, relative outsiders who did not grow up in the town are able to recognize the townspeople's blind acceptance of Hadleyburg's rigid and exploitive ideology. Chief among these outsiders is Barclay Goodson. He attacks the mindless conformity of the common people in Hadleyburg. After Goodson's death, Mary Richards acknowledges that the town has suffered the loss of his honest criticism of its ideology of honesty. "For six months now, the village has been its own proper self once more—honest, narrow, self-righteous and stingy."[6] She implies that Goodson's directness humanized the town. Since his death, the ideology of honesty has made the town psychologically unattractive, moralistic, rigid, unloving. For Twain, the "outsiders" have a strange relationship with the common people. The commoners fear the outspokenness of the *outsiders* because awareness of "the truth" will make following certain rules very difficult. In turn, the rational outsiders criticize and satirize the power structure, with little hope that the commoners will understand. The strong outsiders have empathy for the plight of the commoners, but not much hope.

Mary Richards, one of the common people, has enough common sense to agree with Goodson's view of the town. "It [the town's code of honesty] is what he [Goodson] called [a sham], to the day of his death, said it right out publically, too."[7] The Richardses know the truth of Goodson's opinion of the town and its ideology, but they are afraid to publicly acknowledge their agreement with Goodson. Mary Richards' husband warns her that Goodson "was hated for it."[8] The Richardses fear this public disapproval.

Although Barclay Goodson is the town's "Socrates," he cannot develop a following. People are afraid to identify with him because he has alienated the town's power structure. Even though the townspeople identify him as the kindest man in the town, the only one capable of aiding a stranger, they cannot like him. Goodson poses a threat to those who conform. He speaks his mind based on his independent judgment of the facts, one that is not controlled by public opinion. He follows his own temperamental impulses and that kind of freedom tends to threaten the common people who wish not to think about their lack of freedom.

Years earlier, Goodson had been falsely accused of warning the Reverend Burgess about a mob on its way to attack him for an act of presumed misconduct of which Burgess was, in fact, innocent. Goodson was later confronted about his alleged role in the episode by a representative of the town. Although lacking any evidence that Goodson warned Burgess, people assumed that Goodson was the only one in town with enough moral strength to warn Burgess and face public disapproval.

Confronted about his alleged role in the incident, Goodson met with the disapproving town's representative Sawisberry and made a fool out of him: "Goodson looked him over, like as if he was hunting for a place on him, that he could despise the most, then he says 'so you are the committee of inquiry are you.' Sawisberry said that was about what he was."[9] Goodson identified the town's authoritarian character. The town had sent a mob after Burgess, and then sent Sawisberry to punish Goodson because he was believed to have foiled the mob. Goodson responded with courage:

> Do you require particulars, or do you reckon a kind of general answer will do? If they [the town] require particulars, tell them to go to hell. I reckon that's general enough. And I'll give you some sane advice, Sawisberry; when you come back for the particulars, fetch a basket to carry the relics of yourself home in.[10]

Until his death, which occurred before the action of this story, Goodson's temperament forced him to ridicule the town's false accusations and rebel against its pressure to conform. He knew it made the townspeople into thoughtless robots who carry out the dictates of public opinion. Goodson had the physical courage and the mental strength to rise above the conformity created by the town's ideology. He had the temperamental strength not to need the approval of the town. His sense of self-approval came from his own independent judgment of the realities in the town.

Goodson is not the only person with a strong enough temperament to oppose public opinion in Hadleyburg. Jack Halliday is described by the narrator of the story as an outsider much like Goodson. "Jack Halliday was the good natured, no account, irreverent fisherman, hunter, boy's friend, stray dog's friends."[11] Halliday clearly has empathy, but his good qualities are not respected by the town. He exists on the fringes of society in Hadleyburg. He is like Huck Finn grown up.

Twain describes Halliday as someone who is aware of the realities in the town. "Halliday who always noticed everything; and always made fun of it, too, no matter what it was. He began to throw out chaffing remarks."[12] Halliday, like Goodson, is not afraid to expose what is being ignored by the townspeople.

By challenging the town's illusions, Halliday gives the townspeople an opportunity to recognize the differences between truth and illusion. He tries to have people look at themselves with some objectivity. "He went diligently about, laughing at the town, individually and in mass."[13] Halliday could be a stand-in for Twain himself, and the town, for the human race. Halliday reflects the truth of human nature to the town: "Halliday carried a cigar box around on a tripod, playing that it was a camera, halted all passers and aimed the thing and said, 'Ready—now look pleasant please,' but not even this capital joke could surprise the dreary faces into any softing."[14] Halliday is aware of the town's miserable psychological state, and he tries to change it by helping the townspeople become aware of their feelings.

There is one other person in Hadleyburg who is like Goodson and Halliday—the Reverend Burgess. He is a fair man, but the townspeople hate him. They believe a false charge against him and years earlier wanted to drive him out of town because of it. They had gathered as a mob to ride him out of town on a rail, but Edward Richards did a decent thing and secretly warned Burgess. Although he managed to remain in his home, Burgess' congregation was taken away and he lives as an exile in his own town.

Because of his temperament, Burgess' response to the town's unwarranted persecution is almost Christ-like. He seems never to complain and remains in the town. He appreciates when Edward Richards helps him and is kind to Richards in return. Burgess accepts the fact that he has been falsely accused and he is not bitter about it.

Later in the story, Burgess is able to empathize with Edward Richards about a public lie Richards has told. Burgess tells a lie of his own to protect Richards and, in a note to Richards, takes moral responsibility for having told the lie. He is an example of a person who is honest by temperament. Ironically, those who have internalized an ideology of honesty cannot recognize one who is truly honest.

Burgess is not a rigid moralist. He judges situations based on his perception of the facts and will make moral decisions that help him avoid the occurrence of needless pain—thus, his technical dishonesty in order to protect Richards. He seems to have truly Christian morals that do not depend on direction from church or society. He seems guided by an inner light.

Goodson, Halliday, and Burgess have temperaments that allow them to refuse the group psychology of Hadleyburg, a psychology supported by the local ideology of honesty and public opinion. These men have the temperamental strength to stand outside the group psychology because they identify it as fraudulent. They are able to withstand public disapproval because they understand that they have acted morally according to their own principles, which differ from the rules of the town's ideology. At the same time, they are not judgmental people and are able to feel empathy for some people in the town.

Edward Richards' temperament is the opposite of that of the group of moral outsiders. He is someone who has internalized the dominant ideology. The most important thing for him is public approval. He is a symbol of the common people in Hadleyburg. His behavior is controlled by the town's group psychology. Richards knows that Burgess is innocent of the charge that the town has leveled against him and secretly warns him about the mob. But Richards is afraid to publicly clear Burgess because he is afraid of receiving the wrath of public opinion for doing so.

Richards confesses his temperamental weakness to his wife: "It is a confession. I am ashamed but I will make it. I was the only man who knew he [Burgess] was innocent. I would have saved him, and—and—well, you know how the town was corrupt ... I hadn't the pluck to do it. It would have turned everybody against me."[15] Richards recognizes that he lacks the courage to face the town's disapproval. He also lacks the strength to do what he knows is moral because he is afraid of becoming an outsider.

Richards is the opposite of Burgess in this regard. Burgess lies later in the story to protect Richards because Burgess, although a minister, makes a decision based on his own independent judgment of a situation. In contrast, Richards cannot face public disapproval, although he knew that by not clearing Burgess, he was violating the town's ideology of honesty. Once Richards tried in a limited way to protect Burgess, he immediately regretted warning him that a mob was on its way to Burgess' house. Richards warning Burgess is consistent with Richards' religion, his ideology of honesty, and a weak, but empathic, side of his own temperament. Richards knows that Burgess is innocent of the charge created by the town. Richards' conscience forced him to warn Burgess, but Richards' fear of public disapproval continues to make him wish that he had not acted honestly. "It scares me, yet, to think of it. I repented of it the minute it was done; and I was even afraid to tell you least your face might betray it to somebody ... but after a few days I saw that no one was going to suspect me, and after that I got to feeling glad I did it."[16]

Twain uses ironic language to describe Richards' wish that he had not done a moral act. Twain uses the word "repent" to indicate that the town's real religion is the need to conform to gain public approval. He seems to be indicating that what appears moral to the town is the act of conformity. In contrast, non-conformity is perceived by the town as immoral.

Richards' behavior illustrates how the common people relate to the ideology of honesty in Hadleyburg. They obey its principles when obeying will get them public approval, but they break its rules when breaking its rules will help them keep public approval. The weakness of Edward Richards' temperament, his fear, causes him to conform to the town's will in whatever form that will appears—ideology, religion or any other expression of it.

Richards feels good about helping Burgess only after he feels certain that the act will not alienate him from public opinion. Also, Richards' wife echoes his feelings: "Yes, I am glad; for really you did owe him [Burgess] that."[17] Mary Richards first reacts to the issue that her husband acted honestly. However, then, like her husband, she indicates how much more important public approval is than the honesty. "But Edward, suppose it should come out yet, some day."[18] Her husband reassures her that their secret is safe because the town believes Goodson warned Burgess.

V. The Relationship Between Temperament and Training

In Hadleyburg, people of weak temperaments like the Richardses live according to the ideology of honesty. In normal times, the town is able to make the common people outwardly conform to the code. It creates the illusion of being an incorruptible town: "Hadleyburg was in reality an incorruptible town.... Also throughout the formative years temptations were kept out of the way of the young people, so that their honesty could have every choice to harden and solidify and become part of their very bone."[19]

Twain shows that the town's honesty is a sham. They dislike Goodson for no cause. They try to unleash mob violence against Burgess, without evidence that he is guilty of any wrongdoing. The real code of public behavior in Hadleyburg is seek public approval: Do what will not get one in trouble with public opinion, and hide what appears to be publicly unpopular.

A stranger who has been offended by the town devises a confidence scheme to show the town's dishonesty to itself. He chooses the Richardses as the people with whom to leave forty thousand in gold coin. The reality is that the gold is counterfeit. However, the Richardses and the town think the money is real and are tricked into acts of dishonesty to gain possession of the treasure.

The stranger leaves a letter with the Richardses. He claims that years earlier, a townsperson did him a great favor by giving him twenty dollars. At the time, the townsperson said some words to the stranger. The words are written on a note in the sealed sack of gold; anyone who can identify the words on the note will prove he is the kind citizen who helped the stranger and that person will be awarded the gold coins.

Richards and his wife consider destroying the letter and taking the cash. This thought is motivated by Richards' temperamental desire for wealth and social status in the community. The stranger has created a conflict between Richards' fearful temperament and his wish to be rich even if it requires acting in a dishonest way.

Richards initially resolves the issue by seeking public approval rather than financial wealth. "When I thought what a stir it would make, and what a compliment it was to Hadleyburg, that a stranger should trust it so."[20] As a result of his training, Richards appears able to overcome the dishonest elements in his own nature and not steal the money. He has been influenced by the local ideology of honesty to do the honest thing and publish the search for the rightful claimant of the money. Richards has a sense of self-approval because he has conformed to a set of rules supported by the town's public opinion. Richards' wife Mary is more aware of the potential conflict between their temperamental drives and internalized ideology. However, at first, Richards denies any conflict: "But Mary, you know how we have been trained all our lives long, like the whole village, till it is absolutely second nature to us to stop not a single moment to think when there is an honest thing to be done."[21] For Edward Richards, the dishonest impulses, his desire for wealth and social status in the town have been temporally driven into his unconscious by his need to be loved by the townspeople.

Mary Richards, who is much more in touch with her desire for the money, identifies the town's ideology as an artificial system:

> Oh I knew it—It's been one everlasting training and training in honesty—honesty shielded, from the very cradle, against every possible temptation and so it's artificial honesty.... I never had shade nor shadow of a doubt of my petrified and indestructible honesty until now—and now under the very first big and real temptation.... it is my belief that this town's honesty is as rotten as mine is; as rotten as yours is. It is a mean town, a hard stingy town and hasn't a virtue in the world, but this honesty, it is so celebrated for and so conceited about.[22]

Mary Richards' view of the influence of ideology is close to that of Twain. She uses phrases similar to those that appear in "What Is Man?," phrases like "petrified honesty." Like Twain, she understands that, for a while, ideology can alienate a weak person from some of his temperamental drives; however, under the right conditions, temptation can create conflict between a person's temperamental impulses and his internalized ideology manifested as conscience.

Mary Richards' speech forecasts the downfall of her husband. The stranger who has introduced the first test of Richards' honesty introduces a second temptation, an even greater one. The stranger "con man" sends a letter to nineteen citizens in the town, including Edward Richards. The letter informs the citizens of the quotation which will allow one to identify himself as the individual who gave the stranger the twenty dollars and therefore gets the reward. The catch is that each citizen will have to lie by declaring that he made the statement and gave the stranger the twenty dollars.

In the letter, the stranger identifies the late Barclay Goodson as having named the person who provided the twenty dollars and tells each recipient of the letter that Goodson would have wanted that person to inherit his cash reward. In addition, each of the nineteen is informed by the letter that he did Goodson a good deed, which is the reason he was chosen to receive the late Goodson's reward. All nineteen are willing to lie to collect the reward. However, Richards is the most conflicted about his lie. This creates so powerful an inner conflict for him that his personality begins to dissolve and he becomes paranoid. In describing Richards' behavior, Twain demonstrates a profound knowledge of paranoid symptoms.

Initially, the stranger's second letter to Richards simultaneously activates Richards' selfishness and conscience:

Now, then, if it was you that did him that service, you are the legitimate heir and entitled to the sack of gold. I know that I can trust to your honor and honesty, for in a citizen of Hadleyburg these ventures are an unfailing inheritance, and so I am going to reveal to you the remark [made by the man who had helped the stranger], well satisfied that if you are not the right man, you will seek and find the right one.[23]

Richards wants to claim the money, but needs to soothe his conscience over telling the lie about having helped the stranger by convincing himself that at least he had really helped Goodson. When his wife asks him what he did for Goodson, he lies to her by telling her that he promised Goodson to keep the good deed a secret. Meanwhile, his conscience forces him to search his memory for any trace of good deeds that he might have done for Goodson. Although his imagination finally leads him to a distorted recollection of having helped Goodson, in fact this memory is complete self-deception.

Based on his distorted recollection, Richards submits his claim to have been the man who gave the stranger the twenty dollars and words of advice. When he does this, he does not realize that the letter he received is part of a "con" created by the stranger to expose all nineteen men who have received the letters. The quote given to them in the letters does not match the quote in the sack of gold. Thus, the town will recognize in their written claims that each of the nineteen is a liar, that each man broke the town's code of honesty.

When the Reverend Burgess reads the first eighteen claims for the money at a public meeting, those at the meeting realize that these eighteen are dishonest men. Richards becomes terrified that his letter will be the nineteenth dishonest claim read and this will lead to his exposure by the confidence man's scheme. This fear begins to unhinge Richards' personality. In anticipation of public humiliation, Richards composes a public confession in his imagination: "...for until now we have never done a wrong thing, but have gone our humble way unreproached. We were very poor, we are old and have no chick nor child to help us; we were sorely tempted and we fell ... make our shame as light to bear as in your charity you can."[24]

In his imagined confession, Richards is pleading for the town to understand his temperamental need for security and forgive his breaking of the code. He is driven by his temperamental fear of loss of approval from the town. He is surprised when the Reverend Burgess, who has read the first eighteen letters aloud, does not read the nineteenth which is Richards' dishonest claim for the money. Richards believes that Burgess has lost his letter and that he no longer needs to fear public exposure.

Richards' wife Mary expresses both of their reactions: "Oh, God bless, we are saved—he has lost ours—I wouldn't give this up for a hundred of those sacks."[25] Thus, Mary and Edward Richards realize that public acceptance is more important than money when they feel threatened. Both suffer from fearful and weak temperaments and cannot face the loss of public approval. Richards accepts public approval for his honesty, although he was not honest. One person identifies him as "the cleanest man in town, the one solitary important citizen in it who didn't try to steal the money."[26] Then the town elects Richards "sole guardian and symbol of the now sacred Hadleyburg tradition with power and right to stand up and look the whole sarcastic world in the face."[27] Richards now has the town's acceptance and the con man's as well. The con man tells the townspeople that he could not tempt Richards, the symbol of the town's true honesty. He rigs another confidence game for the town, but this time one that will bring great financial reward to the Richardses for being incorruptible.

This time, Richards' wife warns him that they are being tempted by the stranger's money to acquiesce in another lie. However, Richards' temperamental hunger for security and wealth leads him to accept the money: "Edward fell—that is, he sat still, sat with a conscience which was not satisfied, but which was overpowered by circumstances."[28] Twain uses circumstances in a very specific way. By circumstances, he means that certain unplanned events that activate specific elements in Richards' temperament. Each level of the stranger's offer creates circumstances that were not previously present. In the absence of these tempting circumstances, Richards is driven by his need to blindly conform to the town's code of honesty. Once the circumstances activate Richards' greed, he is caught in a conflict between his need to be loved for obeying public opinion about honesty and his need to gain wealth through dishonesty. This conflict is so severe for Richards that his personality disintegrates and he loses touch with reality, projecting his own manipulative behavior onto others, believing it is they who are trying to manipulate him to expose his guilt.

Thus, Richards' fear of exposure becomes transformed into distrust. When he receives the reward for being honest from the con man, he fears that the checks are a trap. "I have not the pluck to try to market a check signed with a disastrous name [the con man]. It would be a trap. That man tried to catch me; we escaped somehow or other and now he is trying a new way."[29] He does not worry about actually being dishonest, but fears public exposure if found out.

When Richards then realizes that the checks have been signed by the president of the bank, he is overpowered by his temperamental drive for money. He says, "For me, they are the same as gold." Once again, as soon as Richards believes his lies are hidden, his drive for wealth overpowers his conscience. However, just when Richards starts to feel that he is in no danger of public exposure for his dishonesty, the Reverend Burgess writes him a letter that reveals that Burgess knows of Richards' dishonest claim for the reward money. Burgess' letter explains, "You saved me in a difficult time. I saved you last night. It was at cost of a lie, but I made the sacrifice freely."[30] Burgess expresses an honest individual's view of a lie told. Burgess admits that he has lied, but he knows that the lie was told as an expression of empathy. However, this creates terrible fear in Richards.

By this time, Richards has become so unhinged by his own lies and ambivalence that he cannot comprehend or trust Burgess' loving motivation. When Burgess writes to Richards, "none in the village knows as well as I know how brave and good and noble you are,"[31] Richards interprets the words as sarcasm. Richards has projected his own sense of guilt onto Burgess' words. Richards knows that he betrayed Burgess by failing to clear him of the charges years ago; now Richards reverses the situation by anticipating, incorrectly, that Burgess intends to betray him.

Richards begins to imagine things because of his guilt. He begins to, in Freudian terms, project his guilt onto Burgess and others; he does this by imagining that Burgess wants to expose him to the town. Twain intuitively understood the Freudian idea of projection before Freud explained it as part of paranoia. Richards thus projects his guilt everywhere. Upon going to church, he hears the kind of sermon that he has heard for years, but the sermonizing makes him feel guilty:

> At church the morning sermon was of the usual pattern; it was the same old things said in the same old way; they [the Richardses] had heard them a thousand times and found them innocuous, next to meaningless ... but now it was different; the sermon seemed to bristle with accusations; it seemed aimed straight and specially at people who were concealing deadly sins.[32]

Once again, Richards has projected his own guilt onto the "usual pattern" of the sermon and feels that he is the target of that harmless sermon.

As Richards' personality continues to dissolve, he experiences Burgess more and more as a source of persecution. "And by chance they [the Richardses] caught a glimpse of Mr. Burgess as he turned a corner. He paid no attention to their nod of recognition. He hadn't seen them."[33] Twain then turns to Richards' interpretation of the imagined snub. "What could his conduct mean—oh, a dozen dreadful things. Was it possible that he knew that Richards could have cleared him of guilt in that bygone time and had been silently waiting for a chance to even up accounts."[34] Richards' thought process is becoming more and more disordered. At this point in the story, Burgess does not even know of Richards' betrayal of him, because he is unaware that Richards knew of his innocence.

The couple begins to suspect their servant of betrayal. At home, in their distress they imagine that their servant might have been in the next room listening when Richards revealed the secret to his wife that he knew of Burgess' innocence; next, Richards began to imagine that he heard the swish of a gown at that time. The paranoia is shared by the couple, but Edward Richards' emotional disorganization seems to be its source. The couple continues down the path of paranoia.

> When they were alone again, they began to piece many unrelated things together and get horrible things out of the combination.... Richards was delivered of a sudden gasp.... The note—Burgess' note! Its language was sarcastic. He quoted, "At bottom you cannot respect me, knowing, as you do, of that matter of which I am accused."[35]

Burgess means what he said in the note. He thinks that Richards believes that Burgess did something awful, but that Richards chose to warn him of the mob anyway—out of empathic concern. Richards turns Burgess' honest remark into another projection. Richards believes that Burgess "knows that I know [of Burgess' innocence]."[36] Then he imagines Burgess' motivation as hostile. "You see the ingenuity of the phrasing. It was a trap—and like a trap, I walked into it ... he has exposed us to some already."[37] Richards thinks that Burgess has exposed him to the town.

In fact, both the "con man" and Burgess believe in Richards' honesty. It is Richards who has become convinced of his own dishonesty. He is projecting his need to be exposed, punished, onto others. His imagined confession presented early in the story has evolved into an imagined story of people plotting to expose him. His paranoia is growing more serious.

Once Richards has lost his belief that he can obey the code of honesty, his conscience tells him that he must be punished by public opinion. His worse fear will be realized—public disgrace—and this is how the story ends. Richards finally makes a public confession about his dishonesty, but that confession is driven by his paranoid state. He destroys the checks because they come from "Satan." "I knew they were sent to betray me to sin."[38] Richards ends the story by making a public confession because he fears that Burgess has already exposed him. Richards admits that he has lied because he feels humiliated by Burgess. The narrator announces, "The dying man passed away without knowing that once more he had done Burgess a wrong."[39] Richards dies in the grip of a paranoid fantasy.

While the Richardses are examples of townspeople with timid and conforming, if selfish, temperaments, there are others in Hadleyburg with selfish but also strong temperaments. Examples of these are Harkness and Pinkerton. These men pretend to internalize the code of honesty, but their temperamental drive for power expresses itself through their ability to use the town's ideology of honesty to manipulate the common people who follow the code.

V. The Relationship Between Temperament and Training

The narrator of the story identifies them as the aggressive people who emerge as leaders of society, the authority figures who manipulate the culture to control the common people. They pretend to be respectable but are power-hungry, with little fear or conscience. They are the most economically successful people in Hadleyburg. They are also politicians. The narrator is clear about the positions of power held by Harkness, a doctor, and Pinkerton, a banker.

> Dr. Harkness saw an opportunity here. He was one of the two very rich men of the place and Pinkerton was the other; Harkness was proprietor of a mint, that is to say a popular patent medicine.... Both had appetites for money; each had bought a great tract of land with a purpose; there was going to be a new railway, and each wanted to be in the legislature and help locate the route to his own advantage.[40]

These two share a temperamental need to acquire wealth and other forms of power over others in society. They use the "social training" of the society to acquire wealth, but they do not believe in the principles of the society's codes.

Both Harkness and Pinkerton are caught by the stranger's con game and exposed to the town's people as dishonest, but neither cares for they do not need social approval. They are driven by destructive, aggressive temperamental drives. Of the two, Harkness is the more clever. Even after having been exposed, he finds a way of profiting from the stranger's scheme to expose the town as dishonest. He buys the counterfeit gold coins from the stranger and prints a slogan on them which helps him win his contest against Pinkerton for the legislature.

> Three days before the election each of two thousand voters found himself in possession of a prized memento—one of the renowned bogus double-eagles. Around one of its faces was stamped these words, "The remark I made to the poor stranger was—." Around the other face was stamped these: "Go and reform. [signed] Pinkerton."[41]

Harkness is able to take an example of his own dishonesty, his failure to maintain the code of honesty, and turn it against his political opponent. He uses the code as political advertisement to point out Pinkerton's dishonesty. The town is controlled by the advertisement and elects Harkness to the legislature.

The narrator relates: "Thus the entire remaining refuse of the renowned joke was emptied upon a single head, and with a calamitous effect. It revived the recent vast laugh and concentrated it upon Pinkerton; and Harkness's election was a walkover."[42] Harkness is able to control the masses by giving them a laugh. Characters like Pinkerton and Harkness represent what Twain calls that "vague authority" in society that activates the herd instinct of the common people.

In Hadleyburg, Twain integrates much of his thinking about his theory of personality and derives a working model of society from it. He demonstrates how people basically divide into two categories: those with weak temperaments and those with strong. The weak follow authority and are easily misled by those with strong, destructive, aggressive temperaments. The weak internalize the training, while the aggressive and strong control social training and use it for their own benefit. Those with strong positive characters understand this interaction but, like Henry Thoreau, for the most part seem satisfied to exist on the edges of society. They are content to identify society's illusions without being drawn into the power game played by the strong destructive individuals and the weak common people: the game of authority by the powerful used for selfish purposes, and the herd instinct, the majority's need to conform to rules even when created by destructive authority.

People in each of these groups in Hadleyburg translate their temperamental drives through the available cultural codes and symbols. Each is determined by temperamental drives in social settings. The strong constructive individuals are able to express their honesty by criticizing the faults of the culture. Those of strong destructive temperaments are able to use the culture and its belief systems to establish personal power, and the weak are controlled by the cultural norms or, in the case of the Richardses, emotionally destroyed by internal psychological conflict.

Chapter VI

Race and Temperament
Personality and the Ideology of Race in Pudd'nhead Wilson

In *Pudd'nhead Wilson*,[1] Mark Twain's assault on slavery goes beyond the day-to-day practice of this evil to the ideological underpinnings justifying its existence. Here, Twain identifies racism as an ideology composed of a series of illusions that create a position of domination for one group over another. Twain's clear understanding of racism as a destructive tool used by the dominant group of Whites in Dawson's Landing, the small Missouri town setting of the novel, seems to answer the debate over whether Twain himself was racist. In nineteenth-century America, Twain was one of the first writers, literary or political, to recognize the ideological nature of racism and the social unfairness that ideology created, particularly in the form of slavery.

In *Pudd'nhead Wilson*, Twain's view of racism is presented in two ways: first, through the narrator's satiric observations, which ironically critique the illusions of racism; second, through the view of racism as a destructive force in the novel's social environment, shaping the temperaments of three major characters in harmful ways. Twain pays special attention to the environmental forces of political ideology and religious dogma to demonstrate how these forces influence, but do not negate, the temperaments of the novel's major characters by shaping their personalities and, ultimately, their destinies. In addition, true to his philosophy, Twain identifies random circumstance as providing opportunities for the expression of latent temperamental traits; circumstance interacts with temperament and training to shape the destinies of the major characters in the novel—most notably the characters of Roxy, her son Chambers, and Tom Driscoll.

Roxy, who is only one sixteenth Black, is driven by her intelligent, proud, and strong temperament to rebel against the very slave system that defines her. However, like many slaves, she has internalized the racist ideology of her society, which makes her rebellion half-hearted and ambivalent. Her training conflicts with her temperament, and thus her behavior needs to be explained through the framework of Twain's own psychic model.

Driven by her love for her son, a love rooted in the constitution of her temperament, Roxy rebels against the system of slavery by switching her son Chambers de Valet, who is one thirty-second Black, with Thomas a Becket Driscoll, the son of a slave master. Thus, Chambers is raised as Thomas. This switch alters each of these characters' personality developments by changing the social environment of each child. After the real Thomas becomes "Chambers," the usurper Thomas is trained to be a master of slaves. Thus, Twain structures the novel around a psychological experiment involving his psychological system. He takes two children of different temperaments and switches their environments. He then traces the development of their separate personalities as the result, according to Twain's psychological system, of the interaction of temperament and training.

This interaction is most clearly demonstrated by the development of Roxy's real child Chambers, who is switched with the child of the slave-owning family. Chambers assumes the role of Thomas a Becket Driscoll. As part of this new identity, the new Tom Driscoll is conditioned by the racist ideology of the slave owner's culture. This exposure to racist ideology worsens an already destructive temperament. Unlike his mother, Roxy's child has a selfish, criminal nature. He can live by no principle other than that working to his own advantage. As a result of his temperament, he forms no real attachments, and his nature is further corrupted by the slave-owning culture into which his mother moves him.

The slave-owning culture is supported by another ideology beside racism: the aristocratic code of honor. However, Tom's temperament collides with this code. Throughout the story, this conflict causes him many difficulties because his cowardly, selfish temperament is stronger than the influence of cultural training. As a result, he cannot identify with the principles of aristocratic honor. Forming no class attachments, he is driven by the need to follow only his own selfish impulses. His inability to internalize the aristocratic code of honor causes Tom Driscoll to be alienated from his new family.

Chambers de Valet (originally born Thomas Driscoll) is born with a forgiving, loving, Christ-like temperament. As a result, he can attach to those around him and does not rebel against his enslavement. He internalizes the racist culture and becomes an adjusted slave. Furthermore, after the revelation that he is the real Thomas Driscoll, he cannot detach from the slave culture that he has internalized. Thus, his kind and loving temperament is in harmony with his love of others in the slave community. While he does not love his slave master, the real Driscoll views himself, because of his training, as an inferior being who should be a slave. Thus, he cannot adjust to his position as slave owner because of his temperament and training.

Before Twain demonstrates how culture in the form of "training" shapes the temperament of the main characters in *Pudd'nhead Wilson*, he allows the narrator to present a realistic view of the major social forces comprising the culture of Dawson's Landing. As the narrator focuses on ideology as a shaping force of training, Twain through the narrator expresses a modern understanding of the role of ideology in forming character—modern in that the narrator defines ideology as a system of rules that determine the behavior of a given group in a society. The narrator identifies two ideologies that shape the consciousness of people in the society of Dawson's Landing: aristocratic honor and racism. In each case, the narrator illustrates how these ideologies are composed of illusions that justify the domination of Blacks by Whites and the common Whites by the well-born aristocrats. The narrator is most explicit about his description of the operation of aristocratic honor: "In Missouri a recognized superiority attached to any person who hailed from Old Virginia, and this superiority was exalted to supremacy when a person of such nativity could also prove descent from the First Families of that great Commonwealth."[2] Twain's narrator declares that the first aspect of this belief in aristocratic ideology is the establishment of a platform of social superiority based on birth into a certain class. For Twain, however, establishing superiority as a birthright is an illusion.

Twain finds a link between aristocratic honor and racist ideology. Aristocratic honor is the general ideology that shapes the psychology of the dominant class of Whites in the South. The code of honor, simply put, states that the aristocrat must be ready to meet any challenge to his dominance with courage and violence. Thus, any challenge to White superiority is a challenge to aristocratic honor. Twain refers to the linkage between these two ideologies as Sir Walter's disease, the upholding of outdated chivalric codes by Southern aristocrats that cover the drive for domination with the rationalization of honor.

Twain's narrator explains how these aristocratic beliefs and rules work: "It had its unwritten laws, and they were as clearly defined and as strict as any that could be found among the printed statutes of the land."[3] For Twain, the rules of an ideology such as aristocratic honor organize the social behavior of a particular group. "The F.F.V. [First Families of Virginia—those who trace their ancestry to aristocratic Virginia] was born a gentleman; his highest duty in life was to watch over the great inheritance and keep it unsmirched. He must keep his honor spotless."[4] In this way, the definition of aristocratic honor as the watchdog of traditional inheritance dovetails with the racist ideology that justified slavery. The narrator then develops the idea of how the aristocratic ideology becomes a social script shaping the behavior of its followers: "Those laws were his chart; his course was marked on it; if he swerved from it by so much as half a point of the compass, it meant shipwreck to his honour; that is to say, degradation from his rank as a gentleman."[5] This point suggests that failure to follow this belief leads to exile.

In addition to using ideology as a force responsible for character development in *Pudd'nhead Wilson*, Twain shows how ideology shapes mass psychology by influencing the character development of groups of people. The narrator does this by developing the idea that aristocratic honor and racism work together as complementary belief systems with the same goal to insure the domination of others by the aristocracy and, in the case of Dawson's Landing, the domination of Blacks by aristocratic Whites. As he does with aristocratic honor, the narrator also identifies and ridicules racism as a false belief system that uses illusions written into law to establish the right of Whites to dominate anyone of Black birth, no matter how small the genetic influence. The narrator uses the term "fictions"[6] to signify that these ideological beliefs and rules are based on illusions.

"To all intents and purposes Roxy was as white as anybody, but the one sixteenth of her which was black outvoted the other fifteen parts and made her a negro. She was a slave and salable as such."[7] Here, the narrator identifies the difference between ideological illusion and reality. By the laws of the society, Roxy is a slave because of her "blackness" but in reality she is White, and so the illusion triumphs over the reality. Thus, the point of Twain's satirical comment is that one sixteenth is more than fifteen sixteenths. This kind of math is possible only if one is filtering reality through the racist illusion that the inheritance of genes from a Black ancestor is polluting. Thus, this ideological illusion of racism is the target of Twain's satire.

The narrator is very clear about his view of racist ideology and its extension into law. In describing Roxy's child, the narrator comments: "Her child was thirty-one parts White, and he, too, was a slave and by fiction of law and custom, a negro."[8] The use of "fiction" by the narrator is unmistakable proof of his awareness that the racist ideology behind the laws legitimizing slavery is a fiction, based on illusion, whether sanctioned by law or custom. Racist ideology exists, according to the narrator, to support White domination of Blacks in the society of Dawson's Landing. Again, the narrator is very clear: "They [Blacks] had an unfair time in the battle of Life."[9] This unfairness, of course, is caused by the social acceptance of the illusions of racist ideology.

The illusions of racist ideology and aristocratic honor are mutually reinforcing. The concept of aristocratic honor as a code gives identity to those of the dominant group and justifies their oppression of others. This idea of aristocratic honor as a code justifies the use of violence to halt any challenge to aristocratic privilege, including the privilege of owning slaves. "He [Pembroke Howard] was a fine, brave, majestic creature, a gentleman according to the nicest requirements of the Virginia rule ... an authority on the 'code,' and a man always courteously ready to stand up before you in the field if any act or word of his had seemed doubtful or suspicious to you and explain it with any weapon you might prefer."[10] Twain's satiric attack on aristocratic honor is unmistakable. He suggests that the "honor code" is entirely illusory. Twain argues that a challenge to the holder of aristocratic honor will provoke repressive violence directed at the challenger. The honor code rests on training its holders to risk their lives in the service of making the code the dominating force in the society.

Twain, through the narrator, explains how these ideologies as forces in the environment become internalized by individuals and shape their temperaments. When temperament agrees with the behavioral demands of the "code," then the character experiences no inner conflict. However, when the individual's temperament conflicts with ideological demands, that character is in conflict. According to Twain, these conflicts are always resolved in favor of the character's temperament. Thus, following the ways in which temperament and training conflict or agree is critical in *Pudd'nhead Wilson*.

The slave woman Roxy is perhaps the most conflicted character in the novel. Her temperament is described as powerful and intelligent, but she has internalized the racist ideology of her society, which defines her as less than human. Thus, her temperament is shaped in negative ways and limited by the environmental training. Twain describes Roxy as possessed of an extraordinarily powerful temperament. At various places in the novel, her temperament is described as having "splendid common sense and practical everyday ability."[11] Once, the narrator tells the reader: "Her face was shapely, intelligent and comely—even beautiful. She had an easy, independent carriage—when she was among her own caste—and a high and sassy way withal; but of course, she was meek and humble enough where white people were."[12] This description suggests a conflict between her training, which defines her as inferior to Whites, and her temperament, which is described as having "a masterful attitude ... a majesty and grace."[13] In addition to inborn majesty, other aspects of Roxy's temperament allow her to love others and have empathy. She is well regarded as a result of her work on the riverboat—and she willingly sacrifices herself by returning to slavery to protect her child. In that sense, she is almost Christ-like in her caring for her son. In short, Twain has placed a woman of a loving, noble, commanding temperament into the role of a slave. According to Twain's psychic model, temperament will win over training and, in Roxy's case, it does.

Roxy's temperament triumphs over training in two instances in the novel. First, early in the novel, she is able to see through one of the illusions of racism because of her reason and natural intelligence. Her master has cancelled an order to sell the house slaves "down the river." With the exception of Roxy, all of the slaves who were so threatened feel that their master has been as merciful as a god. "The culprits [slaves] flung themselves prone, in an ecstasy of gratitude and kissed his feet, declaring that they would never forget his goodness and never cease to pray for him as long as they lived. They were sincere, for like a god he had stretched forth his mighty hand and closed the gates of hell against them."[14] This reaction illustrates that these slaves had internalized the oppression to which they had been subjected. The danger of their situation led to their accepting the imposed order as reality. They see the slave master as a god who can condemn them to hell.

Because both slaves and slave master have internalized the same racist ideology, there is no difference in the ways either of them interprets the event which Twain, in contrast, clearly presents as an example of the unfairness of racism. "He [the slave master] knew, himself, that he had done a noble and gracious thing, and was privately well pleased with his magnanimity; and that night he set the incident down in his diary, so that his son might read it in after years and be thereby moved to deeds of gentleness and humanity itself."[15] Twain illustrates how the master's racial ideology determines his perception of reality by filtering it through the illusion of racism.

The slave master Percy Driscoll has interpreted the event through illusions created to justify slavery. However, Roxy does not, as her temperamental strength and reason allow her to perceive the reality of her situation. She is aware that in this situation, the slave master has a terrible power over her son and herself, absolute power that allows him to sell them "down the river" to a miserable existence in Mississippi.

Roxy's temperament forces her to respond to her perception of this reality. She first thinks about killing her child rather than allowing the slave-owning culture to exert such power over him. For Twain, Roxy is able to rebel in such a way because of both the strength of her temperament and her capacity to love the child. "A profound terror had taken possession of her [Roxy]. Her child could grow up and be sold down the river."[16] Rather than allow the slave system to have this power, Roxy contemplates killing him and then committing suicide to join him in heaven. "Oh I got to kill my child, day ain't no yuther way.... oh I got to do it, yo' po Mammy's got to kill you to save you, honey."[17] Twain recognizes that killing one's own child can be an act of love in a world where death is the only escape from slavery. A White person's understanding of this protest against racism and slavery was far ahead of its time.

Roxy's temperamental drives leading to her rebellion against slavery are checked by random circumstance. The character Pudd'nhead Wilson makes a chance comment that one cannot tell the difference between her "Black child" and the slave owner's "White child" without the aid of each baby's clothing. Thus, clothing differentiates between slave and slave master. According to Twain, clothing is simply the mask of class which, in Dawson's Landing, is defined by the illusions of racist ideology.

Now armed with the idea of switching the children's clothing, Roxy understands that this would allow her to also switch the children's fates so that her own child could become Tom Driscoll and Tom Driscoll would become the slave Chambers de Valet. Roxy is more easily able to do this because the "White" child's father pays no attention to him, whereas Roxy, the "Black" parent, is most concerned about sparing her child the horrible destiny of becoming a slave.

Roxy's switch transforms how the racist ideological system of Dawson's Landing defines each child. By changing clothes, the boys' positions and consequent power have changed within the system. Thus, Roxy has gained a victory over ideology. In addition, she has reversed roles; her "Black" child now has power over the "White" child. Roxy can vicariously enjoy this role reversal as she watches the two children grow up.

Roxy faces one problem, however. Her temperamental capacity to love creates a feeling of guilt over the impact her action will have on the "White" child, Thomas Driscoll. She knows that her action is condemning him to a slave's destiny. However, she turns to yet another ideological system that justifies her action in the face of this guilt. Roxy invokes Calvinism to provide God's justification of her action.

Roxy refers to the Calvinistic teachings she has learned in church. As she attends to the White Driscoll infant, soon to be raised as the slave Chambers, Roxy raises a religious question that shows her use of Calvinist thought to trump the system of racist ideology. "What has my po' baby done, tat he couldn't have yo' luck. He hain done nuth'n. God was good to you; why won't he be good to him?"[18] Here, Roxy refers to God's power to predestine all humans, Black or White. In essence, she asks why God has made her child a slave and Tom Driscoll a master. In so doing, Roxy has shifted her focus from racist ideology justifying slavery on genetic grounds to slavery as fate within the framework of Calvinistic predestination. She recognizes the source of her theological education:

> Now I's got it; now I 'member. It was dat ole Nigger preacher dat tole it, de time he come over here fum Illinois en preached in de nigger church. He said

dey ain't nobody kin save his own self—can't do it by faith, can't do it by works, can't do it no way at all. Free grace is de only way en dat don't come from nobody but jus he Lord.... He kin give it to anybody he please—saint or sinner—he don't care ... he select out anybody dat suit him and put anuther one in his place, en make the first one happy for ever en leave t'other one to burn wid Satan.[19]

Thus, Roxy equates her temperamental impulse to switch the babies with God's will acting through her to save her child from a life of slavery.

Twain understands Roxy's problem and her solution to it. Her temperament leads her to rebel against the slave system by changing her child's destiny. However, her temperament also leads her to empathize with the "White" child, whose destiny she alters by switching him to slave status. She turns to her understanding of Calvinism to explain why she does not need to feel guilty about changing the destiny of the "White" Tom Driscoll. According to Calvinism, Roxy believes God has already willed Tom Driscoll's change of status. God's will is also responsible for changing Roxy's son's destiny. Thus, God's will alone moves Roxy's hand, absolving her of guilt.

Roxy's use of Calvinism demonstrates Twain's awareness of how ideologies in a culture interact with an individual's temperament to shape his or her choices. Because of her own experience in slavery, Roxy comprehends that by switching the children, she is dooming the real Tom Driscoll to a painful life as a slave. With her empathic temperament, she needs to rationalize her guilt feelings which grow out of her ability to identify with the White child whose destiny she is changing. Therefore, she utilizes all of the ideological constructs her culture offers to provide such rationalization. She refers to a minister's authority and employs the racist-aristocratic honor ideology of her society. Her position is that her actions of switching the children are justified because her minister said White aristocrats have done a similar act and, according to racist belief, if White aristocrats do it, it must be right. "A preacher said it ... it ain't no sin, 'ca'se White folks done it—yes dey don it; en not only jus common White folks neither, but de biggest quality dey is."[20] Roxy's sense of morality then is drawn from her own society.

Twain demonstrates how Roxy's temperament is modified and shaped by the system of social training presented to her by the society of Dawson's Landing: a system of slavery and racist ideology. However, her temperament based on an emotional predisposition to act in a given way is stronger than her training; in fact, one can argue that Roxy equates her irresistible temperamental drive with Calvinistic predetermination. From Twain's point of view, Roxy's temperament creates the impulse to rebel against the slave system, but she rationalizes that rebellion and its consequences because of the guilt produced by her training and her temperamental capacity to love. In any event, her temperament leads to her altering the slave system, replacing a potential "White" slave master Tom Driscoll with a "Black" one, her own child Chambers.

Although her temperament-driven rebellion succeeds, Roxy is not spared the influence of her social training. She believes in the idea of "Black inferiority" and "White aristocratic superiority." In short, she is torn by the conflict between her temperament and culture. Roxy's temperament also determines her sense of guilt, created by robbing the real Tom Driscoll of his place as slave master and saddling him with a slave's destiny. Roxy's temperament prevents her from feeling any sense of victory from punishing a "White" child. Instead, her inborn capacity to love forces her to recognize that she has damaged Tom Driscoll and she can empathize with his new condition, since she herself is a slave.

Twain explains that while Roxy uses Calvinism to rationalize her rebellion against racist ideology in one place, she falls victim to racist ideology in another. She exhibits the influence of racist ideology in refusing the advances of a suitor because he is too Black: "You is, you black mud-cat! Yah-yah-yah. I got somep'n better to do din social'n wid niggers as black as you is."[21] Twain's awareness of Roxy's internalized prejudice clearly shows his own understanding of how racism works to plant the seeds of inferiority feelings within the victim. In illustrating how racism works, he suggests that the seeds of hatred are planted in one's consciousness through the process of social training.

As Twain demonstrates how this process shapes the thought of both Black and White characters, readers should not confuse Twain's personal belief system with that of fictional characters whose conscious perceptions of race are shaped by the ideology of their own society. Roxy's behavior repeatedly illustrates such conditioning. In yet another example, Twain shows how she identifies her biological child's lack of courage as resulting from his inherited "drop" of negro blood, instead of recognizing that his actions are caused by his individually inherited temperament. "En you refuse to fight a man dat kicked you, stid o' jumpin' at the chance.... It's de nigger in you, dat's what it is. Thirty-one parts o' you is white, en on'y one part nigger, en dat po' little one part is yo' soul."[22] Twain's awareness of Roxy's training, her internalization of the racist's code, reveals his insight into how racism affects its victims by planting feelings of inferiority within their unconscious through social training.

For Twain, Roxy's son's failure to fight is explained not by racial inferiority but by Twain's psychological model of personality development. In his model, each individual inherits a temperament as an event separate from racial inheritance. Temperament, like fingerprints, makes one unique and not, in Twain's words, part of a group. This explains how parents like Pap Finn and Roxy can have children whose temperaments are so markedly different from their own. According to Twain's model, Roxy's son has inherited his unique temperament which accounts for his cowardice. Twain does not explain his character according to racial inheritance since for him, temperamental inheritance, not race, is the dominant force in personality formation. Thus, Twain does not ascribe personality to racial inheritance as Roxy does—or as any racist would.

At another point in her dialogue, Roxy presents an equation between race and personality. Her belief has been determined by her internalized prejudice, although this proves not to be Twain's belief.

> Whatever has come o' you' Essex blood [White inheritance]. En it ain't on'y just Essex blood dat's in you, not by a long shot. My great, great, great gran' father en yo great, great, great, great gran' father was ole Cap'n John Smith, de highest blood dat Ole Virginny ever turned out ... en yet here is you, a slinkin' outta a duel en dis giving our whole line like a ornery low-down hound! Yes, it's de nigger in you.... Ain't nigger enough in him to show in his finger nails.... Yet day's enough to paint his soul.[23]

Roxy does not understand Twain's meaning, that her son's inheritance of temperament is independent of race, and that each individual inherits the stuff of his individuality.

Twain's handling of Roxy's rebellion against slavery offers proof that race in this novel is a cultural illusion. After she switches her "slave" child with the master's child, she observes: "Now who would b'lieve clo'es could go de like o' dat? Dog my cats if it ain't all I kin do to tell t'other from which, let alone his pappy!"[24] In switching the children, Roxy hopes to alter the destiny of her slave child by altering external circumstance. However, she does not realize that her child's destiny is very much determined by the inheritance of his individual temperament. According to Twain, while changing one's social environment can shape his temperament, it does not change it radically. Roxy's biological son has inherited a selfish, criminal, cowardly temperament, one that will in the main determine his personality. Still, Roxy believes that switching her child is giving him the advantages of the training of the slave-owning culture. "With all her splendid common sense and practical everyday ability, Roxy was a doting fool of a mother—and she was also more than this; by the fiction created by herself, he was become her master."[25]

Twain thus details the process of how internalizing racist ideology becomes part of Roxy's consciousness. This process becomes a fixture in her consciousness through the formation of mental habit, then moves into her unconscious. "The necessity of recognizing this relationship outwardly and of perfecting herself in the forms required to express the recognition, had moved her to such diligence and faithfulness in practicing these forms that this exercise soon concreted itself into habit; it became automatic and unconscious."[26]

This brilliantly describes how training in the form of racist ideology becomes internalized and part of character.

Roxy ultimately becomes a victim of her own rebellion against slavery. She comes to perceive her own son as her master:

> The little counterfeit rift of separation between imitation-slave and imitation-master widened and widened and became an abyss and a very real one—and on one side of it stood Roxy, the dupe of her own deceptions and on the other stood her child, no longer a usurper to her, but her accepted and recognized master.[27]

Roxy's treatment, and that of the culture itself, spoil her boy and make him believe he is a deity in relation to Blacks. This training shapes his temperament, which is by inheritance already negative.

Through the vehicle of the narrator, Twain presents a bleak view of the temperament of Roxy's biological son. Called by the name of the child he replaced, Thomas a Becket, this individual is described as "a bad baby, from the very beginning. ...He would cry for nuthing; he would burst into storms of devilish temper without notice...."[28] Twain illustrates how this impulsive, selfish temperament is reinforced by the child's circumstances: "He was indulged in all his caprices...."[29]

This boy's nasty temperament produces a child who is self-centered and fixed on gratifying his every impulse. "What he preferred above all other things was the tongs. This was because his 'father' had forbidden him to have them."[30] His temperament produces in "Tom," Roxy's child, a perverse criminal character, one incapable of living according to rules. Twain then shows how the institution of slavery further accelerates the child's destructive temperament. Through the conditions of the slave culture, Roxy treats her own child—in reality a slave—like a god; this treatment only aggravates his already selfish, arbitrary temperament. "He was her darling, her master, and her deity all in one, and in her worship of him she forgot who she was and who he had been."[31]

Tom is spoiled by Roxy and by the rules of the slave system which grant him the role of master over slaves, an ironically granted power given the facts of his birth. In turn, given his temperament and training as slave master, he mistreats Chambers, the real child of Percy Driscoll, whom Roxy switched with her own child. "In babyhood Tom cuffed and banged and scratched Chambers unrebuked."[32] Twain does not allow the reader to forget that Thomas a Becket's behavior is conditioned by his environment but determined by his temperament. "Tom was fractious, as Roxy called it and overbearing; Chambers was meek.... Tom did his humble comrade these various ill turns partly out of native viciousness...."[33] Tom's cultural influences aggravate an inherited destructive, selfish temperament, instead of modifying it as much as possible.

By the age of nineteen, "Tom was petted and indulged and spoiled."[34] This treatment worsens his destructive temperament, but suits him as a slave master. Thus, basically, his criminal temperament and racist ideology are in harmony. However, there is another belief system connected to slavery which conflicts with an aspect of Tom's temperament. His cowardly nature collides with the gentleman's code of the aristocratic slave-owning culture. Tom refuses to fight a duel with a man who has physically assaulted him. He is temperamentally unable to follow the code of his family, the code of aristocratic honor. Instead, Tom settles the matter in court.

Tom's uncle, Judge Driscoll, tells him that he has violated the code of honor: "You cur! You scum! You vermin! Do you mean to tell me that blood of my race has suffered a blow and crawled to a court of law about it."[35] Tom's lack of courage brings him into direct conflict with the slave-owning culture and strengthens his temperamental detachment. Tom's temperament is even more exposed after his mother Roxy informs him that he is her child and, in reality, a slave, thus identifying him as a "Black" man. Initially stunned by his reversal of status, Tom's temperamental lack of identification with principle allows him to handle this reversal of fortune. After a brief period of disorientation, he reverts to thinking only of his survival through the manipulation of his mother and others in the environment.

At first, Tom accepts the meaning of the Black identity in the Dawson's Landing society. "If he [Tom] met a friend, he found the habit of a lifetime had in some mysterious way vanished—his arm hung limp instead of involuntarily extending the hand for a shake. It was the 'nigger' asserting its humility."[36] Twain places the term "nigger" in quotes because he is using it to identify the designation for Blacks used by the racist White society of the town. Twain understands that this ideology implants a sense of inferiority and impotence within "Blacks." "Tom" dons this sense like a mask and then, because of his temperamental incapacity to attach to his mother or her identified race, removes it like a mask. Ultimately, he thinks about his survival and a strategy to insure it.

Twain uses his concept of training to explain how Tom deals with the knowledge of his slave birth. "For as much a week after that Tom imagined that his character had undergone a pretty radical change. But that was because he did not know himself."[37] Twain notes that Tom "did not know himself" since he does not understand his own detached, criminal temperament nor that temperament does not change radically. Therefore, Tom does not understand that the change in how he perceives his real social status cannot alter his temperament.

Twain explains this reality to the reader: "In several ways his opinions were totally changed and would never go back to what they were before, but the main structure of his character was not changed and could not be changed."[38] Twain is suggesting a separation between Tom's consciousness, represented by his changed opinions, and his unconscious character, shaping influences rooted in an unchanging temperament. Since his temperament determines his behavior, Tom easily returns to his way of acting like a slave owner who is determined by a coward's temperament. "He dropped gradually back into his old frivolous and easy-going ways and conditions of feelings..."[39]

The third major character in the novel is Chambers de Valet, who is born Thomas a Becket before Roxy switches him with her child and makes him a slave. Chambers' temperament is naturally loyal but shaped by the "training" of racist ideology, so he becomes a devoted slave who follows the laws of slavery as well as he can. Twain makes it clear that he is trained to be an obedient slave through the cultural process outlined in his psychological model of mind.

Born to be master, Chambers instead receives the training of a slave. "He [Percy Driscoll] told Chambers that under no provocation whatever was he privileged to lift his hand against his little master."[40] Thus, the master is taught to be the slave, and Tom, Roxy's real son, treats him as an object. "He [Chambers] was Tom's patient target when Tom wanted to do some snowballing but the target couldn't fire back."[41] Twain carefully defines a master-slave relationship according to the racist ideology of the time, specifically the relationship between slave-made-master and master-made-slave. Thus, Twain illustrates that the superiority of the masters is created by cultural training and is not rooted in genuine superiority.

Because Chambers' temperament is described as "patient" and "humble," one can conclude that it is possible for an individual born to be master to have a temperament that allows him to adapt to slavery. Tom's temperament leads him to sell his mother "down the river" to preserve his identity as slave master and to murder Judge Driscoll because he threatens Tom's inheritance. Tom is driven by a corrupt temperament, the opposite of his mother's loving nature. Temperament continues to rule the situation until the character Pudd'nhead Wilson employs the use of reason to defeat him. Through the science of fingerprinting, Wilson identifies Tom as Judge Driscoll's murderer. Thus, his aggressive, unprincipled temperament is controlled by reason. Although Twain's psychic system permits the operation of reason, one character imposes it on another through the use of scientific methodology. Thus, for Twain, reason does not operate that well as an inner force capable of controlling temperament.

The outcome of the story transforms the slave into the master. The community becomes aware that Chambers de Valet is really Thomas a Becket. However, his training as a slave has blended with his loving nature. Following his model, Twain demonstrates how training can shape temperament. Given both temperament and training, the real Thomas a Becket cannot adjust to being a master according to the racist ideology of slavery. "The real heir suddenly found himself rich and free, but in a most embarrassing situation. He could neither read nor write and his speech was the basest dialect of the negro quarter. His gait, his attitudes, his gestures, his bearing, his laugh—all were vulgar and uncouth, his manners were the manners of a slave."[42] Twain traces the influence of training on the formation of the true White heir's temperament. In view of the fusion between his loving temperament and his training as a slave, he can never feel comfortable as a slave master.

Through Chambers' case, Twain illustrates that slave ideology can shape anyone's individual temperament, White or Black. This ideology is a tool that controls the behavior of individuals for the benefit of the dominant group. Chambers has a Christ-like temperament, leading him to love others and bond with the slave community and Roxy, whom he believes to be his natural mother. Even after he realizes how she has changed his life by switching him with her natural child, he remains loyal to her because of his nature. The slave ideology has affected Chambers by making him feel inferior. He has internalized this code and cannot adjust to his new status. "The poor fellow could not endure the terrors of the white man's parlour, and felt at home and at peace nowhere but in the kitchen."[43] As this internalized training blends with Chambers' loving nature, he cannot give up his emotional attachments. This is symbolized in his act of rewarding Roxy with a pension, another loving, Christ-like gesture.

A careful reading of *Pudd'nhead Wilson* reveals how carefully Twain follows his psychic model in constructing his characters. Roxy has inherited a temperament that makes it difficult for her to tolerate slavery, but she has internalized the teachings of slavery and racism. Thus, she feels inferior and identifies with her society's power structure. However, while her temperament leads her to rebel, her training shapes that rebellion. She switches babies so her biological child will be a slave master, allowing her to vicariously enjoy her son's escape from slavery.

Roxy's biological child has inherited a temperament that impedes attachment to others. Selfish and cowardly, he can operate with the slave culture as master, but cannot internalize his family's code of honor since it requires courage that his temperament does not allow. The conflict between his temperament and the aristocratic code results in his inability to adjust to his life. His criminal temperament would allow him to be a slave master, but his family's aristocratic code creates a conflict for him.

The real Thomas a Becket is born into slavery, but his temperament allows him to adjust to slavery in the most constructively human way possible. He internalizes his attachment to the other slaves and his mother as part of his personality. However, this honest identification with the slave culture also creates a conflict for him when he is thrust into the slave-master's role. He remains unhappy because identification and attachment to his slave family have become a permanent part of his personality through training.

According to Twain, for each character, White or Black, the inheritance of temperament is an individual experience. Thus, only individuals, not races, have temperament. The development of that temperament is a result of the training to which it is exposed and the circumstance that determines one's opportunities to express personal temperamental traits. In this sense, Twain is definitely an individualist and his thinking in *Pudd'nhead Wilson* is not racist. He treats each person as an individual who inherits a temperament as unique as his fingerprints.

CHAPTER VII

Religion and Civilization
The Democratic Demagogue *in* Christian Science

During the first part of the twentieth century, Mark Twain and Sigmund Freud independently addressed the question of what psychological causes drive the need for religious belief, and how that belief becomes internalized from the external social environment in a way similar to the internalization of other cultural and political ideologies such as racism and the aristocratic code. Twain attempted to answer this by studying the operation of only one religion, Christian Science. In 1901, he published an article on the subject in *Cosmopolitan* magazine and did further journalistic research for a book-length study, *Christian Science*,[1] that was published in 1907. In contrast to Twain's narrow study of religion in *Christian Science*, Sigmund Freud sought answers to the same questions, but turned his attention to the universal practice of religion by using the principles of psychoanalysis. He published his findings in a number of works, including *The Future of an Illusion, Civilization and Its Discontents,* and *Totem and Taboo.*

Interestingly, both writers reach similar conclusions about some of the psychological needs for religion. Each utilizes his own psychic model of human nature to explain how the psychological needs of the individual for security and protection lead him to accept and internalize religious dogma. Twain's model of the human psyche into temperament, training, and reason mirrors in some ways Freud's id, superego, and ego. Given their parallels, a number of their conclusions about religious belief reached through the use of these models are similar. Their differences stem from variations between the models.

In general, Twain's investigation suggests that the belief system underlying Christian Science, like that of many other religions, resembles the features of political ideology. Each usually has a leader or founder to whom followers surrender their rational judgment because the leaders have promised them protection and/or happiness. Adherents of both religious doctrine and political ideology, according to Twain, internalize the principles, values, and ideals of the leader and his ideology or doctrine, which, in turn, shape the followers' view of the world.

In Twain's view, the parallel between religious dogma and political ideology is important because both operate as social institutions that shape group psychology in a way that renders individual judgment difficult, if not impossible. Much religious or political ideology is based on illusions, the prejudices of those who create the religious dogma or principles of ideology; therefore, internalization of the belief system interferes with the believer's ability to perceive reality without the prejudices of the internalized system. Thus, Twain argues that religious systems, like other instruments of culture, manipulate human nature, primarily in negative ways.

Freud's view of religion both resembles and differs from Twain's. Both see religion as a tool of civilization internalized by the individual. For Freud, religion is stored in the superego component of the mind, while for Twain, it lies in training. Freud argues that religion acts to tame the aggressive aspect of human nature which he labeled id. In contrast, Twain is ambivalent about the civilizing influence of religion. If religious dogma trains people to be loving, then it can have a positive effect in modulating the temperament. However, Twain believes that many religions shape the temperament of the individual in negative ways and have the potential to alienate individuals from positive elements of inborn temperament. In addition, religious institutions tend to divide people into separate groups and encourage the groups to treat each other as enemies.

Both writers agree that much of religious belief is made up of illusions. These are encouraged by civilizations to maintain control and accepted by individuals because of a regressive element in human nature, the wish for protection from an authority figure against the harsh realities of nature. Adopting a psychological point of view of religion, each writer explains how it shapes the human psyche as part of personality formation. Of all the writing addressing these issues, nowhere does Freud present a clearer discussion than in *The Future of an Illusion*,[2] published in 1928, twenty-one years after Twain's study of Christian Science.

As a journalist and satirist, Twain uses rational investigation to identify and expose the illusions utilized by Christian Science, while as a scientist, Freud employs his psychoanalytic theory to analyze the universal human need for religious illusions. In both cases, the writers believe in rationality as a path to reality and as a tool capable of both identifying religious illusions and separating them from the scientific facts they obscure. This trust in reason as a path to the truth provides common ground for Twain the satirist and Freud the scientist.

However, Freud and Twain disagree on the beneficial effects of religious illusions on the human psyche. Freud believes that these religious illusions tame the destructive impulses of the id, while Twain believes that for those who are aggressive and anti-social by temperament, some religious illusions can weaken these destructive impulses. In other cases, for individuals with constructive temperaments, some illusions can alienate those persons from the positive aspects of their natures.

Thus, although Twain and Freud do not exactly agree on the influence of religious illusions, they both draw a parallel between the ways in which religious dogma and political ideology shape human thought. Both religious and political ideas allow groups to be controlled by a select, small group of individuals. This influence occurs as a result of the individual's internalization of this religious dogma or political ideology and, in this way, individual by individual, a group psychology is formed that reflects the ideas of the leader's political or religious philosophy. Since the individual usually absorbs these ideas unconsciously, he is not aware of how powerfully they influence his thinking.

For Twain, religion contributes to shaping the individual's perception of the world, and hence his consciousness of it, by inculcating opinions that are based on the authority of the religion's leaders or dogma. He illustrates this general view in his book *Christian Science* by noting how the followers of Mary Baker Eddy have identified with her as a parent figure and internalized her teachings without testing these beliefs empirically through the use of reason. In so doing, her followers have been reduced to the position of children obeying a parent's authority. In the case of Christian Science, its followers are programmed by the religious dogma created by Mrs. Eddy, dogma that fixes her authoritarian control over them. Twain explains this process of programming by identifying it as training, a component in his psychological model of personality development.

According to Twain's psychological system, training—the impact of the environment on temperamental predisposition—involves more than the influence of external systems of beliefs and values such as religion. Chance and circumstance play a role in determining the opportunity to express temperament. For example, an individual with a temperamental predisposition to lead must have the opportunity to express this trait—an opportunity provided by chance or circumstance. Before one can be influenced by religion, circumstance must expose him to it.

In his study of Christian Science, Twain explains how training, as elements internalized from the environment, shapes the temperaments of those who follow the religion. He illustrates how the members of the religion follow its dogma, which determines their behavior. Because of this influence, followers surrender their own capacities to rationally analyze Christian Science. They "cannot competently examine either a religious plan or a political one. A scattering few of them do examine both—that is they think they do. With the results as when I examine the nebular theory and explain it to myself."[3] For Twain, an internalized religious belief system interferes with the individual's capacity to objectively analyze that system.

Twain believes internalization of religious belief results from acculturation involving many other institutions of society, such as the family. The process is mostly emotional and unconscious for the person receiving the training. "They [Christian Science followers] get a little of it [dogma] through minds, more of it through their feeling."[4] According to Twain, this way of internalizing religion is irrational:

> Environment is the chief thing to be considered when one is proposing to predict the future of Christian Science. It is not the ability to reason that makes the Presbyterian or the Baptist or the Methodist.... it is the environment. If religion were got by reasoning, we should have the extraordinary spectacle of an American family with a Presbyterian in it and a Baptist, a Catholic, ... [a] Presbyterian family does not produce Catholic families or other religious brands, it produces its own kind and not by intellectual means but by association.[5]

Twain further identifies association as an encounter with a determining force found in the environment. This force comes in contact with the individual through circumstance or chance and usually does not involve choice. Twain explains how this process works within the context of the Christian Science family and how the religion is spread by one family in the community to others.

> There are families of Christian Science in every community in America and each family is a factory; each family turns out a Christian Science product at the customary intervals and contributes it to the cause in the only way in which contributions of recruits to churches are ever made ... by the puissant forces of personal contact and association. Each family is an agency for the cause.[6]

Twain's view of how religion is internalized from the external environment is close to Freud's. Each believes the process takes place as a result of a strong identification with an authority figure, an emotional identification that leads to the acceptance of the figure's values and beliefs without much rational analysis. Freud describes this process in terms of the child's identification with the parents. "It is in keeping with the course of human development that external coercion gradually becomes internalized for a special mental agency, man's superego, takes it over and includes it among its commandments. Each child presents this process of transformation to us. Only by that means does it become a moral and social being."[7] For Freud, the internalization of religion is part of the process by which individuals become socialized.

Freud clearly sees the benefit of religion in providing moral rules to help people understand how to live in society. The human drives of aggression and sex tend to be restrained by religious rules, thus civilizing the individual. Freud recognizes that this process often involves a civilized minority imposing civilizing moral rules on the majority. Twain is less optimistic about the role of religion in shaping human nature. He does believe that it can teach positive values such as the Golden Rule of Christ and help socialize those with aggressive temperaments. However, Twain, unlike Freud, is wary of the power created by religious organizations and suggests that the few who direct religions often want to impose their authority over the masses for personal gain. Twain accuses Mary Baker Eddy of this in his analysis of Christian Science. His account warns that the religion is as dangerous for its followers as any cult; it serves the interests of those who control it by programming the followers to obey the leaders.

Twain believes that Mary Baker Eddy uses principles of Christian Science to manipulate her followers so that she can take their money. In fact, he blatantly refers to her as "the queen of frauds" and compares her to a "con artist." As victims of her confidence routine, her religious followers are blinded by the illusions embedded in the faith. They desperately desire the protection these religious illusions offer; moreover, they lack the education to analyze the scientific validity of such promises. Twain directs this charge against most religions, and specifically against Christian Science.

For Twain, the average person's lack of training in how to rationally evaluate religious dogma or ideology makes him or her even more vulnerable to its illusions.

> They [most people] are not capable, for the reason that their minds, however good they may be, are not trained for such examination.... But indeed the truth is almost all men and women of our nation or any other get their religion and their politics where they get their astronomy—entirely at second hand. Being untrained, they are no more able to intelligently examine a dogma or a policy than they are to calculate an eclipse.[8]

By "second hand," Twain means the individual accepts the belief system only through an emotional identification with the leader of the religion. In this sense, the believer is placed in the role of a child.

Like Twain, Freud believes the need for religious belief stems from a regressive need in human nature. Freud too uses his psychological model to identify the human need for religious illusions. "Religion would thus be the universal obsessional neuroses of humanity, like the obsessional neuroses of children, it arose out of the Oedipus Complex, out of the relation to the father.... [Religion] comprises a system of wishful illusions...."[9] For Freud, a human has certain needs related to his conscious or unconscious psychological wishes, which blind the individual to illusions within the religion. Although Freud sees value in the moral principles of religion, he recognizes that these principles are reinforced by supernatural beliefs rooted in the regressive elements of human nature. Science can be the tool that separates these supernatural illusions from reality: "...scientific work is the only road which can lead us to a knowledge of reality outside of ourselves."[10] However, the human need for a regressed relation with an authority figure is rooted in an intrinsic inability of most people to face the hard truths of life. Initially, a child identifies with the parent as a powerful protector armed with magical powers to protect the child against harm. With normal development, the maturing child comes to realize that the parent does not possess these magical powers. However, even in adulthood, this individual retains a need for "the magical parent" to protect against the dangers of nature and, according to Freud, that need leads to the creation of the concept of God, a figure who can control the forces of nature.

> It will be found if we turn our attention to the psychical origin of religious ideas ... the secret of their strength lies in the strength of those wishes [for protection from nature]. As we already know, terrifying impressions of helplessness in childhood aroused the need for protection—for protection through love—which was provided by the father; and the recognition that this helplessness lasts throughout life made it necessary to cling to the existence of a father but this time a more powerful one.[11]

Thus, the individual is willing to follow the principles representative of religion in return for the illusory protection from God.

Twain and Freud share the position that the individual turns to religions like Christian Science in search of a protective parent. For Twain, Mary Baker Eddy capitalizes on this need and on her followers' vulnerability by selling that protection, trading illusions for cash donations to her church:

> The Christian Scientist believes that the Spirit of God (life and love) pervades the universe; that who will so study *Science and Health* (Mary Baker Eddy's Bible) can get from it the secret of how to inhale the transforming air; that to breathe it is to be made anew.[12]

Twain believes this claim is hogwash.

According to Twain, scientific explanation, not religious illusion, can account for the magical claims of Christian Science. He argues that Mrs. Eddy's claims of natural healing are nothing but the normal biological power of the imagination to fix self-induced illness. "How much of the pain and disease in the world are created by the imagination of the sufferer.... Four-fifths."[13] Twain indicts Christian Science for taking credit for this natural process. He believes that Mrs. Eddy utilizes natural healing, a normal biological process, to build a claim of supernatural power for her religious dogma and then uses that dogma to exert control over her followers.

Twain returns to the idea of the con game to explain Mrs. Eddy's motivation. "The dollar is hunted down in all sorts of ways; the Christian Science mother church and Bargain Counter in Boston peddles all kinds of spiritual wares to the faithful, and always on the one condition—cash, cash in advance."[14] Twain explains that Mrs. Eddy offers all this to those who buy her book and follow its principles. In Twain's view, she is offering the illusion of freedom from disease for money and obedience to her teachings. Twain believes that Mary Baker Eddy preys upon her followers' wish fulfillment need.

Twain also focuses on the psychological need of Christian Scientists to imbue their leader with supernatural power. "How long do you think it before it is claimed that Mrs. Eddy is a Redeemer, a Christ and Christ's equal? Already her army of disciples speak of her reverently as 'Our Mother.'"[15] Here, Twain clearly connects the ideas of worship to the regressive need for a parent figure, and unites the psychological need for a parent figure with the need to worship that figure.

> It is inferable, then, that in the near by and by the new Church [Christian Science] will officially rank the Holy Family in the following order:
> 1. Jesus of Nazareth. 1. Our Mother (Mary Baker Eddy)
> 2. The Virgin Mary[16]

While Twain limits his analysis to Christian Science and not religion in general, one can draw an inference from his analysis. He believes that religions overall depend on the deification of a human authority figure.

> That a commonplace person should go climbing aloft and become a God or a half-god or a quarter-god and be worshipped by men of average intelligence is nothing. It has been millions of years since the first of these supernaturals appeared and by the time the last one—in that inconceivable remote future—shall have performed his solemn little high jinks on the stage and closed the business.... [17]

Twain believes that Mary Baker Eddy's followers must see her as divine before they can internalize her teachings. After people have worshipped Mrs. Eddy and internalized Christian Science, individual judgment is lost and they blindly follow her religious ideology. In this sense, the internalization of a religious ideology has the same effect as the internalization of a political ideology: the loss of individual judgment. Twain describes the consequences of internalizing a religious ideology in much the same way he would describe the influence of internalizing a political ideology. In short, both result in blind allegiance.

> When these people [Christian Science followers] talk about Christian Science, ... they do not use their own language but the books [e.g., Mary Baker Eddy's *Science and Health*]. They pour out the book's shadowy incoherences and leave you to find out later they were not originating but merely quoting. They seem to know the book by heart and to revere it as they would a Bible—another Bible, perhaps I ought to say.[18]

In his analysis of religion, Twain also employs his concept of temperament to explain the need of a religious leader to command the obedience of the followers. In Twain's view, the power-seeking temperament of the leader is all important. It drives that individual to use religion to exert his need for control over the masses by inducing the internalization of the leader's illusions in the form of religious dogma. By explaining Mary Baker Eddy's role in the development of Christian Science, Twain demonstrates how a powerful temperament functions in the development of a religion.

> The man born ambitious of power and glory may live long without finding it out, but when the opportunity comes he will know, will strike for the largest thing within the limit of his choices at the time ... but he will not stop with that start; his appetite will come again ... it will at last begin to drawn upon him that what his Napoleon soul wants and was born for, is something away higher he dare not quite know what, but circumstance and opportunity will indicate the direction and he will cut a road through and find out.[19]

Twain applies his idea of a great man's temperament to help him understand Mary Baker Eddy's rise to religious power.

> I think Mrs. Eddy was born with a far-seeing business eye but did not know it; and with a great organizing and executive talent and did not know it, and with a large appetite for power and destruction and did not know it. I think the reason that her make [her temperament] did not show up until middle life was that she had General Grant's luck—circumstance and opportunity did not come her way when she was younger. The qualities that were born in her had to wait for circumstance and opportunity.[20]

Twain chooses the example of Mrs. Eddy to illustrate how the powerful temperament of one individual can lead to the domination of many others. Temperamental drive for power propels the leader to create illusions which the followers internalize as a result of identifying with the leader. Twain then defines the psychological process involved in internalizing those illusions by the masses who follow the teachings of Christian Science:

> From this stage onward—Mrs. Eddy being what she was—the rest of the developmental stages of the growth of Christian Science would follow naturally and inevitably. But if she had been anybody else there would have been a different arrangement of them, with different results. Being the extraordinary person she was, she realized her position and its possibilities; realized the possibilities, and had the daring to use them for all that they were worth ... a splendid dream; and by force of the qualities born in her she is making it come true. These qualities and the capacities growing out of them by the nurturing influence of training.[21]

Thus, Twain identifies her special skill, rooted in her temperament. She possesses "a knowledge of the weaknesses and poverties and docilities of human nature and how to turn them to account which has never been surpassed, if ever equaled."[22]

Aware of one of human nature's basic weaknesses—the need for a strong parent in both childhood and adulthood—Twain feels that Mary Baker Eddy is equally aware of that need and takes advantage of it by fostering a belief in her own divinity. "We have seen what her methods were after she passed the stage where her divine ambassadorship was granted ... in the hearts and minds of her followers."[23] Twain finds that Mrs. Eddy cultivates the idea that she is divine and has supernatural powers to establish control over her followers. Mrs. Eddy is similar to others who have created images of themselves as divine to extend control over the masses.

> In a room in the First Church of Christ, Scientist, there is a museum of objects which have attained to holiness through contact with Mrs. Eddy.... The fitting up of that place as a shrine is not an accident, not a casual unweighted idea; it is imitated from age-old religious custom. In Treves the pilgrim reverently gazes upon the Seamless Robe; and does the same in that other continental church where they keep a duplicate; and does likewise in the Church of the Holy Sepulchre in Jerusalem where memorials of the Crucifixion are preserved; and now by good fortune we have our Holy Chair and things and a market for our adorations nearer home.[24]

Mary Baker Eddy's followers view their leader as divine because of their own need to be dominated by an individual of strong temperament. Twain feared that this need to surrender one's judgment and follow the leadership of a strong individual was rooted in the civilization process, and thus that civilization's institutions often lead to the loss of an independent perception of the world. The inability on the part of Mrs. Eddy's followers to rationally analyze her teachings supports Twain's concept:

> To ask them to examine with a microscope the character of such a benefactor; to ask them to examine it at all; to ask them to look at a blemish which another person believes he has found in it—well, in their place, could you do it? ... They are prejudiced witnesses ... they sincerely believe that Mrs. Eddy's

character is pure and perfect and beautiful, and her history without stain or blot or blemish."[25]

Thus, he means that each person has in a lifetime internalized a series of belief systems and expressed them as opinions. Since these systems are composed of psychologically-needed illusions, each person does not perceive reality but a subjective belief system. However, each person sees this shortcoming only in observing others, not himself.

> That is a simple rule and easy to remember. When I, a thoughtful and unbiased Presbyterian, examine the Koran, I know that beyond any question every Mohammedan is insane; not in all things, but in religious matters. When a thoughtful and unbiased Mohammedan examines the Westminster Catechism, he knows beyond any question I am spiritually insane, because you can never prove anything to a lunatic—for that is part of his insanity and the evidence of it. He cannot prove to me that I am insane for my mind has the same deficit that afflicts him. All Democrats are insane but no one of them knows it; none but the Republicans and Mugwumps know it. All the Republicans are insane but only the Democrats and Mugwumps can perceive it. The rule is perfect: in all matters of opinion, our adversaries are insane.[26]

According to Twain, an individual can recognize that another's belief system is based on emotional identification, but he cannot apply the same rational analysis to his own ideological opinions. Thus, Twain believes that "in disputed matters political and religious, no one man's opinion is worth more than his peer's; and hence it follows that no man's opinion possesses any real value."[27] By real value, Twain means a value established by empirical verification, the reality principle.

Twain does hold some hope that individuals can be trained to apply rational methods to test the validity of evidence or political ideology and religious dogma. He finds support for this hope in the effective use of reason in training individuals to function in technical and professional areas. "Men are usually competent thinkers along the lines of their specialized training only."[28] However, Twain argues that in any "civilized" group, only a few people will be temperamentally suited or experientially shaped to test reason against the validity of religious doctrine.

> In a church assemblage of five hundred persons there will be a man or two whose trained minds can seize upon each detail of a great manufacturing scheme and recognize its value or its lack of it promptly, and can pass the details in intelligent review, section by section ... and probably not one man in the entire lot will be competent to examine, capably, the intricacies of a political or religious scheme, new or old, and deliver a judgement upon it.[29]

Nevertheless, Twain remains optimistic that training in reason can qualify an individual to pass a rational judgment on an ideology, if that person also possesses the right temperament and has not identified with the leader nor internalized the belief system.

Unlike Twain, Freud trusts the civilizing role of religious illusions. Religion in the form of moral rules becomes the weapon of the superego against the antisocial drives of the id. Thus, for Freud, religion allows leaders to civilize the masses by offering them illusions of an all-powerful parent who supports moral behavior. Religion should not be abandoned, according to Freud, until late in the process of civilization. Only by that stage in human history, he hopes, will the ego be well enough developed to control the id.

> The doctrines of religion are not a subject one can quibble about like any other. Our civilization is built upon them and the maintenance of human society is based on the majority of men's believing in the truth of these doctrines. If men are taught that there is no almighty and all-just God, no divine world order and no future life, they will feel exempt from all obligation to obey the precepts of civilization. Everyone will, without inhibition or fear, follow his asocial, egoistic instincts and seek to exercise his power.[30]

Thus, Freud believes that religious doctrine is composed of many necessary illusions. "Countless people find their one consolation in religious doctrine and can only bear with their help."[31] Thus, unlike Twain, Freud finds that religion provides illusions that help humans function in a civilized way as part of a process of controlling their antisocial impulses rooted in the id.

For Freud, powerful leaders protect the civilization that they have built from the masses who do not want to relinquish their instinctual drives. "All is well if these leaders are persons who have risen to the height of mastering their own instinctual wishes. But there is a danger that in order not to lose their influence they may give way to the mass more than it gives way to them, and it therefore seems necessary that they shall be independent of the mass by having means to power at their disposal."[32] Freud distrusts the masses and believes that civilization must be protected against them and their instinctual drives. Thus, he turns to the strong leader who can impose rules leading to a renunciation of instinctual behavior.

Freud is more trusting of leaders who impose civilization, including religious illusion, on the masses. "Thus civilization has to defend against the individual and its regulations, institutions and commands are directed to that task."[33] In contrast to Freud's position on civilization, Twain distrusts the role of leaders and belief systems in civilizing the masses. He feels that the temperamental drive of the average leader causes him to desire control of the masses for his own selfish gratification, not the betterment of mankind. At the same time, the temperament of the average man pushes him in the direction of following the leader and his belief systems. Thus, for Twain, the masses need to be protected against the aggressive temperaments of most leaders, including religious leaders.

Twain views the American civilization of his own time as corrupted and governed by political and religious leaders and their illusions. "My idea of our civilization is that it is a shoddy, poor thing and full of cruelties, vanities, arrogances, meannesses, and hypocrisies."[34] This corrupted civilization is, for Twain, the result of the few controlling the many. He believes that the hope for civilization lies in the development of the self-governing individual—in short, in republican government run by leaders who are motivated by loving temperaments, Christ-like leaders chosen by the people. Twain's hope for a republic that can help people realize the best in their natures is stated in *A Connecticut Yankee at King Arthur's Court*. "There is plenty good enough material for a republic in the most degraded people that ever existed."[35] That material is the side of human nature that allows one to love and identify with the public good as one loves oneself.

According to Twain, however, as long as the masses are governed by selfish leaders and the illusions they create, there is little hope for civilization. Hope can only come from a belief that the average person can recognize that government run from the top through the use of illusion is not necessary. Even Freud speaks of a time when illusions such as religious doctrine will not be necessary for civilization, when they will be replaced by the growth of an individual's reality principles. For Freud, that would take place during a highly developed stage of civilization.

Unlike Freud, Twain does not accept the values of religious or political illusions at any stage in the process of civilization. For Twain, this view becomes clear in his fiction, exemplified by characters who preserve their individuality and judgment by following the truth wherever it leads them. Often, that is away from a civilization controlled by political and religious illusions. In Twain's novels, the characters who remain in society are often misled by its illusions. In a corrupt society, even those with positive temperaments have these temperaments shaped by the social illusions of their civilizations. Thus, they are directed by unrealities and suffer the consequences. In contrast, the rare individual who uses reason to identify these illusions often is separated from society by his or her allegiance to the truth. At best, this individual is forced into an isolated rebellion against the civilization's leaders and their sheep-like followers.

Twain does not believe that all religious teaching is based on illusion. He supports that aspect of it that follows the teaching of Christ's Golden Rule, to love the other as oneself. That aspect of religion also clearly supports Twain's idea of what is necessary for republican government.

CHAPTER VIII

History and Character

Temperament and Training in Two Historical Periods: A Connecticut Yankee at King Arthur's Court

In his book *Christian Science*,[1] Mark Twain described how a strong leader, Mary Baker Eddy, created an ideology, the religion of Christian Science, that blinded its followers to their own abilities to rationally judge her miraculous claims. Although written eighteen years earlier than *Christian Science*, Twain identified a similar theme in his fictional work *A Connecticut Yankee at King Arthur's Court*.[2] In this novel, the church leaders create the ideology of the divine right of kings that alienates the populace from its ability to assess its own self-interest, causing them to blindly follow the dictates of clergy and royalty. Using his main character, Hank Morgan, as spokesman, the novel also provides Twain's analysis of the group process underlying this social phenomenon—a process involving a number of parallels to Freud's principles of group psychology. However, *A Connecticut Yankee*, in addition to addressing these themes of group psychology and the development of ideology, uses Twain's theory of individual developmental psychology in its depiction of character.

In many of his works, Twain employs the separate components of his model of personality to realistically portray the development of character. In novels like *The Adventures of Huckleberry Finn* and *Pudd'nhead Wilson*, Twain skillfully interweaves the dynamics of his psychological theory to demonstrate how the personalities of characters like Huck and Roxy are shaped through the interaction of inborn temperament, cultural training, rational problem-solving, and circumstance. However, in *A Connecticut Yankee at King Arthur's Court*, Twain utilizes these elements of personality more explicitly than in many other of his novels.

In *A Connecticut Yankee*, Twain uses his model of human nature to explain how the main character, Hank Morgan, is shaped by the forces of late-nineteenth century New England culture as these interact with his aggressive temperamental drives. At the outset of the novel, Morgan's inborn temperament has been exposed to and molded by the forces of late-nineteenth century America: democracy, capitalism, Protestantism, and post–Industrial Revolution technology. As a result, he has learned to value individualism, technological understanding, problem-solving reasoning, and economic mobility.

Through the literary device of time travel, Twain then transports Morgan from America to sixth-century Camelot. In so doing, Twain uses history as a laboratory for his theory of personality development. In that laboratory, Morgan's personality—shaped by nineteenth-century American ideals, values, and ideas—is then exposed to the new world of Camelot with a new overlay of culture to interact with his temperament. Here, he encounters monarchy, feudalism, primitive technology, and widespread magical thinking. As a result of these new cultural influences, key shifts take place in how Morgan's temperament expresses itself.

Moving Morgan through history allows Twain to fully illustrate his own model of personality development and to explain its workings by using Morgan as both an example of and spokesman for his theory. Although Morgan is not completely aware of the influence of time travel on his own personality, he is interested in how Camelot's aristocratic ideology, supported by the church, has molded the common people into a group who worships the authority of the aristocracy to the detriment of their own self-interest. He observes that once individuals in Camelot fall prey to group thinking, they tend to lose touch with their individualistic temperamental drives. Using Morgan as his spokesman, Twain develops the idea of how "petrified thinking" in the form of ideology locks people into rigid, scripted patterns of thought and makes them easily controllable by those with power in the society. Those who internalize the ideology of their time lose the ability to rationally test the environment and make independent judgments based on a realistic perception of experience. These people are ruled by the existing ideology.

Morgan understands how the people's loss of ability to make independent judgments leads to a reliance on magical thinking by all levels of society in Camelot. Those in power claim the ability to perform miracles that keep the common people safe and the commoners' belief in this power of royalty and clergy reduces the commoners to a regressive child-like dependency on those who rule them. Twain recognizes that the religious and political leaders take advantage of this dependency by creating illusions that they are controlling the forces of nature as agents of God. Although Morgan does not approve of Camelot's politics, he learns from his observations and takes advantage of a herd instinct among the populace by creating the illusion that he also has magical powers over nature.

Soon after his arrival in Camelot, Morgan is captured by a knight and sentenced to death. While in captivity, he is befriended by the knight's page, Clarence. Clarence understands the public's gullible need for miracles and describes this to Morgan: "It was but a dull lie, a most indifferent invention, but you should have seen them seize it and swallow it, in the frenzy of their fright, as it were salvation sent from heaven; and all the while was I laughing in my sleeve the one moment to see them so cheaply deceived and glorifying God the next."[3] However, although Clarence sees through many contemporary political illusions, he is taken in by Morgan's claim to magical power that leads to Morgan's release from captivity.

Unlike Clarence and the rest of the people in Camelot, Morgan does not believe in magic, but he understands that it can be used to make the common people identify with and follow a strong leader. He observes that the commoners worship King Arthur and have internalized his aristocratic ideology. Morgan argues that the internalization of this aristocratic ideology renders them helpless to assert their own economic and political interests against the ruling aristocrats. His acceptance of the rationalist-scientific culture of nineteenth-century America allows him to perceive the falseness of the ideology of Camelot. He then explains how the cultural indoctrination in Camelot occurs by applying Twain's ideas about the formation of group psychology. Morgan notes how much of an individual's perception of social reality is formed by the system of political ideas internalized by that individual.

Although Morgan is aware of the influence of ideology on others, he does not fully understand how his own exposure to Camelot's cultural forces has shifted the development of his character by reinforcing certain authoritarian tendencies in his own temperament, which had been tempered by the culture of democratic America. Morgan's inherited temperament is one source of deterministic forces in *A Connecticut Yankee*, and the strongest force in the development of his personality. In both cultural worlds, Morgan's reason allows him to develop technology that helps him establish some level of command over others, thereby meeting his temperamental needs.

After arriving in Camelot, Morgan's ability as the cultural outsider to understand social reality through reason gives him an advantage over the residents. At all levels of sixth-century society, the people believe in magical illusions to control nature. Because of the aristocratic ideology of the time, many people in Camelot believe that the royalty and clergy possess supernatural powers granted by God. Thus, the common people accept the authority of the church and aristocracy as an extension of God's power. Once they have internalized this belief, the people are guided by a herd instinct and follow the leaders. As the rational observer, Morgan is able to explain how this group psychology has been created: the people follow the monarchical ideology without using reason to test its claims. Morgan asserts that the use of critical reason would destroy the society because the relationship between leaders and the herd is based on superstitious belief. "There did not seem to be brains enough in the entire nursery, so to speak, to bait a fishhook with, but you didn't seem to mind that after a little, because you soon saw that brains were not needed in a society like that."[4]

Morgan's perceptions of the political and psychological conditions in Camelot are shaped by Twain's three-part model of human nature, a model which Twain has incorporated into Morgan's views. Thus, in applying Twain's model, Morgan understands that the people in Camelot have the capacity to analyze their own cultural environment but have not employed it. Instead, they view the world through the internalized ideology of the time, the divine right of kings and, as such, are reduced to the position of children. "They were a child-like and innocent lot ... ready and willing to listen to anybody else's lie and believe it too."[5]

Morgan further describes the effects of Twain's concept of social training, pointing out that the people of Camelot are imprisoned by the aristocratic ideology they have internalized. "However modified, any kind of aristocracy, however pruned, is rightly an insult, but if you are born and brought under that sort of arrangement you probably never find it out for yourself and don't believe it when somebody else tells you."[6] Morgan proceeds to describe how the commoners in Camelot have internalized the monarch as a protective father figure. He identified magical thinking as the key to the ideology of Camelot. He realizes that the church has functioned as a pseudo parent figure and offered the people a belief system involving passive submission in return for the promise of protection against the vicissitudes of nature and eternal happiness in the afterlife.

> But then the church came to the front, with an axe to grind, and she was wise, subtle and knows more than one way to skin a cat—or a nation; she invented divine right of kings ... she preached to the commoner humility, obedience to superiors, the beauty of self-sacrifice ... she introduced heritable ranks and aristocracies and taught all Christian populations of the earth to bow down to them and worship them.[7]

Thus, the church manipulates the people to associate King Arthur's power with that of God and the commoners are led to believe that the king is a vessel for God's power to control nature. For example, "A priest pronounced the words 'they shall lay hands on the sick and they shall recover.' Then the king stroked the ulcers, while the reading continued."[8] In this way, the people are led to accept the illusion that the king's power can protect them against disease. Once the people worship the magical leader, it is only a short step for them to accept an ideology that grants the leader vast political power.

The tradeoff is simple. The people obtain illusory protection from their political and religious leaders and, in turn, the leaders acquire the people's obedience and admiration. In the previous example, Morgan admits that the patient may have recovered, but he believes it is the result of the patient's own psychosomatic power to cure himself that was triggered by the illusion of divine intervention through the king's magical power over nature. Morgan uses the laws of nature to explain the king's power, but the clergy and royalty in Camelot use illusions of magic to distract the people from rational explanations, reducing them to the position of dependent children who rely on the king's authority for protection against nature.

Morgan is an objective observer of this process and explains its reality to the reader. "Would you think that this [the king's intercession] would cure? It certainly did. Any mimicry will cure if the patient's faith is strong in it."[9] Like Twain, Morgan believes that faith healers take credit for what can be explained through natural science. In the case of the patient helped by the king, the identification with the authority figure's magic stimulates the natural process of psychosomatic healing. The aristocrats and clergy of Arthur's time take advantage of the illusion of the authority figure's magical power. They use the illusion of divine power to develop political power over the common people.

Morgan knows that identifying with the king and internalizing his ideology depend on a belief in the king's magical authority. Here, Morgan demonstrates an understanding of group behavior that comes close to Freud's theory of group psychology. Freud uses the model of the strong leader who activates the primitive instinct in the primal horde to obey parental authority and surrender individual adult judgment of reality. In Camelot, once the common people believe that the king is an extension of God, they regress to the level of children who feel protected by the illusion of an all-powerful parent. Thus, Twain depicts the society of Camelot as an extended family. Its spokesman, Morgan, understands that as a child internalizes his parents' belief system, the commoners internalize the belief system of its political and religious leaders.

Morgan identifies the central element in the process of the formation of group psychology in Camelot by using a concept later developed by Freud, "identification with the aggressor." Morgan explains how identification with the aggressor leads the common people to surrender their rights to aristocratic authority figures. This identification with the aggressor occurs because of the common people's internalization of the aristocratic ideology created by the church and royalty in Camelot. "The painful thing observable about all this business is the alacrity with which this repressed community have turned their cruel hands against their own class."[10] According to Morgan, the common people identify with the aristocratic leaders and follow their commands, even though the belief system is damaging to their own well-being. Morgan contrasts the process with nineteenth-century democracy, adding, "And what of greatness and position a person got, he got mainly by achievement, not by birth."[11] He characterizes a democracy by the economic mobility it provides for people and its ability to maintain equality before the law.

Morgan's sense of democracy is derived from his experience in late-nineteenth century New England. Because of his exposure to capitalistic democracy, he stresses the competitive elements of capitalism and omits the democratic trait to identify one's welfare with that of the community. Morgan believes that a democracy must allow for economic mobility, rewards according to merit, not birth, and equality before the law. His view of democracy is strongly colored by the economic liberalism of nineteenth-century America. Because of this American conditioning, Morgan condemns the political structure of Camelot.

Despite his disapproval of Camelot's political structure, Morgan's circumstances and temperament lead him to adapt its magical ideology for his own purpose. First, he employs the superstitious belief system of the people to save his own life. As a result of his capture by a knight named Sir Kay, he is sentenced to be burned at the stake. Because of Morgan's knowledge of the future, he recognizes that an eclipse of the sun will happen on the day of his execution. He warns all the people of Camelot that he is a magician who has the power to blot out the sun forever. Morgan, armed with fore-knowledge of this event, claims the power of nature for himself. In this sense, he imitates the church's use of magical thinking to create personal power over the people. Once the eclipse has begun, the king treats Morgan like a magician who has proven his power over nature: "Now sweep away this creeping night and bring the light and cheer again that all would bless thee."[12] The king suggests that if Morgan uses his magical power to protect his people from the forces of nature, they will worship him.

After Morgan succeeds in escaping his planned execution, he continues to hide his scientific knowledge to gain power for himself. The king is so frightened by Morgan's illusion of controlling nature that he offers Morgan great political power. "Name any terms, reverend sir, even to the halfing of my kingdom."[13] The king himself is acting like one of his subjects by trying to appease Morgan's power over nature.

Once Morgan has convinced the people in Camelot that he can control the sun, he makes an interesting observation. "There was another thing that troubled me a little. Those multitudes began to agitate for another miracle. That was natural."[14] Those who begin to worship Morgan for his supernatural power also identify with him as an all-powerful parent, a kind of God. Morgan says they want "to carry back to their far homes the boast that they had seen the man who could command the sun riding in the heavens."[15] Morgan continues to use his practical knowledge of nature to create illusions of control, reinforcing the belief among the people of Camelot that he can protect or destroy them.

As a result of creating such illusions of power over nature, Morgan is given great political power by the people and King Arthur. Morgan announces, "Inasmuch as I was now the second personage in the kingdom, as far as political power and authority were concerned, much was made of me."[16] Because of his temperamental need to control others, he relishes his power. However, unlike the clergy and royalty in Camelot, he understands that this power rests on the illusions he has created.

In contrast to the people of Camelot, Morgan uses reason to help him understand the political and psychological realities of their society. However, he cannot apply that reason to himself to understand his own internal contradictions. Morgan's conflict results from his democratic conditioning manifested in his conscience and his temperamental drive for power and dominance. Because of his democratic training, part of him empathizes with the suffering inflicted on the masses by the church and royalty in Camelot. He sees that they are exploited by the very authority figures they worship and trust. "As if they [the people] had any more occasion to love and honour King and Church and noble than a slave has to love and honour the lash."[17]

Nevertheless, his temperament leads him to relish power and look down on the exploited commoners as herd-like animals who need a strong leader, such as himself, to lead them to democracy. Morgan tries to resolve his conflict by becoming a democratic demagogue, a despotic leader with socially desirable democratic goals.

In creating Morgan, Twain demonstrates the emergence of the archetypal political leader, who is driven by a sense of personal destiny, a will to dominate originating in personal temperament. In search of this dominance over others, the leader creates illusions of great power that compel people to identify with him. Ultimately, the identification takes place because of their regressed need for a strong parent figure. Once the common people have identified the leader as having magical powers, they submit to the leader as a child would to a dominant parent.

Twain uses Morgan's experience in Camelot as a case study of the rise of a political leader driven by temperamental need for power. Ironically, when

Morgan first arrived in Camelot, he did not know if he was in a new historical period or a mental asylum. However, he was aware of being in a new political environment. In this new situation, he expresses his temperamental need to dominate.

> One thing at a time, is my motto—and just lay that thing for all it is worth, even if it's only two pair and a jack. I made up my mind to two things; if it was still the nineteenth century and I was among lunatics and couldn't get away, I would presently boss the asylum or know the reason why; and if on the other hand it really was the sixth century all right, I didn't want any softer thing; I would boss the whole country inside of three months.[18]

Morgan needs to politically control people. In Camelot, he has escaped the limitations of democratic capitalistic culture and been transported to an authoritarian culture organized by an aristocratic ideology. "I was fast getting adjusted to my situation and circumstances."[19] Twain uses the twin terms "situation" and "circumstances" to alert the reader to the fact that Morgan's personality is being reshaped by his exposure to a new "training" provided by the new culture and a new fate created by "circumstance." Situation and circumstance play an important role in Twain's view of character formation and its relationship to an individual's destiny.

Morgan himself comments on the significance of the change of environment. "For a time, I used to wake up mornings and smile at my 'dream' and listen for the Colt's factory whistle; but that sort of thing played itself out, and at last I was fully able to realize that I was actually living in the sixth century."[20] Morgan identifies the new culture of Camelot as suiting his temperamental drives more than the culture of America. "After that, I was just as much at home in that century as I would have been in any other and as for preference, I wouldn't have traded it for the twentieth."[21] He explains why he prefers his new culture. "Look at the opportunities here for a man of knowledge, brains, pluck and enterprise to sail in and grow up with the country. The grandest field that ever was, and all my own; not a competitor; not a man who wasn't a baby to me in acquirements and capacities."[22] He recognizes that his power-driven temperament was limited in nineteenth-century America. "Whereas what would I want to be in the twentieth century. I should be foreman of a factory, that is about all; and could drag a seine down street any day and catch a hundred better men than myself."[23]

In America, Morgan's power-driven temperament had expressed itself through capitalism; it has been limited by the rules of corporate structure and the profit motive. He was a foreman in a factory supervising two thousand men. By contrast, in Camelot, Morgan can express his temperament through an authoritarian political system organized by an aristocratic ideology. This political system places very few limits on those who can establish power over the common people. Morgan begins to understand that his inherited temperament was in conflict with the democratic culture of America. He resented having been one of many. In his new world, he proclaims, "I was no shadow of a king; I was the substance. ... my power was colossal. I was a unique."[24] Morgan's temperamental drive for power encounters one huge obstacle—the aristocracy of Camelot—and he becomes aware that his will to power is limited by having been born a commoner. Morgan perceives that the aristocratic ideology in Camelot prevents the people from fully recognizing him as a great leader because he was not born into aristocracy and lacks a title.

Morgan uses Twain's model of human nature to explain how ideology in Camelot keeps the people from worshiping him as intensely as they do the aristocracy. "Inherited ideas are a curious thing, and interesting to observe and examine. I had mine, the king and his people had theirs. In both cases, they flowed in ruts worn deep by time and habit and the man who should have proposed to divert them by reason and argument would have a long contract on his hands."[25] The people cannot worship him fully because of their training. Because of the aristocratic ideology, his birth limits his wish for absolute power.

In explaining his situation in Camelot, Morgan becomes Twain's spokesman, again describing how Twain's idea of "training" shapes the consciousness of people through the internalization of a given political ideology. He laments that the aristocratic ideology of Arthur's England limits his temperamental drive for power. While on one level Morgan has achieved much power through his control of natural phenomena like the eclipse, that power is limited by Camelot's aristocratic ideology. "I was not even respected. I had no pedigree, no inherited title; so in the king's and nobles' eyes, I was mere dirt; the people regarded me with wonder and awe, but there was no reverence mixed with it; through the force of inherited ideas they were not able to conceive of anything being entitled to that, except pedigree and lordship."[26] This ideology of Camelot limits Morgan's drive for power.

Morgan is caught between two aspects of the aristocratic ideology. His aggressive temperament has been freed by his transition to its undemocratic culture, but the aristocratic ideology of that culture limits his will to power to the role of a court magician. Furthermore, Morgan becomes conscious of yet another conflict: his temperamental drive for power is blocked in another direction. The democratic training he received in America has been internalized as a democratic conscience, making him feel guilty about wishing to exercise arbitrary power over the people of Camelot. "I had inherited the idea that human daws who can consent to masquerade in the peacock shams of inherited dignities and unearned titles are no good but to be laughed at."[27]

Morgan's dilemma is clear. His temperament drives him to wish for aristocratic reverence while his training makes him ridicule such power.

Morgan is correct; he does carry a democratic conscience as part of his psychology. Because of his temperament, he envies the position of the aristocracy in Camelot, but his democratic conscience leads him to hate the arbitrary use of that position to suppress the people. Morgan realizes that all of the people in Camelot are crippled by the very aristocratic ideology they have internalized. This ideology determines the political behavior of both the dominant aristocracy and the exploited common people. He identifies the political cruelty of the time as coming from its ideological script. One can observe the impact of Morgan's democratic conscience in certain situations. For example, when visiting the dungeon of Morgan DeFey, the king's sister, Hank Morgan sees people imprisoned unfairly. "It was the stubborn unreasoning of the time. It was useless to argue with her. Arguments have no chance against petrified training."[28] "Petrified training" has been Twain's phrase for ideological determinism. Morgan attributes the injustice of the time to the ideology that determines Morgan DeFey's views: "Her training was everybody's."[29] Morgan seems to understand that training can alienate a person from his ability to render individual judgment, once that person has been indoctrinated by a group psychology created by the dominant political ideology: "Oh it was no use to waste sense on her. Training, training is everything."[30] By this, Morgan means that training is the principal medium through which temperament can be expressed.

Morgan recognizes that the training of Morgan DeFey's time has intensified her temperamental aggressiveness, thus determining her cruel and sadistic behavior. As an aristocrat, she feels that her aggressive impulses are justified by her position. However, Morgan does not fully recognize the impact of training on his own behavior. He cannot see that his own aggressive temperament has been shaped by the democratic training that he experienced in nineteenth-century America. It is his democratic conscience that leads him to identify with the exploited common people in Morgan DeFey's prison.

Morgan's democratic conscience eventually drives him to take action. "I had had enough of this place by this time and wanted to leave but I couldn't because I had something on my mind that my conscience kept prodding me about and wouldn't let me forget."[31] Morgan identifies the goal of his conscience: "I set forty seven prisoners loose out of those awful rat holes."[32] Morgan now senses that his democratic conscience creates an internal conflict for him. "There is no real difference between a conscience and an anvil—I mean for comfort. I have noticed it a thousand times. And you could dissolve an anvil with acid, when you couldn't stand it any longer, but there isn't any way that you can work off a conscience."[33] Morgan's view of his conscience is similar to Huck Finn's struggle with his conscience, with one major difference: while Huck has internalized a slave owner's ideology, his loving temperament overcomes his training. For Morgan, the conflict is caused by a clash between a democratic conscience and his domineering temperament. His temperament makes him complain about his democratic conscience.

At times, Morgan seems to be aware of his domineering temperamental drives, comparing himself to Robinson Crusoe, a person driven by a sense of destiny to build a version of the society he has left behind. Also like Crusoe, he uses an advanced sense of technology to conjure a sense of magical power among those he wishes to reform. "I was just another Robinson Crusoe cast away on an uninhabited island with no society but some more or less tame animals and if I wanted to make life bearable I must do as he did—invent, contrive, create, reorganize things, set brain and hand to work and keep them busy. Well, that was in my line."[34] Morgan suggests he is aware that his identification with Crusoe is based on a temperamental similarity: Both feel superior to the humans that they want to lead; both feel like outsiders who use scientific knowledge to establish superiority over those in whose society they find themselves. Crusoe imposes British civilization on his island and fuses his sense of identity with his project. In like manner, Morgan identifies himself with his democratic project in Camelot. Yet, this identification creates a conflict for Morgan because he wants to create a democratic society which ultimately will limit his temperamental drive for authoritarian control of that society.

The conflict between Morgan's aggressive temperament and his democratic training is symbolized by the title a blacksmith gives Morgan in Camelot: "The Boss." This title, recognized by the common people, endows Morgan with a sense of being special. Morgan explains how he received the title and what it means to him. "This title fell casually from the lips of a blacksmith one day, in a village, was caught up as a happy thought and tossed from mouth to mouth with a laugh and an affirmative vote; in ten days it had swept the kingdom and was become as familiar as the king's name."[35]

The title in fact has a dual message. As Morgan explains, "The title, translated into modern speech, would be the boss. Elected by the nation, that suited me and it was a pretty high title. There were very few 'the's' and I was one. If you spoke of the duke or the earl or the bishop, how could anyone tell which one you meant. But if you spoke of the king or the queen or the boss, it was different."[36] Morgan's drive for equality with royalty rather than with the people is obvious. Still, he wants to be identified as an individual whose great power is bestowed by the people. Again, he is caught between his temperamental drive for superiority and his democratic training.

Morgan's drive to establish two contradictory goals—absolute power and democratic leadership—may reveal Twain's opinion of nineteenth-century American democracy. Morgan's need to see himself at the head of a democratic machine may explain why Twain chose the term "Boss" for Morgan. By the time of *A Connecticut Yankee*, "Boss" was already a term designating the corruption of the democratic process by a political machine.

Morgan recognizes his need to lead the masses, but he soothes his democratic conscience by planning to create a democracy in Camelot. He expresses this need for power and for that power to be endorsed by the people: "to be vested with enormous authority is a fine thing but to have the onlooking world consent to it is finer."[37] However, he believes that to obtain that public consent, he must, once again, use the illusion of magic to appeal to the herd instinct of the masses. The high point of demonstrating his magical power is by defeating Merlin. Morgan destroys Merlin's tower through the use of scientific means, but pretends to have employed magic to destroy it. Morgan is aware of his use of this device to gain his political control. "The tower episode solidified my power and made it impregnable."[38]

Morgan has a temperamental need to destroy the old aristocratic order in Camelot because that order stands between him and his goal of establishing his rule over the country. He wishes to replace the aristocracy with a democratic order for two reasons. It satisfies his democratic conscience at the same time that it allows him to lead a democratic revolution. Leading the revolution meets his temperamental need for authoritarian power, while the revolutionary goal of improving the commoners' lives allows him to comply with his democratic training.

> That most of King Arthur's British nation were slaves, pure and simple ... the truth was, the nation as a body was in the world for one object, and one only: to grovel before king and church and noble; to slave for them, sweat blood for them, starve that they might be fed, work that they might play ... and for all this, the thanks they got were cuffs and contempt; and so poor spirited were they that they took even this sort of attention as an honor.[39]

Morgan knows that leading a democratic revolution will be difficult. He can understand that the common people have been trained by the aristocratic ideology to accept their political lot. While he views the ideological hold of the nobles and clergy as unfair, he knows the commoners are unaware of any other reality.

Morgan draws a historical generalization from his observation of the exploitation of the commoners. In history, aristocratic classes have created the ideologies that justify the royalty's exploitation of the common people, and the only way to change such psychological brainwashing is through political revolution or evolution. The commoners need to internalize a new belief system. Morgan compares the plight of these people in Camelot with that of the peasants in France before the French Revolution. In both cases, the aristocracy dominated and exploited the people.

Morgan's inborn reason tells him that internalized training can be replaced only as a result of an evolutionary process, not a revolutionary one. His temperament may favor immediate rebellion, but his reason limits his impulse. "I knew that the Jack Slade or Wat Tyler who tries such a thing [revolution] without educating his materials up to revolutionary grade is absolutely certain to get left [fail]."[40]

Morgan's reason tells him that he needs to gradually retrain the common people of Camelot. His mechanical problem-solving ability leads him to the idea that he can fashion a republican machine, which draws on principles of capitalism that reflect Morgan's American training. He wants to rebuild Camelot into a version of American democratic society. His wish to introduce democracy to Camelot is driven by an altruistic imperialism, a wish to recreate Camelot into a version of his own culture. Like Robinson Crusoe, Morgan believes it is his destiny to create this political and social change.

Morgan's temperament allows him to view himself as a man chosen to change the course of history. He has an overwhelming sense of his own authority, and feels, further, that he needs to become "a despot" to effect democratic change. In imposing his will on history, he sees himself as a great leader, like Napoleon. His arbitrary use of power, he feels, is justified by the political ends of his policy, the creation of democracy. As Crusoe identified his own drive for greatness by creating a Calvinistic society in the wilderness, Morgan fuses a sense of his own identity with his plan to create democracy in sixth-century England.

Morgan's democratic dream is consistent with Twain's formula for personality development. Morgan wants to create a democracy because he has internalized the beliefs, values, and ideals of late-nineteenth century America, and is conscience-driven to do this. However, it is his temperamental drives that make him believe he can successfully implement this plan and lead people to accomplish his goal. Finally, his reason leads him to understand that he needs to evolve his democratic plan gradually because the common people of Camelot need retraining. To do this, he attempts to create institutions that foster economic mobility, majority rule, and equality before the law. At the same time, he sees himself as the absolute master of this project. Morgan does not detect the contradiction between his need for despotic authority over the plan and the creation of democratic reform. Thus, although all three components of his personality play a role in shaping his behavior, his temperament dominates.

In a chapter entitled "Beginnings of Civilization," Morgan demonstrates his grandiosity. "I was pretty well satisfied with what I had already accomplished. In various quiet nooks and corners I had the beginnings of all sorts of industries under way—nuclei of future factories, the iron and steel missionaries of my future civilization."[41] Morgan appears god-like as he describes himself as the creator of a new civilization: "I stood with my hand on the cock, so to speak, ready to turn it on and flood the midnight world with light."[42] Furthermore, he creates an interesting metaphor: "the iron and steel missionaries of my future civilization"[43] suggests that the new democracy is a kind of religious movement ushered in by the creation of capitalism. Morgan's vision of democracy is not exactly consistent with more conventional views of classical republics. Rather, it is determined by his capitalistic conditioning and his own temperament.

Because of this temperament, Twain views Morgan as a flawed character. "He is boss of a machine shop; he can build a locomotive or a Colt revolver, he can put up and run a telegraph line, but he's an ignoramus nevertheless."[44] Morgan simply is an ignoramus for Twain because he feels no empathy for others. He is, like Robinson Crusoe, interested only in building little worlds with the help of his own scientific understanding, his reason. He is interested in recreating the world in his own image, distinguished by the American culture which produced that image.

Morgan believes that his motives are pure; he does not suspect his own unconscious drives but states, "unlimited power is the ideal thing when it is in safe hands."[45] He asserts that while this does not apply to other mortals, it does apply to himself. He fools himself into thinking that he can become a despot to usher in democracy, and a true democratic leader once the democracy is born. As he says, "My works showed what a despot could do."[46] However, he is not aware that his temperament conflicts with the role of a true democratic leader.

Morgan's drive for democratically sanctioned power is blocked by the clergy and aristocracy. As a result, he is rejected by the majority of people in Camelot. However, Morgan does not understand that his real goal is the establishment of his own power. Democracy is not as important to Morgan as is his need to govern as the absolute leader of that democracy. By the end of the novel, Morgan's temperamental drive for power becomes clear. Although the people have chosen not to follow his leadership, he does not accept their decision because he rationalizes that the masses have been ideologically brainwashed.

> Ah, what a donkey I was! Toward the end of the week I began to get this large and disenchanting fact through my head—that the mass of the nation had swung their caps and shouted for the republic for about a day, and there an end. The church, the nobles and the gentry then turned one grand, all disapproving frown upon them and shriveled them into sheep. From that moment

the sheep had begun to gather to the fold—that is to say, the camps and offer their valueless lives and their valuable wool to the "righteous cause." Imagine such human muck as this: conceive of this folly.[47]

Morgan misses a simple point about democracy: the majority rules. When that majority does not vote his way, he refers to them as "human muck." He lacks empathy, true understanding of human frailty. When his temperamental drive to lead is challenged, he responds with rage and disdain. Morgan cannot accept the clear voice of the people. "Yes, it was now 'death to the republic' everywhere—not a dissenting voice."[48] Nor can he value the voice of the people. Instead, he belittles them for being driven by the herd instinct.

Morgan uses his capacity for scientific problem-solving to analyze the psychology of his own revolutionary soldiers. He does not know if he can trust them. He seeks signs of weakness in them: "I watched my fifty-two boys narrowly; watched their faces, their walk, their unconscious attitudes: for all of these are a language; a language given us purposely that it may betray us."[49] Morgan wants to "read" the unconscious motivation of the people to help him successfully impose his will. In this case, he wants to be certain that he has successfully trained his fifty-two supporting soldiers, to be sure of their support in the coming battle.

Morgan's powers of observation allow him to formulate a theory of the unconscious that resembles the ones of both Twain and Freud. Morgan comprehends that each individual has a conscious level of thought, but like Twain and Freud, he recognizes that certain deterministic elements register in the unconscious, which are forces symbolically revealed by "the language given us purposely that it may betray us."[50]

Morgan's reading of the unconscious of his fifty-two men allows him to trust them, but he feels betrayed by the remaining people of Camelot who supported republican principles one day and reverted to their aristocratic training the next. Morgan believes that the commoners have reverted to the herd instinct and are being led by the aristocratic masters. As a result, he senses the failure of his democratic project and is enraged. He ultimately lacks an empathic connection to the people of Camelot. Turning his own sense of failure into rage, he directs that rage against the populace.

Towards the end of the novel, Morgan is isolated and murderous, more Captain Ahab than Walt Whitman. Morgan's temperament, his Napoleonic side, takes over. He inspires his remaining soldiers to fight. "While one of these men remains alive, our task is not finished, the war is not ended. We will kill them all (loud and long-continued applause)."[51] Morgan has turned his followers into a killing machine instead of a democratic machine, and armed them with powerful modern technology to carry out his aims.

Morgan's temperament dictates his reaction to his sense of popular betrayal. When the masses reject him, he comments, "Truly this was more than I had bargained for."⁵² Then, his temperamental drive takes over in the battle with the English knights: "Within ten short minutes after we had opened fire, armed resistance was totally annihilated, the campaign was ended, we fifty-four were masters of England."⁵³ He again sounds like Robinson Crusoe who proclaims himself master of his own island universe. Morgan has become the master of England and fulfilled his unconscious goal driven by his temperament. After the battle, however, his democratic conscience returns and he feels some guilt about the carnage that he has created.

In understanding Morgan, one can apply Twain's tripartite model of mind. Morgan's reason allows him to create technology; his "will to power" originating from his inborn aggressive temperament drives him to conquer those who oppose is will; his training provides him with an ideological model to rationalize his temperamental will to power. He uses the rationalization of providing democratic government to justify his own need to dominate the process of creating a democratic system in Camelot. He believes he needs despotic power as a means to a democratic end. As the despotic leader, he will have the power to retrain the people to be receptive to democratic capitalism. He views himself as creating a democratic machine to train the commoners and providing the will to energize the machine.

In America, Morgan's drive to conquer was translated by capitalist training into a drive to climb the corporate ladder. As time passes in sixth-century Camelot, Morgan's temperament is re-conditioned by the authoritarian culture of the land. Thus, his split between democratic training and aggressive temperament becomes less of a conflict as he pursues power for his own ends and not that of democracy. Increasingly, Morgan creates a military technology to impose his own despotic will, and when the common people turn away from democratic government, Morgan feels justified in using his weapons to enforce his will to impose democracy. Of course, the imposition of democracy is a contradiction, but Morgan does not realize this. According to Twain's model of personality, strong temperaments will always be more powerful than training, and Morgan's aggressive temperament is further strengthened by his scientific ability.

By the end, Morgan's aggressive style is obvious; one can see that his need for democratic government has been a means to exercise his despotic temperament. In this sense, Twain portrays Morgan, like Mary Baker Eddy, as an early type of democratic demagogue, a type who would reappear in twentieth-century American literature. Morgan resembles Willie Stark in *All the King's Men* and other figures such as Citizen Kane. The creation of these characters points to a weakness in republican government noted as far back as classical theory, the rise of the tyrant who feeds his own need for power rather than serves the public good. This figure uses democracy as a set of illusions to help him establish his own power and, as such, is a democratic demagogue. In *A Connecticut Yankee,* Twain also uses the character of Morgan to demonstrate how the same person expresses his basic temperamental drives differently in different cultures. In this sense, the novel may be read as "a tale of two cultures."

Chapter IX

Politics, Patriotism, and Leadership

The Democratic Leader in Personal Recollections of Joan of Arc

The work of both Freud and Twain goes beyond individual and group psychology to reflect on the evolution of civilization. In doing so, both writers used their respective theories of personality to fashion a bridge linking the individual to the moral and political structure of his civilization. In essays like "What Is Man?," "Corn-pone Opinions," "The Fall of the Great Republic," "As Regards Patriotism," and "Monarchical and Republican Patriotism," Twain employs his ideas of temperament, training, and reason to explain how leaders in a society develop the rules of civilization to either oppress the masses through authoritarian policies or facilitate the practice of a democratic process. In addition to exploring his psychological ideas in his essays, Twain translated his theory of personality with all of its components into his historical novels such as *The Prince and the Pauper*, *A Connecticut Yankee at King Arthur's Court*, and *Personal Recollections of Joan of Arc*. In each of these works, he utilizes history as a laboratory for the demonstration of his model of human nature: the intervention of historical "circumstance," internalized "training," and inherited "temperament," forces which determine an individual's personal destiny as well as his relationship to the society in which he lives.

In *A Connecticut Yankee*, Twain moves Hank Morgan from one historical period to another, exposing his leader's temperament to the historical and cultural forces of two different periods. In *The Prince and the Pauper*, Prince Edward through an accident exchanges places with a pauper, thus exposing each character to a new set of cultural circumstances. In *Personal Recollections of Joan of Arc*, Joan is a democratic leader and introduces democratic training to monarchical France, inspiring the growth of republican patriotism among the masses. Twain believes that democratic leaders are the hope of humanity. However, he also believes that democratic leaders are rare and that their influence is often overshadowed by more selfish, destructive leaders.

Unlike Twain, who was often skeptical of the role of leaders in society, Freud maintained a generally optimistic view of the leaders of civilization. He believed that leaders tend to be more rational than the masses and, as a result, help citizens develop a social superego and repress the primitive urges of the id. In books like *Group Psychology and the Analysis of the Ego*, *The Future of an Illusion*, *Totem and Taboo*, and *Civilization and Its Discontents*, Freud credits the political leaders of a society with its moral progress.

The differing attitudes of Twain and Freud about the evolution of civilization result from their respective analyses of the political and psychological relationship between leaders and citizens. Each examines this through the lens of his own theory of individual and group psychology. For each, this is based on a familial model in which the masses' identification with the leader underlies the leader's ability to impose the rules of civilization. Both writers see this process as parallel to that occurring within the nuclear family in which the child's need for psychological safety and physical protection motivates his identification with the powerful parent figure. Thus, for both writers, political leaders, like parents, socialize and transform the masses.

Twain's explanation of the relationship between leaders and citizenry is based largely on his personality concepts of temperament and training. Using these concepts, he argues that the temperament of the leader determines how the leader will train the masses in political and moral areas, including the meaning of patriotism—whether in support of an autocratic or democratic social order. For a number of reasons, Twain believed that autocratic or "monarchical" patriotism is the most common because of both the tendency of individuals with aggressive, power-driven temperaments to assume leadership roles and because of the tendency of most individuals to seek physical protection from powerful leaders and the psychological protection of social approval.

Twain believed that the average person's temperament lacked the strength to stand alone when confronted by a person of truly powerful temperament or the pressure of group opinion. Thus, in groups, most individuals will identify with the group leader, internalize his "teachings," and follow uncritically. Twain referred to this as the herd instinct, which he believed is exploited by leaders with aggressive, power-driven temperaments. Such leaders train the masses to be passive and uncritically obedient by creating a series of illusions about the meaning of patriotism—what Twain called "monarchical patriotism."[1]

Citizens who have internalized monarchical patriotism (love of the powerful father/leader) accept unquestioningly their leader's decisions, believing that to do otherwise is unpatriotic and makes them vulnerable to charges of treason. They have been taught to surrender their rational judgment and live according to the ideology, "my country right or wrong."[2] Thus, the average citizen in an authoritarian civilization relinquishes his reason and individuality because of the greater need for the illusion of government protection and social approval.

Twain contrasts this theory of the operation of monarchical patriotism with his concept of republican patriotism. Once again, the masses' view of the meaning of "love of country" derives from the temperament of the leaders—in this case, leaders who seek only the independence of the nation and the welfare of its citizens. In republican patriotism, the masses identify with a leader who trains them directly by example to assert their individuality and apply their reason to decide whether or not particular government policies are appropriate and worthy of their support.

Freud's theory of the role of political leaders in civilizing a society rests on his model of personality structure: id, ego, and superego. As a result, he views the development of civilization as a linear process. He believes that, in the main, leaders tend to be rational and they, in history, have tended to impose rationality on the id-driven masses. In Freudian terms, the leaders represent the ego functions and the masses represent the id. Freud views history as a story of the ego replacing the id. "It is not true that the human mind has undergone no development since the earliest times and that, in contrast to the advance of science and technology, it is the same today as at the beginning of history. ... it is in keeping with the course of human development that external coercion gradually becomes internalized."[3]

Freud claims the leaders of civilization are responsible for this progress of the human race. "One gets the impression that civilization is something which was imposed by a minority which understood how to obtain possession of the means to power and coercion."[4] Freud admits that there are occasional setbacks in the human march toward ego-driven civilization because of leaders who abuse their power, but the general upward direction is a fact for him.

For Twain, history tells a different story. Twain believes that republics exist for only a brief period in history because leaders with loving temperaments are rare and the conditions that support such leaders are difficult to maintain. Twain turns to the fall of Rome to illustrate this point: "The teacher pointed to Rome's stern virtue, incorruptibility, love of liberty and self-sacrificing patriotism—this is when she [Rome] was young and poor."[5] He continues by showing that the development of wealth in Rome corrupted the leaders and they, in turn, corrupted the common people. Thus, Twain illustrates his conviction that the development of civilization is cyclical, depending upon the temperaments of the leaders.

According to Twain, the fall of any republic is caused by internal corruption of the citizens' relationship to their leaders. In his historical fantasy called "The Fall of the Great Republic,"[6] a narrator describes the fall of a mythical republic in the ninth century. The republic was an ideal democracy: "her just and gentle government" respected the liberties of the people and produced "her stainless history."[7] This republic's citizens practiced a "lofty patriotism ... which won our liberties ... and has preserved them unto this day."[8] For Twain, that republican patriotism produces a kind of republican virtue which protects the nation against "the monarchies which hem her in on every side."[9] However, the accumulation of wealth among the few within the society distorts the commitment to the common welfare and facilitates the emergence of selfish, power-driven leaders. "The government was irrevocably in the hands of the prodigiously rich and their hangers-on."[10] Not infrequently, such leaders embark on imperialistic wars to enhance their wealth and status. Initially, citizens may protest such a policy "by an impulse natural to their [democratic] training."[11] Over time, such republican patriotism is transformed by the leadership which creates illusions to justify the imperialistic invasion and other undemocratic policies—"a politician's trick."[12] The leaders induce a new kind of patriotism among the masses, one based on uncritical support of government, "our country right or wrong."[13] Twain's narrator concludes that such a phrase is "an insult to the nation."[14] This corruption produces the alternating cycle of history, moving a nation from a republic to tyranny, "the drift toward monarchy in some form or other."[15]

Twain translates his cyclical vision of history into his historical novel, *Personal Recollections of Joan of Arc*.[16] In this work, Twain illustrates his conviction that the conflict between monarchical leaders and republican leaders produces the history of nations and their civilizations. Joan of Arc and her followers represent the forces of an emerging democratic society and the monarchy and clergy are manifestations of monarchical civilization. While Joan is useful to the monarchy, her republican tendencies are tolerated, but when she emerges as a powerful republican leader, she is betrayed and destroyed by the monarchy and clergy.

In *Joan of Arc*, Twain illustrates his philosophy of history, a belief that the history of nations is determined by a conflict between leaders driven by democratic temperaments and those by authoritarian temperaments. Joan is an example of a leader with a democratic temperament whose impulses bring her into conflict with the forces of royalty and clergy that ruled France during her time. At first, Joan is useful to King Charles, but eventually she begins to lead her followers in a democratic direction; then she is betrayed by the King and his advisors.

Joan's behavior is driven by her temperamental impulses, and Twain illustrates her temperamentally-caused behavior from childhood to adulthood. As a child, Joan acts as a democratic, loving leader in relation to the other children. In a series of experiences, Joan shows fairness, courage, and empathy; she leads the other children in her village.

Joan's first encounter is with a superstitious authoritarian Catholic priest named *Père* Fronte. This priest banishes the wood nymphs worshiped by the children of Joan's village. The children turn to Joan to present their arguments to the priest to reverse his banishment of the wood fairies. The priest, at first, does not take Joan's arguments seriously and, to placate her, admits that his banishing the fairies was a mistake. He foolishly, as part of a game he thinks he is playing, tells Joan he will punish himself. "*Père* Fronte turned away his face for it would have hurt her to see him laugh."[17] He insincerely tells her that he "will put on sackcloth and ashes"[18] unless she grants him forgiveness. In a Christ-like gesture, motivated by her temperamental impulse of empathy for the suffering of another, Joan tell him to forgive himself.

Next, the priest tries to convince Joan that her interests are different from those of her friends who want the "fairies" returned. "He asks her what loss have you suffered by it [the banishment]."[19] The novel's narrator comments on Joan's inborn nature: "Was he never going to learn that things which concerned her own gain and loss she cared nothing about ... to rouse her up was to show her where some other person was going to suffer."[20]

The narrator of the novel, Lewis de Conte, describes Joan's temperamental response to the priest in a way that demonstrates that, even in childhood, she had the temperamental traits that would make her an outstanding republican patriot and leader. She is selfless, empathic, just, and fearless. In addition, she possesses a strong sense of realism and logic and a rebellious nature against those who oppress the masses.

At other times in her childhood, Joan again demonstrates republican traits inherited from her temperament. Unselfishly, she shows great courage in protecting village children against a dangerous madman who has escaped from prison and she offers her own food to a starving man. In Twain's appendix to the novel, he applies his theory of personality explicitly to the character of Joan of Arc, leaving no doubt that Joan's inherited temperament allowed her to defy the monarchical training of her own time and identify her own well-being with that of all members of her society.

In a prologue to the novel, Twain describes the conflict between Joan's temperament and the training of her time. "The character of Joan of Arc is unique.... She was truthful when lying was the common speech ... full of pity when a merciless cruelty was the rule."[21] Here, Twain draws a distinction between Joan's temperamentally-driven republican traits and the climate created by the monarchical training of the day that shaped the personalities of most others. Joan's temperamental traits make her a democratic leader and the novel's narrator argues that these traits motivate her to inspire the masses and redirect French history for a brief time. "She had laid her hand upon the nation, this corpse and it rose and followed her. ... She turned back the tide of the hundred years war."[22] Twain suggests the people's identification with Joan as a republican leader creates a new form of patriotism in France.

> We can comprehend how she could be born with these great qualities but we cannot comprehend how they became immediately usable and effective without the developing forces of a sympathetic atmosphere and the training.... All the rules fail in this girl's case.[23]

She is an exception to the rule of personality formation, an exception that proves the rule. She inspired a nation to drive out the British through the strength of her temperamental patriotism.

Joan's patriotism resembles Twain's description of a republican patriot-leader. The republican patriot, for Twain, introduces the example of individual judgment to a society conditioned by authoritarian rule to unquestioningly accept direction. Joan's patriotism, although inspired by religious voices, resembles the decision of a republican patriot who acts out of a sense of his own perception of reality and conscience. She decides to act out of a sense of inner conviction informed by the facts. "Neither the government nor the entire nation is privileged to dictate to any individual what the forms of patriotism should be."[24]

Twain traces Joan's patriotic leadership to her temperamental traits which allow her to provide a perfect example of republican leadership for her followers. For Twain, the traits on which a republican civilization is built reside in the inborn temperaments of democratic leaders like Joan. Unlike Freud's concept of individuals who force the masses to be civilized, Twain's leaders "train" the masses through providing models of virtue. They do not oppress the instinctual selfishness of the masses, but instead elicit their constructive temperamental traits.

Joan leads the French Army through a demonstration of her inspiring temperamental republican traits. Twain defines the central issue for the republican patriot. She is a rebel with a cause: "a patriot is ... a rebel at the start ... a scarce man and brave and ... scorned. ... when his cause succeeds, the timid join him."[25] As a republican patriot, Joan goes to war to repel the invader and her decision is one that she makes as a result of her own judgment, fed by religious values. In Twain's view, Joan is the perfect republican, a Christ-like patriot. "She loved her home and friends and her village life; she was miserable in the presence of pain and suffering; she was full of compassion ... on the field of her most splendid victory she forgot her triumphs to hold in her lap the head of a dying enemy."[26]

Joan's example of republican leadership allows not only her troops but the masses to identify with her as a leader and internalize her democratic behavior. "For Joan was a mirror in which the lowly hosts of France were clearly reflected."[27] Here, Twain employs his theory of personality to explain how Joan was able to assert a positive influence over the masses by training them in republican behavior through her own example of leadership. The masses respond to her leadership naturally and offer her a symbol of their devotion. "The common people had had leaden medals struck which bore her effigy ... these they wore as charms."[28]

Joan's leadership begins to teach her troops as well as the masses political virtue, and the soldiers internalize her republican ideology of patriotism. The troops recognize Joan is commander in chief and they respect her for her military leadership and courage. On the other hand, they view her as an equal. "It made one shiver, sometimes, to see how calm and easy and comfortable they [her troops] were in her presence."[29] Her republican leadership inspires the troops with a love of France that gives them the spirit to be victorious over the British invaders.

The narrator of the novel explains Joan's success in reviving the fighting spirit of the French. He attributes it to her being of the people. "She was of the people and knew the people." In contrast, the royalty "moved in loftier spheres."[30] Sieur Louis de Conte goes on to recognize that the source of French patriotic energy is the masses and Joan activates that spirit. The narrator compares her positive influence over the masses to that of a virtuous country priest. "Whatever the parish priest believes the flock believes ... they love him, they revere him; he is their unfailing friend, their dauntless protector."[31] Like the priest, Joan is like a good parent. Both her troops and the common people have internalized her democratic message about the value of each human life.

Twain is conscious that the leaders of a civilization appear to the citizens as parents who provide an ideology for the masses to follow, either for good or destructive purposes. In this case, Joan is providing a positive model of leadership for the French masses and introducing a form of democracy into French history. As a result, she threatens the monarchy and clergy who rule the masses through the use of monarchical patriotism.

There are two battles in Twain's *Joan of Arc*, the one between the forces of monarchy and democracy, and the other, the battle between French patriotism and the English invaders. The French monarch and his advisors fear

Joan's democratic leadership as much or more than they do the British invaders. The king's chief advisor, La Tremouille, is afraid of Joan's growing popularity in France and counsels the king to disband her army. "The King disbanded the noble army of heroes ... La Tremouille wore the victor's crown; Joan of Arc, the unconquerable, was conquered."[32]

The main force of Joan's army is disbanded because the monarchy is more concerned about its own control of the masses than it is about its patriotic duty to drive the British out of France. "Joan of Arc, who had never been defeated by the enemy, was defeated by her own king. She had said once that all she feared for her cause was treachery.... Tremouille wanted to keep her where he could balk and hinder her."[33]

Once the king and his advisors gain control of Joan and her troops, France signs a treaty and the king agrees to leave Paris. The king uses the temporary peace to allow him and his court to experience their own pleasures. "Now followed about eight months of drifting ... gay and showy and dancing ... and dissipating court."[34]

Joan continues to battle for France. Although she no longer is the commander of the army, she commands troops and attempts to defend the people of Compeigne against British aggression. During the battle, Joan is captured and taken to the Duke of Burgundy. The monarchy takes this opportunity "to blight her influence and valor-breeding inspiration."[35] The monarchy does not pay the ransom demand of Joan's captors. The narrator indicts the monarchy in France for not providing the ransom to free Joan. Without her leadership, the army reverts to its former condition, lacking inspiration. "With her gone, everything was done ... the army and all of France became what they had been before, mere dead corpses ... incapable of thought, hope, ambition or motion."[36] Because of the monarchy, the army loses the republican patriotism and leadership provided by Joan of Arc.

Like the monarchy, the French church wants to destroy Joan's influence over the common people, so it allows the British to use the French clergy and its courts against Joan. "The church was being used as a blind, a disguise.... If the church could be brought to take her life, or to proclaim her an idolater, a heretic, a witch sent from Satan, not from heaven."[37]

The common people of France attempt to support Joan, but the combined forces of the French monarchy, the church, and the British defeat the popular reaction and Joan is martyred for her true patriotism. "With Joan of Arc, love of country was more than a sentiment—it was a passion. She was the genius of patriotism."[38] Joan's temperament made her a republican leader who did not seek power or glory for herself; she struggled to establish the well-being of her nation.

When Twain looked into the mirror of history, he saw a contest between leaders like Joan who seek the truth and love their fellow man and those who use illusions to dominate others as part of a search for personal advantage. Some contend that Twain's picture of this conflict was too melodramatic, with Joan representing the forces of good and the monarchy and clergy representing the forces of evil. According to Everett Emerson, George Bernard Shaw believed Twain was guilty of oversimplifying this historical conflict to illustrate his own political views. "In 1924 ... George Bernard Shaw ... lamented ... Mark Twain's theory of progress had obstructed an understanding of why Joan was burned and that his lack of appreciation of medieval churches and chivalry made him unqualified to deal with her epoch."[39] Perhaps Shaw was correct in his assessment of Twain's political bias in presenting Joan of Arc as a republican hero. In any event, in *Joan of Arc*, as he would do in *A Connecticut Yankee at King Arthur's Court* and *The Prince and the Pauper*, Twain used history to depict the clashes among temperamentally-driven leaders who compete to win over the masses to their vision of civilization. In this sense, Twain employs his theory of personality to explain why there are so few successful lasting republics while oppressive governments seem to be in the majority.

Perhaps Twain's perception of history as a conflict between leaders who are determined by differing temperaments is an oversimplification. However, one should not dismiss Twain's view too quickly. Most civilizations do fail to serve their citizens because the masses are drawn to power-driven leaders who manipulate them with patriotic illusions that do not serve the well-being of the majority or the nation.

CHAPTER X

Leadership, Ideology, and the Church

Temperament and Religion in the Eseldorf Version of "The Mysterious Stranger"

In his introduction to "The Mysterious Stranger,"[1] William Gibson identifies four versions of the novel that survive in three manuscripts. Gibson labels version A as "The Saint Petersburg Fragment," version B as "The Chronicle of Young Satan," version C as "The Schoolhouse Hill," and version D as "The Mysterious Stranger."[2] I have chosen to analyze the second version, "The Chronicle of Young Satan," because its themes and European setting place it within the context of Twain's historical novels like *A Connecticut Yankee at King Arthur's Court* and *The Personal Recollections of Joan of Arc*. Moreover, in this second version of "The Mysterious Stranger," Twain deals with the deterministic forces of group psychology in ways which tie this version to "What Is Man?" as well as to the historical novels.

"The Chronicle of Young Satan" is set in Eseldorf, Austria, in 1702. Twain's description of this European town and its society reminds one of the societies he created in *A Connecticut Yankee at King Arthur's Court* and *Personal Recollections of Joan of Arc*, worlds organized by the domination of royalty and religious leaders who use superstition to blind and control the common people. Like Freud, Twain has definite ideas about the interaction between leaders and groups and the impact of this dynamic on civilization. However, in contrast to Freud, who is aware of the potential for abuse of power by leaders but views their role as ultimately moving civilization in a positive direction, Twain's more pessimistic position is evident in "The Chronicle."[3]

In an ironic masterstroke, Twain introduces a Satan figure whose primary function is to provide truths about human nature to a young boy named Theodor Fischer. Twain calls this young Satan Philip Traum. Although *traum* is the German word for *dream*, this figure is often realistic about the economics and politics that underpin the civilization of Eseldorf. This supernatural figure identifies for Theodor how the dominant group in the town combines political, economic, and religious illusions into an ideology that justifies its control of the common people. Central to this ideology is what this ironic devil calls the human "moral sense." By it, Traum means the ideological use of morality by the rich and powerful of Eseldorf to justify their exploitation of the poor as part of God's plan for humanity.

Like the Old Man in Twain's "What Is Man?," the young devil in "The Chronicle of Young Satan" defines the deterministic forces which shape human nature. Also like the Old Man, the young devil educates an innocent, Theodor Fischer. However, while the Old Man in "What Is Man?" focuses on individual psychology, the focus of Traum in "The Chronicle" is on group psychology, and his explanations serve to strip away the illusions that had informed Theodor's perception of society. In doing this, the devil relies on "Twainian" concepts of group psychology formation such as the human "herd instinct" and need for a "moral sense," which are often used to dominate the masses by those who have a temperamental need for power.

In a letter to W. D. Howells, Twain admits that his mission in writing "The Chronicle" matches the devil's reason for coming to Eseldorf. "I believe I can make it tell what I think of man and how he is constructed and what a shabby, poor, ridiculous thing he is and how mistaken he is in his estimate of his character and powers and qualities...."[4] In this letter, Twain's stated purpose in "The Chronicle" echoes the young devil's goal of educating Theodor so that the young boy can understand the truths of how human nature operates in the world of Eseldorf. In this sense, the young Satan becomes a spokesperson for Twain's point of view on group psychology.

Before the devil's arrival in Eseldorf, the narrator Theodor describes the civilization of the society as one in which the people have internalized the ideology of church and royalty. As a result, they are like trusting children. "Yes, Austria was far from the world and asleep and our village was in the middle of that sleep.... It drowsed in peace.... It was still the Middle Ages in Austria and promised to remain so forever ... by the mental and spiritual clock, it was still the Age of Faith."[5] This false paradise described by Theodor is really a kind of hell in which the ideology of the clergy and monarchy maintain a group psychology that accepts the exploitation of the common people by those in power. William Gibson identifies the destructive underside of this commomplace ideology governing Eseldorf: "Mob cowardice and mob cruelty, often abetted by the orthodox figure again and again ... eleven girls of Eseldorf are burned together as witches because of 'witch signs' or flea bites on their bodies."[6]

Orthodox clerical and political thought do more than abet this cruelty. The aggressive leaders use it to manipulate the masses into mindless compliance prior to young Satan's arrival. At this time, the common people are more or less dominated by a corrupt, power-driven priest named Father Adolf who controls them through the use of religious and political dogma to serve his own selfish motives. By playing upon the primitive instincts of the masses, Father Adolf is able to create situations that take advantage of the townspeople's fear and greed to build his own personal power and that of the church. This manipulation of the masses in the story occurs because of Father Adolf's power-driven temperament combined with the herd instinct in group psychology. The operation of the herd instinct causes the people of Eseldorf to accept the priest's manipulations as the justified establishment of a moral order.

Father Adolf's behavior is driven by his aggressive temperament which interacts with the group psychology of the average people in the town. These people, who comprise "the masses" of the town, are shaped by the priest's appeal to the herd instinct. Twain believed that this "herd instinct" which allows leaders to manipulate the masses is a central flaw in the psychology of most people. As a group, they need a leader of strong temperament and are therefore vulnerable to the individual who is temperamentally power-driven and corrupt. Theodor describes to the reader the aggressive and devious behavior of Father Adolf. However, early in the story, Theodor does not let himself realize how dishonest and self-serving Father Adolf is.

Father Adolf feeds lies to the townspeople of Eseldorf to magnify his own stature and play on their fears of the unknown. He is an example of Twain's concept of the aggressive leader who distorts the truth to manipulate the herd instinct in his followers. To foster the masses' belief in his own supernatural power, Father Adolf brags that he has confronted the devil and driven him away from the town. He uses this kind of religious mythology to frighten the masses into obeying his oppressive religious leadership. Theodor explains that "There have been better priests in some ways than Father Adolf ... but there was never one in our commune who was held in more solemn and awful respect. This was because he had absolutely no fear of the Devil.... People stood in deep dread of him [Father Adolf] ... for they thought there must be something supernatural about him, else he could not be so bold and so confident."[7]

In one incident, Father Adolf steals the flock of Father Peter, the other priest in the town, by claiming that he heard Father Peter say "that God was all goodness and would find a way to save all his children."[8] This loving, comforting portrayal of God contradicted the conventional church practice of threatening potential sinners with damnation. Although Father Adolf's charge against Father Peter is not corroborated by anyone else, the local bishop turns Father Peter's flock over to Father Adolf, adding to his power.

On other occasions, Father Adolf takes advantage of the masses' fear of natural forces to reinforce his power. Theodor says, "it was fine to see him make procession through the village in plague-time with our saints, relics and candles to the Virgin for her help in abolishing the pest."[9] There is no end to the superstitious beliefs Father Adolf provides his followers to intensify their need for illusions of protection.

Father Adolf uses religion as an ideology that allows him to invoke a fake morality to help him exploit the common people. This includes moralistic threats of eternal damnation to maintain their blind obedience to the rules of the church and monarchy. "Whenever there was a suicide, he [Father Adolf] was active. He was on hand to see that the government did its share and turned the family into the road and confiscated its small belongings and didn't smouch any of the church's share."[10]

Twain analyzes this clerical-political confidence game through the filter of his theory of group psychology. The most influential leaders of Eseldorf, like Father Adolf, are driven by aggressive temperaments which determine their behavior. Because of their temperaments, they lack empathy for the masses and want only to acquire power over them. In turn, the common people are shaped by sheep-like temperaments that cause them to seek powerful figures to protect them against uncertain and supernatural forces. For Twain, this destructive interaction empowers leaders like Father Adolf, so that he has no difficulty defeating decent leaders like Father Peter, a priest capable of Christian traits like empathy and honesty. Twain blames the timid temperaments of the average citizens of the town for their vulnerability to herd behavior. He sees this as a defect in the nature of most people.

Twain identifies the interaction between leaders with strong temperaments and the masses with weak temperaments as a problem in the evolution of civilization. The leaders are like wolves who are driven by instinct or temperament to dominate the sheep-like masses. In his essay "Does Man Love a Lord?"[11] Twain characterizes this dynamic of group psychology as an intrinsic element of civilizations. "As a race, we [common people] do certainly love a lord—let him be a croker or a Duke, or a prize-fighter, or whatever other personage shall chance to be the head of our group."[12] Thus, Twain reduces people in a given society to one of two groups: those whose temperaments cause them to lead and those whose temperaments make them followers. The leaders in Twain's model are like powerful parents and the followers like children who believe that they require protection from the powerful authority figures.

In "Does Man Love a Lord?" Twain continues to describe the psychological relationship between leaders and followers in any civilization. "The human race [the masses] clearly envies a lord's place."[13] This envy leads the common people to lose sight of their own strength. Rather, their awareness of the power of the lord causes them to worship him. "An Englishman (or any other human being) does clearly love a lord (or other conspicuous persons). It includes us all. We love to be noticed by a conspicuous person; we love to be associated by such."[14] The masses' craving for the approval and affection of their leaders causes them to forfeit any rational examination of the quality of that leadership. The average citizens hope that their worship of and obedience to the lord will induce the powerful leader to protect them against the forces of nature and the powerful of other societies. This analysis certainly applies to the political world of Eseldorf.

In Twain's view, the temperaments of the townspeople in Eseldorf and elsewhere lead them to seek the approval of leaders who become like parent figures. Although these political parent figures can potentially lead the masses toward democracy, as Joan of Arc strove to do in *Personal Recollections of Joan of Arc*, Twain believes that such constructive leadership is the rare exception; rather, the leaders in most societies cause much more harm than good. Twain contends that most leaders are motivated only by the desire for personal and material advantage and therefore convince the common people to betray their own interests. Thus, for Twain, the typical leader damages civilization through the undemocratic use of religious and political ideology to manipulate the citizenry.

Unlike Twain's negative view of religion's role in the development of civilized behavior, Freud's *The Future of an Illusion*[15] is a portrayal of religion as a source of illusions that are necessary for the development of the civilization. Freud contends more explicitly than Twain that the leaders of civilization acquire influence over the masses because most people seek parent figures who create the illusion of being able to protect them. However, in contrast to Twain, Freud views this domination by religious authority figures as necessary for the development of civilization because he believes that most leaders use the religious illusions to create more or less rational rules of social behavior for the common people to live by. Furthermore, because the masses identify with the powerful leaders and internalize the leaders' rules and values, they eventually repress their own primitive impulses which are incompatible with life in a civilized society.

In Freud's view, the common people's need for "a father figure" can be used by religious and political leaders to help civilize the masses by facilitating their transition from primitive instinct-driven behavior to rational behavior, a transition from id through superego to ego. "Religion has clearly performed great services for human civilization. It has contributed much toward the training of social instincts."[16] For Freud, civilization needs religion to create moral rules that constitute a social order for the masses to internalize. Freud believes that this socio-moral order based on supernatural illusions is a step toward the development of a civilization based on a rational order.

Twain's view of the role of religion in the development of civilization is more dichotomous than Freud's. For Twain, some civilizations are based on a genuine moral foundation such as "the golden rule" and an egalitarian, democratic ethic. However, he believes that such a truly moral order is a rare situation introduced by leaders with loving temperaments who base their relationship with their followers on truth and genuine concern for the social welfare. In contrast, he believes that civilizations based on religious illusions, while more common, are undemocratic and power-driven. He views the "moral order" based on such illusions as a disguised form of ideology that favors the rich and powerful in a society. Such a false moral system damages any civilization by manipulating the common people to identify with leaders who exploit them rather than to behave in ways that enhance the common welfare of all citizens.

Thus, unlike Freud, Twain does not accept religious illusions as a path leading to rationality through the use of a moral sense to repress primitive instincts. Twain will accept morality as a civilizing tool only if it is a true morality that teaches the individual to identify with the social good as an extension of his own welfare. This is certainly not the case in Eseldorf, where Father Adolf uses religion to build his power and that of the church and monarchy at the expense of the welfare of the townspeople.

Before the devil's arrival in Eseldorf, Theodor's descriptions of the society of Eseldorf and Austria in general leave little doubt that Father Adolf and other political and religious leaders use religion to justify their domination of the common people. In short, there is the illusion of civilization in Eseldorf, but not the reality. "Mainly we are trained to be good Catholics ... to hold the monarch in awful reverence ... regard him as the gracious provider of our daily bread ... ourselves being sent into the world with only one mission, to labor for him, die for him."[17]

Theodor does not understand the injustice that he observes, for, as he says, he has been "trained to be a good Catholic." His training blinds him to the realities that he describes for the reader. Like the other townspeople, Theodor has internalized an ideology which merges religion and politics. In this ideology, the monarch is a representative of God and rules by the divine right of kings. As a result, the common people confuse the Holy Father God with the political father, the king. They are ready to sacrifice anything for the king because they feel that by being loyal to one father figure, they gain both his political protection and the supernatural protection of the other.

In "The Chronicle," Twain introduces the devil Traum to deliver Theodor from his ideological innocence, to help him understand the political realities that underpin the ideological dream which determines the behavior of the townspeople. In this sense, the Satan figure in "The Chronicle" has a similar role to that of the stranger in "The Man Who Corrupted Hadleyburg." The missions of both Traum and the stranger are to identify the forces that shape human nature as manifested in their respective towns. In both settings, these figures employ Twain's theory of personality development and group psychology to explain how the townspeople allow themselves to be "hoodwinked" by the aggressive leaders who control their communities. Before the devil educates Theodor, Theodor describes this process without awareness of its destructive influence on the common people. "The priests said that knowledge was not good for the common people, and could make them discontented with the lot which God has appointed for them."[18]

Like Huck Finn, Theodor describes the world in realistic terms but does not, early in the story, demonstrate awareness of the satiric content of his realistic descriptions. He reports that Father Adolf "was a very loud and zealous and strenuous priest and was always working, working to get more reputation, hoping to be a Bishop one day."[19] Father Adolf's treatment of a widow in the town, Frau Marx, provides another illustration of his aggressive, power-driven motives and those of the church hierarchy in the town of Eseldorf. Father Adolf discovers that Frau Marx has been exposed to a liberal religious influence that contradicts his interpretation of Catholic teaching. This liberal influence is introduced by an outsider, a newcomer to the town, a Hussite woman named Frau Adler. Theodor, indoctrinated into Father Adolf's religious orthodoxy, describes her as "a cunning woman" who "sought out those few who could read ... she gradually got them together, and these she poisoned nightly with her heresies ... she gave them Bibles and hymn books ... and persuaded them that it was no sin to read them."[20]

When Father Adolf discovers that Frau Adler is encouraging townspeople to interpret the Bible personally and apply their independent judgment to religion, he warns, "I will attend to this woman."[21] He accomplishes this by using superstitious religious beliefs to turn Frau Marx against Frau Adler and her liberal Christianity. He tells Frau Marx, "You are on the road to Hell. The Virgin will punish you for this."[22] When Frau Marx's horse dies, Father Adolf tells her it was punishment for her independent religious thought. "Father Adolf ... went on storming at her and telling her what the Virgin would do with her, until she was ready to swoon with fear."[23] Upon the death of her second horse, Frau Marx is convinced that Father Adolf is an instrument of God's wrath: "I told you the Virgin would punish you."[24] Frau Marx is so frightened by Father Adolf's manipulation of her superstitious religious fears that she persuades the other followers of Frau Adler to abandon her and burn their books. "They all burned their books and returned repentant to the bosom of the church."[25]

Throughout the description of the events with Frau Marx, Twain makes it clear that Father Adolf's behavior is motivated by his fear of losing his religious control over Frau Marx and the other townspeople. The authority of Father Adolf and others in the church hierarchy is clearly based on the townspeople's blind acceptance of the orthodox clerical interpretations of the Bible. Thus, any personal or independent reading and interpretation of the Bible would represent a threat to the religious and political leadership of the Eseldorf.

The repentance of Frau Marx and the other brief followers of Frau Adler reinforces for the rest of the townspeople Father Adolf's assertion that he is capable of reading and enforcing God's will. "For they thought there must be something supernatural about him."[26] Because of this illusion of his possessing special power, Father Adolf continues to convince the common people of Eseldorf to follow the religious rules of the church. In reality, the religious rules imposed by Father Adolf constitute an ideology that uses the illusion of God's will to justify the control of the common people by the church and royalty. Twain's young Satan understands the ideological nature of the church in Eseldorf and uses an intervention along with Twain's theory of human nature and personality to illustrate and explain this misuse of power to Theodor.

As part of the devil's education of Theodor, young Satan makes him aware of the workings of human nature, particularly the reasons for the average person's vulnerability to aggressive, dominant leaders. The devil Traum also exposes the aggressive, dishonest temperament of Father Adolf, throwing into doubt the priest's claim of special religious-altruistic motives for the rules he imposes on the townspeople of Eseldorf. Reminiscent of the outsider in "The Man Who Corrupted Hadleyburg," Traum accomplishes this by introducing a large sum of money for honest Father Peter to find. Although poor and in need of the money, Father Peter is honest and reports his newly found fortune to the local authorities. Once Father Adolf hears about Father Peter's good luck, Father Adolf claims that the money is his and was stolen from him by Father Peter. In response to Father Adolf's accusation, the local police arrest Father Peter for theft.

At Father Peter's trial, the devil, acting through Wilhelm Meedling, Father Peter's lawyer, proves Father Adolf's claim that he once owned the money is a lie. He does this by demonstrating that some of the money bore a mint date later than that when Father Adolf claimed to have acquired it. As a result of this intervention by Traum, Father Adolf is exposed as a fraud, a religious con man who is driven by selfish, dishonest motives. He is like the other frauds exposed by the stranger in "The Man Who Corrupted Hadleyburg."

As the incident with the money unfolds, the devil uses Twain's model of human nature to explain to Theodor that what civilization calls the "moral sense" is merely rationalization for those driven by aggressive temperaments—often those within the clergy, aristocracy and/or wealthy classes—to exploit others for their own gain. Traum proceeds to describe Twain's model of personality involving the interaction of temperament, training, random circumstance, and limited human reason to explain why the typical leader as well as the average citizen are determined by forces beyond their control. As a result of Traum's teaching, Theodor begins to understand that most leaders conceal their intentions with illusions to hide their real power-driven motives, while the average citizenry's more timid, approval-seeking temperaments make them highly vulnerable to such leaders' manipulations.

The devil goes on to explain that the clergy falsely interprets divine will as supporting the status quo of the unfair economic system that governs Eseldorf. "God would not endure discontentment with his plan."[27] Traum connects this use of religious illusions to the church's use of group psychology to train the masses to be passive in the face of economic and political domination by the church and monarchy. According to the devil, the church teaches both the rich and the poor that it is moral for the rich to exploit the poor. Both groups internalize this teaching as being God's will, accepting the economic system as divine will. Traum illustrates how this enables factory owners to misuse the idea of morality to sanction the exploitation that takes place in the factories of the time. "It is more moral sense, the proprietors are such and very holy, but the wage to these brothers and sisters is only enough to keep them from dropping dead with hunger. It is the moral sense which teaches the factory proprietors the difference between right and wrong."[28]

The young Satan is able to see through these human shams and illusions because he is "not limited like you [humans]." He "can measure and understand ... human weaknesses."[29] He is able to perceive the truths of human nature and the civilizations that it produces. Theodor begins to respond to the devil's teaching about the use of the moral sense by so-called leaders of civilization: "I had a dim sense of what the moral was."[30]

Traum completes Theodor's education about the political use of the moral sense: "monarchies, aristocracies and religions ... these institutions will always remain, always flourish and always oppress you, affront you and degrade you [the common people] because you will always be and remain slaves of minorities."[31] For the devil, the misuse of the moral sense takes place because the leaders of civilization tend to be individuals with power-driven temperaments. The common people have a temperamental tendency to worship such leaders. "Two centuries from now ... the Christian civilization will reach its high mark. Yet its kings will still be then, what they are now, a closed corporation of land thieves."[32]

According to young Satan, the common people pay a high prices for internalizing "the moral sense" taught to them by their leaders and civilization. They are kept ignorant about the forces which actually determine the workings of human nature—as a result, the average person lives with "continuous and uninterrupted self-deception."[33] It is this self-deception from which the devil hopes to free Theodor. In this sense, he hopes to retrain Theodor by teaching him how the interaction of temperament, training, circumstance, and reason shape human destiny.

Traum promises Theodor his education will provide the truth about the human psyche. The devil completes Theodor's education about human nature by turning to the workings of individual psychology—"what man calls his mind."[34] To link individual psychology to group psychology, the devil teaches Theodor the dynamics of personality formation. Using Twain's model of human nature, he shows Theodor how temperament, training, circumstance, and reason link the development of the individual to the civilization in which he lives. He begins with the individual's temperament as the driving force of personality formation.

Young Satan begins to introduce Theodor to Twain's tripartite theory of personality with an example of how the temperament of man works. Referring to temperament as a man's "make and disposition," he tells Theodor, "Sometimes a man's make and disposition are such that his misery machinery is able to do all the business."[35] In Twainian terms, this means that an individual can be made to be miserable all his life, if his temperament causes him to not allow himself to be happy. "Such a man gets through life almost ignorant of what happiness is."[36]

Next, the young devil explains the relationship between an individual's temperamental disposition and the "training" that he receives from his community. "In any community, big or small, there is always a fair proportion of people who never do unkind things except when they are overmatched by fear or when their self interest is greatly endangered."[37] Frequently, the latter occurs as a reaction to political or religious manipulation. When this happens on a broad scale, the herd instinct overrides individual temperament. The devil explains this experience to Theodor: "I know your race. It is made up of sheep ... it suppresses its feelings and beliefs and follows the handful that makes the most noise. The vast majority of the race ... are secretly kind hearted ... but in the presence of the aggressive and pitiless minority, they don't dare to assert themselves."[38]

The next component of personality which the devil teaches Theodor is the influence of random circumstance. "The man's circumstance and environment order it [destiny]. His first act determines the second and all that follow after."[39] Theodor comes to understand that circumstance shapes the training to which a temperament is exposed. Theodors echoes Twain's deterministic model of personality. Then, Traum explains the limits of human reason to Theodor in words that are very similar to those used in "What Is Man?": "Man's mind clumsily and tediously and laboriously patches little trivialities together and gets a result."[40] For Twain, for the old man in "What Is Man?," and for the young Satan character, the average man's reason is weak and not able to detect the illusions frequently contained in such traits as patriotism.

The devil demonstrates for Theodor how training can be misused to manipulate people into wanting an unjust war: "The loud little handful as usual will shout for the war."[41] He then explains that some people will try to train the masses to behave morally. "The pulpit will ... object—at first ... a few fair men ... will argue and reason against the war...."[42] Traum then concludes that leaders, driven by aggressive temperaments, will sway the masses. "Those others will outshout them and presently the anti-war audiences will thin out ... and now the whole nation pulpit and all—will take up the war cry...."[43]

After being educated about human nature by the devil, Theodor concludes that "It shows how foolish people are when they blame themselves for anything they have done. Satan knows...."[44] Theodor has learned that all human behavior is determined by the interaction of temperament, training, circumstance, and reason.

By the end of "The Chronicle," young Satan has shown himself to be no conventional devil. Rather than lure Theodor into evil, this young devil has exposed the evil Father Adolf and others in Eseldorf who have sold their souls to gain power. More importantly, he has educated Theodor by teaching him the "Twainian" truths of human psychology and giving the boy the gift of self-awareness. By the story's end, Theodor can observe his own experience and understand the forces that shape his personality. Thus, he comes to agree with young Satan that "Monarchies, aristocracies and religions are all based upon that large defect of your race—the individual's distrust of his neighbor, and his desire, for safety's sake or comfort's sake, to stand well in his neighbor's eyes."[45] This vantage point does not free Theodor from the deterministic influences that mold him. However, it does allow him to separate truth from illusion and neither deceive himself nor be easily deceived by others.

Conclusion

What makes Mark Twain one of the most intensely American writers this culture has produced? It is his belief that people are born with unique temperaments that can only be modified—not changed—by society's institutions. Twain has incorporated two American biases into this formulation. The first is that each person is unique and inherits his or her nature, be it positive or negative. The second is his distrust of the effects of social influence on temperament.

In describing his concept of temperament, Twain commented, "The human family cannot be described by any one phrase; each individual has to be described by himself."[1] That is, each person has his own unique combination of traits making up his or her temperament. The same cannot be said, however, of Mark Twain's works; patterns exist among them and the search for the meaning of those patterns has generated an industry of criticism and produced a number of frameworks for reading him. I have to confess to the crime of having added one more to the list. I do not, however, believe that there is only one way to read the works of any truly great writer. A multitude of approaches deepens the reader's understanding of the work. In that spirit, I have used Twain's own theory of personality as a lens through which to view his construction of character and society in some of his fiction.

Twain applied his psychological theory to his construction of character and society in some of his most famous novels, ranging from *The Adventures of Huckleberry Finn*[2] to *Pudd'nhead Wilson*.[3] Although he viewed his psychological theory as scientific, it was in many ways impressionistic, and his explanations of it were, at times, unclear. Nevertheless, in developing his theory of personality, Twain was to a great degree ahead of his time. It was a number of years after Twain published "What Is Man?"[4] that Freud presented his structural model of personality. I have found no evidence to suggest that Twain's work influenced Freud or the reverse. However, while there are important differences between Twain's tripartite and Freud's structural model of personality, there are also some strong parallels. These can be found in some aspects of their understanding of certain mechanisms of socialization—such as internalization and identification—as well as in their application of their understanding of individual psychology to a theory of social organization and group psychology. Moreover, despite their differences, Freud's more precise and systematic models of individual and group psychology have enhanced my understanding of Twain's psychological thought.

In contrasting aspects of Twain's thought with that of Freud, certain elements of both men's theories can be traced to the influence of their respective cultures. Thus, they differed considerably in how they evaluated the impact of social organization on individual development and expression. Twain, the American, focused on the potentially negative effects of social training in suppressing individuals with positive temperaments and reinforcing those with certain negative temperamental traits. Freud, the European, began with the idea that inherited instincts are uniformly aggressive and socially destructive, leading him to generally value the socialization process by which they are repressed.

In addition to his distrust of the influence of social training on the individuality of character, Twain distrusted the psychological mechanisms through which the institutions of society—its customs, rules, and belief systems—influence individual temperament. A significant concern for him was that the psychological mechanisms involved in the socialization process work in favor of those with strong temperaments, allowing them to dominate others for selfish ends. He observed that once in power, those strong individuals often used ideological justifications to establish their oppressive control. Unlike Twain, Freud accepted the necessity for control of society by the strong, and believed that such control was essential for the evolution of civilization.

While Freud illustrated his understanding of the relationship between the individual and society using didactic analysis and case studies, Twain conveyed his primarily through the dramatic conflict in his novels. In Twain's characters, individual behavior is always determined by the main characters' unique temperaments, and a central theme of the plots involves an exploration of the relationship between those individual temperaments and the social environment. Moreover, in certain works, the narrator or an important character actually articulates the psychological theory or important terms from it to highlight this relationship. As a result, a close reading of many of Twain's novels reveals that his characters' relationships to society can be defined according to certain patterns. These include those observed in the thinking and behavior of the democratic outsider, the conformist, the amoral social climber, the democratic demagogue, the democratic leader, and the con man.

Examples of the first group of characters, the democratic outsiders, include Huck Finn in *The Adventures of Huckleberry Finn* and Barclay Goodson in "The Man Who Corrupted Hadleyburg."[5] These are individuals with strong temperamental traits of empathy, leading them to identify with social norms involving genuine fairness and concern for the common welfare, but to see through and reject the more prevalent (according to Twain) norms of materialism and blind conformity. Huck Finn—the quasi-orphan—grew up on the periphery of society, while Goodson had not been raised in the town of Hadleyburg. These circumstances may have facilitated both characters' abilities to withstand social pressure and, for the most part, to remain true to their temperaments. This is not to say that the democratic outsider is free of all negative social influence. Huck, in particular, struggles at several points in his relationship with Jim to overcome the negative stereotypes he has internalized about Blacks as slaves.

Yet another example of a democratic outsider is Roxy in *Pudd'nhead Wilson*. Born a slave, she was subjected to the most negative form of social indoctrination. However, she too possessed strong temperamental traits of empathy, leading her to switch her fair-skinned infant son with the master's infant son at birth, thereby sparing her son the fate of a slave. Beyond her attachment to her son, Roxy felt compassion for and guilt about the fate of the other infant, now consigned to slavery, and was further able to recognize, when other slaves did not, that minimally humane behaviors of their master, such as relenting and not selling them all down the river, did not qualify him as a great, God-like human being. However, unlike some of Twain's other democratic outsiders, Roxy's slave upbringing and status did result in some limitations on her independence of thought, as well as significant limitations on her options for independent action. She had internalized much of the slave master's ideology of Black inferiority, leading her to eschew romantic contact with darker Blacks and to attribute negative aspects of her biological son's behavior to his one thirty-secondth of Black blood. However, given the pervasiveness of the oppressive socialization to which Roxy, as a slave, had been subjected, her capacity for empathy and exercise of independent judgment are remarkable.

Standing in contrast to the relative independence of the democratic outsider is Twain's conformist who complies blindly with societal dictates. Twain's concept of the dynamics of socialization and group psychology—including the internalization of cultural values so that self-approval is based on beliefs and behaviors associated with social approval—leads him to view most people as potentially falling into this pattern. These include the commoners in *A Connecticut Yankee at King Arthur's Court*,[6] the majority of Hadleyburg's citizens, and most of the residents of the different communities along the

Mississippi in *The Adventures of Huckleberry Finn*, as well as the non-fictional followers of Mary Baker Eddy. However, Twain explores the dynamics of the conformist still further in his development of certain fictional characters, such as Mary and Edward Richards in "The Man Who Corrupted Hadleyburg" and Buck Grangerford in *The Adventures of Huckleberry Finn*—characters whose inborn temperaments include an exceptionally strong need for social approval.

As such, the characters are very fearful of social punishment, particularly public humiliation or isolation. Mary and Edward Richards in "Hadleyburg" are prototypical conformists. Essentially decent people, they have internalized the town's rigid, narrowly defined ideology of honesty. When circumstances activate other aspects of their temperaments—aspects that were suppressed for years by social training—the psychological conflict that is generated becomes so intense that they fall ill and, finally, die. Another example of a conformist is Buck Grangerford. Socialized into an aristocratic ideology of honor, he acts in blind allegiance to a code which requires him to engage in a feud with members of a rival clan. Though admittedly ignorant of the reason for the enmity between the two families, he continues to participate in the feud until killed by a member of the "enemy" family. Thus, Twain's conformists are individuals whose temperaments are so dependent on avoiding social disgrace that they sacrifice their self-interest, their capacity to exercise independent judgment, and in some cases, their very lives in the service of maintaining social approval.

Related to the conformists in some respects but distinctive in others are the amoral social climbers. These are individuals in whom the impact of socialization has been counterbalanced somewhat by strong traits of greed or selfishness in their inborn temperaments. They essentially accept the norms and values of their culture and feel most comfortable behaving in accordance with these as long as their conformity is not at the cost of personal gain. As a result, they become particularly astute at "working the system" from the inside to procure their own advancement, while maintaining their positions as model citizens. In communities characterized by Twain's concept of the corrupted republic, these individuals are often among the town's leading citizens, while within his feudal societies they are found among the aristocracy. Twain illustrates these dynamics more fully in his development of the characters of Harkness in "The Man Who Corrupted Hadleyburg" and Miss Watson in *The Adventures of Huckleberry Finn*.

Even after having been exposed (along with eighteen others) as attempting to violate the town's ideology of honesty for personal gain, Harkness, already a wealthy citizen, manages to manipulate the situation to discredit his primary rival for elected office and obtain a position that gives him access to yet another source of wealth. Miss Watson, another amoral social climber, adheres fully to norms that advance her social standing or wealth, while oblivious to the inherent contradictions in the Christian value of concern for human welfare when it conflicts with an opportunity for profit through the slave trade. Thus, Miss Watson is an active church member and insists that Huck strictly obey social conventions. At the same time, she clearly lacks any loyalty to her faithful slave Jim and his family, whom she sells to a slave trader—not out of financial need, but merely because the price is so good.

While the amoral social climber works within the social structure for personal advancement, those falling into yet another pattern—the democratic demagogue—stand above and lead the group. Their strongest temperamental need is for dominance and control, but they also have a temperamental need for social approval. As a result, they seek ways to dominate others in the context of values they unconsciously internalize from the societies in which they are raised. Thus, they incorporate these values into their quest for power and are unaware of the absence within their personalities of much genuine capacity for empathy, fairness or concern for others' welfare. While they tell themselves that their purpose is to uplift, protect or reform the masses, their unconscious motivation is fulfillment of their temperamental need for dominance. Classical republican writers identified this type as one who in a democracy flatters the variety of the people to gain power over them.[7]

An example of Twain's description of the dynamics of the democratic demagogue is the fictional character of Hank Morgan in *A Connecticut Yankee at King Arthur's Court*. Twain portrays Morgan as an individual who seems to be a champion of the common people to help them overcome feudal oppression. He believes his intentions are altruistic and for the most part lacks awareness of his temperamental need to dominate. He uses political ideology to manipulate the people into following him, while hiding from even himself his own true, selfish motivation.

In contrast to the democratic demagogue, the democratic leader is an infrequent figure in Twain's literature, even less common than the democratic outsider. Unlike the democratic outsider, this figure does more than criticize and personally resist the tyranny created by social conformity. He or she, for at least a brief period of time, rises to a position of power in the society by inspiring the masses with democratic ideals such as honesty, empathy, fairness, and social equality. In *Personal Recollections of Joan of Arc*,[8] Twain depicts Joan of Arc as just such a democratic leader who is driven by a temperamental love of the common people. She is different from democratic demagogues in that she has no personal political ambition, but only wishes to train the people to recognize and protect their own rational self-interest against the political manipulation of ambitious leaders. As in the case of Joan of Arc, Twain's democratic leaders are often betrayed by the common people, who are easily led astray. Thus, for Twain, genuinely democratic societies are often short-lived.

Unlike his concept of the democratic demagogue, Twain's concept of the con man is of the individual without any self-deception about altruistic goals. His con men are people with selfish, criminal temperaments who are fully aware of their intent to cheat and defraud. As such, they can be ruthless and violent. The con man has been exposed to social training, but failed to internalize its values; he is without conscience. In that sense, he lives on the edge of society, entering it only intermittently to steal something from its residents. Moreover, because he understands the illusions by which society is organized, he is able to use those to manipulate or defraud its citizens. Examples of con men in Twain's fiction include the Duke and the King in *The Adventures of Huckleberry Finn* and the stranger who calls himself Howard Stephenson in "The Man Who Corrupted Hadleyburg." The Duke and the King seek the more conventional selfish goal, personal wealth, by successively posing as aristocrats, medical salesmen, and heirs to a deceased wealthy citizen in their attempts to defraud. The stranger, in contrast, out of anger and the quest for revenge, seeks to destroy the town of Hadleyburg's reputation for honesty, and in the process destroys the mental and physical health of its prototypical conformist citizens, the Richardses.

Twain's identification of different character patterns proves his talent for probing the American soul. He was so adept at mapping American character formation that many of his character patterns have found their way into modern American fiction. Thus, writers such as John Steinbeck, Sinclair Lewis, Robert Penn Warren, Joseph Heller, and Ernest Hemingway went on to create characters consistent with Twain's patterns. Penn Warren's Willie Stark,[9] for example, illustrates the democratic demagogue; Lewis' George C. Babbitt,[10] the conformist; and Steinbeck's Tom Joad,[11] the democratic outsider. Hemingway's famous statement, "All modern literature comes from Mark Twain's *Adventures of Huckleberry Finn*,"[12] may be a broad overstatement of Twain's influence. Nonetheless, one has to concede that Twain has had a demonstrable impact on the modern imagination.

Afterword

One may wonder if Twain's deterministic theory of human nature, so steeped in mechanistic imagery, has any relevance for the modern age. Many critics have answered "very little," seeing it as a worn-out restatement of theories of determinism rooted in Twain's own time. Charles Johnson characterizes Twain's psychological thought as not "original or groundbreaking."[1] However, this as well as other critiques of Twain's theory of human nature miss its central contribution, which is to identify the psychological role of political leadership in shaping the historical destiny of societies. Viewed from this angle, Twain's model of human nature is very important for our times.

Twain's literature issued a warning to his own time, the then-recently-turned twentieth century: do not trust leaders who use ideology to manipulate and control those they govern. Freud also recognized the potential for abuse by leaders, but viewed them as generally more rational than the masses even in their use of ideology. In contrast, Twain called ideology "petrified thought" and understood how it transforms thoughtful individual reflection into "groupthink." In Twain's view, once these systems of "petrified thought" are wed to the aggressive, power-driven wills of certain leaders, tyrannies are born, tyrannies which hypnotize the citizenry through the use of group psychology. Simply put, Twain's model of human nature seems to anticipate the coming of the age of "isms" and the wreckage wrought by leaders whose ideologies opposed educating the common people to use their capacities for reflective and rational thought.

Twain's insight into the weaknesses of human nature and the ways political leaders could take advantage of those weaknesses make him a political prophet who anticipated writers like Erich Fromm and George Orwell. Like Fromm and Orwell, Twain understood that ideology is the opponent of democratic societies, for any ideology requires that the masses accept it as a matter of faith without putting its premises to the pragmatic test. Twain knew that "petrified thought" homogenizes individual thought and, through the process of group psychology, turns people into "mass men" no longer capable of making individual decisions based on a rational examination of evidence.

Is Twain's theory of human nature relevant to our own times? I think so. His distrust of political leaders who offer simplified, ideological solutions to complex problems is badly needed today. His understanding that democracy requires its citizens to treat each other as they wish to be treated is badly needed today. His idea that democracy requires people to identify their own welfare with the general well-being is badly needed today. As my good friend and noted scholar of American civilization, the late Carey McWilliams, once said, "No one can read Mark Twain without becoming more decent as a result of the experience."[2]

Appendix

"What Is Man?" by Mark Twain

Annotated and edited by Edith Frank; from the 1917 edition published by Harper & Brothers, New York and London.

Mark Twain identified "What Is Man?" as "my book on psychology."[1] However, perhaps because it is also a satiric critique of human vanity and social institutions such as political systems and organized religion, its terminology is somewhat idiosyncratic and its arguments are at times exaggerated. As a result, some readers may find it confusing and conceptually inconsistent. The 1917 edition has been annotated with the goal of clarifying some of the idiosyncratic terminology and apparent contradictions in Twain's psychological theory. In addition, some sections that are repetitious or less relevant to his psychological thinking have been deleted. It is hoped that these annotations will make the value of Twain's psychological thought more evident.

I.
a. MAN THE MACHINE.   b. PERSONAL MERIT.

[The OLD MAN and the YOUNG MAN had been conversing. The OLD MAN had asserted that the human being is merely a machine, and nothing more. The YOUNG MAN objected, and asked him to go into particulars and furnish his reasons for his position.]

Y. M. You have arrived at man, now?

O. M. Yes. Man the machine—man the impersonal engine. Whatsoever a man is, is due to his *make*, and to the *influences* brought to bear upon it by his heredities, his habitat, his associations. He is moved, directed, COMMANDED, by *exterior* influences—*solely*. He *originates* nothing, not even a thought.

[Twain, via the Old Man's words, uses the term "exterior" because he views these influences as beyond the actual control (versus perceived control) of the individual, whether their source is intrinsic/hereditary (e.g., temperament) or environmental (training, culture, circumstance, etc.). However, for the first few pages of the following section, the focus is on environmental influences.]

Y. M. Oh, come! Where did I get my opinion that this which you are talking is all foolishness?

O. M. It is a quite natural opinion—indeed an inevitable opinion—but *you* did not create the materials out of which it is formed. They are odds and ends of thoughts, impressions, feelings, gathered unconsciously from a thousand books, a thousand conversations, and from streams of thought and feeling which have flowed down into your heart and brain out of the hearts and brains of centuries of ancestors. *Personally* you did not create even the smallest microscopic fragment of the materials out of which your opinion is made; and personally you cannot claim even the slender merit of *putting the borrowed materials together.* That was done *automatically*—by your mental machinery, in strict accordance with the law of that machinery's construction. And you not only did not make that machinery yourself, but you have *not even any command over it.*

Y. M. This is too much. You think I could have formed no opinion but that one?

O. M. Spontaneously? No. And *you did not form that one;* your machinery did it for you—automatically and instantly, without reflection or the need of it.

Y. M. Suppose I had reflected? How then?

O. M. Suppose you try?

Y. M. *(After a quarter of an hour.)* I have reflected.

O. M. You mean you have tried to change your opinion—as an experiment?

Y. M. Yes.

O. M. With success?

Y. M. No. It remains the same; it is impossible to change it.

O. M. I am sorry, but you see, yourself, that your mind is merely a machine, nothing more. You have no command over it, it has no command over itself—it is worked *solely from the outside.* That is the law of its make; it is the law of all machines.

Y. M. Can't I *ever* change one of these automatic opinions?

O. M. No. You can't yourself, but *exterior influences* can do it.

Y. M. And exterior ones *only*?

O. M. Yes—exterior ones only.

Y. M. That position is untenable—I may say ludicrously untenable.

O. M. What makes you think so?

Y. M. I don't merely think it, I know it. Suppose I resolve to enter upon a course of thought, and study, and reading, with the deliberate purpose of changing that opinion; and suppose I succeed. *That* is not the work of an exterior impulse, the whole of it is mine and personal: for I originated the project.

O. M. Not a shred of it. *It grew out of this talk with me.* But for that it would never have occurred to you. No man ever originates anything. All his thoughts, all his impulses, come *from the outside.*

Y. M. It's an exasperating subject. The *first* man had original thoughts, anyway; there was nobody to draw from.

O. M. It is a mistake. Adam's thoughts came to him from the outside. *You* have a fear of death. You did not invent that—you got it from outside, from talking and teaching. Adam had no fear of death—none in the world.

Y. M. Yes, he had.

O. M. When he was created?

Y. M. No.

O. M. When, then?

Y. M. When he was threatened with it.

O. M. Then it came from the *outside*. Adam is quite big enough; let us not try to make a god of him. *None but gods have ever had a thought which did not come from the outside.* Adam probably had a good head, but it was of no sort of use to him until it was filled up *from the outside.* He was not able to invent the triflingest little thing with it. He had not a shadow of a notion of a difference between good and evil—he had to get the idea *from the outside.* Neither he nor Eve was able to originate the idea that it was immodest to go naked: the knowledge came in with the apple *from the outside.* A man's brain is so constructed that *it can originate nothing whatever.* It can only use material obtained *outside.* It is merely a machine; and it works automatically, not by will-power. *It has no command over itself, its owner has no command over it.*

Y. M. Well, never mind Adam: but certainly Shakespeare's creations—

O. M. No, you mean Shakespeare's *imitations.* Shakespeare created nothing. He correctly observed, and he marvelously painted. He exactly portrayed people whom *God* had created; but he created none himself. Let us spare him the slander of charging him with trying. Shakespeare could not create. *He was a machine, and machines do not create.*

Y. M. Where *was* his excellence, then?

O. M. In this. He was not a sewing-machine, like you and me; he was a Gobelin loom. The threads and the colors came into him *from the outside;* outside influences, suggestions, *experiences* (reading, seeing plays, playing plays, borrowing ideas, and so on), framed the patterns in his mind and started up its complex and admirable machinery, and *it automatically* turned out that pictured and gorgeous fabric which still compels the astonishment of the world. If Shakespeare had been born and bred on a barren and unvisited rock in the ocean his mighty intellect would have had no *outside material* to work with, and could have invented none; and *no outside influences*, teachings, moldings, persuasions, inspirations, of a valuable sort, and could have invented none; and so Shakespeare would have produced nothing. In Turkey he would have produced something—something up to the highest limit of Turkish influences, associations, and training. In France he would have produced something better—something up to the highest limit of the French influences and training. In England he rose to the highest limit attainable through the *outside helps afforded by that land's ideals, influences, and training.* You and I are but sewing-machines. We must turn out what we can; we must do our endeavor and care nothing at all when the unthinking reproach us for not turning out Gobelins.

[The previous paragraph highlights Twain's awareness of the influence of culture on human behavior. However, it also reflects his differential valuations of certain cultures, valuations derived from his own training and other experiences. Twain's references here suggest that despite his ability in other works like The Adventures of Huckleberry Finn *and* Pudd'nhead Wilson *to criticize and satirize aspects of U. S. racist culture, he had not fully transcended cultural bias in his own thinking.]*

Y. M. And so we are mere machines! And machines may not boast, nor feel proud of their performance, nor claim personal merit for it, nor applause and praise. It is an infamous doctrine.

O. M. It isn't a doctrine, it is merely a fact.

Y. M. I suppose, then, there is no more merit in being brave than in being a coward?

O. M. *Personal* merit? No. A brave man does not *create* his bravery. He is entitled to no personal credit for possessing it. It is born to him. A baby born with a billion dollars—where is the personal merit in that? A baby born with nothing—where is the personal demerit in that? The one is fawned upon, admired, worshiped, by sycophants, the other is neglected and despised—where is the sense in it?

Y. M. Sometimes a timid man sets himself the task of conquering his cowardice and becoming brave—and succeeds. What do you say to that?

O. M. That it shows the value of *training in right directions over training in wrong ones.* Inestimably valuable is training, influence, education, in right directions—*training one's self-approbation to elevate its ideals.*

Y. M. But as to merit—the personal merit of the victorious coward's project and achievement?

O. M. There isn't any. In the world's view he is a worthier man than he was before, but *he* didn't achieve the change—the merit of it is not his.

Y. M. Whose, then?

O. M. His *make*, and the influences which wrought upon it from the outside.

Y. M. His make?

[Here, that other group of "exterior" influences—those derived from intrinsic, hereditary, temperamental sources—is introduced.]

O. M. To start with, he was *not* utterly and completely a coward, or the influences would have had nothing to work upon. He was not afraid of a cow, though perhaps of a bull: not afraid of a woman, but afraid of a man. There was something to build upon. There was a *seed*. No seed, no plant. Did he make that seed himself, or was it born in him? It was no merit of *his* that the seed was there.

[The concept of "seed" foreshadows Twain's personality construct of temperament, to be developed later in this essay, as a biologically-based component of personality. Twain goes on in this section to describe how environmental influences may interact with this "seed" to motivate the individual in a particular direction. He identifies some specific environmental influences including general cultural norms (e.g., the value of "bravery"), significant individuals in a person's life (e.g., a girlfriend), and personal experiences/circumstances (e.g., military training, examples set by fellow soldiers, experiences of survival in combat). He also identifies the common human need for social approval which may motivate the individual to struggle to develop one aspect of his temperament and suppress another.]

Y. M. Well, anyway, the idea of *cultivating* it, the resolution to cultivate it, was meritorious, and he originated that.

O. M. He did nothing of the kind. It came whence *all* impulses, good or bad, come—from *outside*. If that timid man had lived all his life in a community of human rabbits, had never read of brave deeds, had never heard speak of them, had never heard any one praise them nor express envy of the heroes that had done them, he would have had no more idea of bravery than Adam had of modesty, and it could never by any possibility have occurred to him to *resolve* to become brave. He *could not originate the idea*—it had to come to him from the *outside*. And so, when he heard bravery extolled and cowardice derided, it woke him up. He was ashamed. Perhaps his sweetheart turned up her nose and said, "I am told that you are a coward!" It was not *he* that turned over the new leaf—she did it for him. *He* must not strut around in the merit of it—it is not his.

Y. M. But, anyway, he reared the plant after she watered the seed.

O. M. No. *Outside influences* reared it. At the command—and trembling—he marched out into the field—with other soldiers and in the daytime, not alone and in the dark. He had the *influence of example*, he drew courage from his comrades' courage; he was afraid, and wanted to run, but he did not dare; he was *afraid* to run, with all those soldiers looking on. He was progressing, you see—the moral fear of shame had risen superior to the physical fear of harm. By the end of the campaign experience will have taught him that not *all* who go into battle get hurt—an outside influence which will be helpful to him; and he will also have learned how sweet it is to be praised for courage and be huzza'd at with tear-choked voices as the war-worn regiment marches past the worshiping multitude with flags flying and the drums beating. After that he will be as securely brave as any veteran in the army—and there will not be a shade nor suggestion of *personal merit* in it anywhere; it will all have come from the *outside*. The Victoria Cross breeds more heroes than—

Y. M. Hang it, where is the sense in his becoming brave if he is to get no credit for it?

O. M. Your question will answer itself presently. It involves an important detail of man's make which we have not yet touched upon.

Y. M. What detail is that?

O. M. The impulse which moves a person to do things—the only impulse that ever moves a person to do a thing.

Y. M. The *only* one! Is there but one?

O. M. That is all. There is only one.

Y. M. Well, certainly that is a strange enough doctrine. What is the sole impulse that ever moves a person to do a thing?

O. M. The impulse to *content his own spirit*—the *necessity* of contenting his own spirit and *winning its approval.*

[Here, Twain introduces his concept of man's need to "content his own spirit" and win self-approval as the central determinant of individual behavior.]

Y. M. Oh, come, that won't do!

O. M. Why won't it?

Y. M. Because it puts him in the attitude of always looking out for his own comfort and advantage; whereas an unselfish man often does a thing solely for another person's good when it is a positive disadvantage to himself.

O. M. It is a mistake. The act must do *him* good, FIRST; otherwise he will not do it. He may *think* he is doing it solely for the other person's sake, but it is not so; he is contenting his own spirit first—the other person's benefit has to always take *second* place.

Y. M. What a fantastic idea! What becomes of self-sacrifice? Please answer me that.

O. M. What is self-sacrifice?

Y. M. The doing good to another person where no shadow nor suggestion of benefit to one's self can result from it.

II
Man's Sole Impulse—The Securing of His Own Approval

Old Man. There have been instances of it—you think?

Young Man. *Instances?* Millions of them!

O. M. You have not jumped to conclusions? You have examined them—critically?

Y. M. They don't need it: the acts themselves reveal the golden impulse back of them.

O. M. For instance?

Y. M. Well, then, for instance. Take the case in the book here. The man lives three miles up-town. It is bitter cold, snowing hard, midnight. He is about to enter the horse-car when a gray and ragged old woman, a touching picture of misery, puts out her lean hand and begs for rescue from hunger and death. The man finds that he has but a quarter in his pocket, but he does not hesitate: he gives it to her and trudges home through the storm. There—it is noble, it is beautiful; its grace is marred by no fleck or blemish or suggestion of self-interest.

O. M. What makes you think that?

Y. M. Pray what else could I think? Do you imagine that there is some other way of looking at it?

O. M. Can you put yourself in the man's place and tell me what he felt and what he thought?

Y. M. Easily. The sight of that suffering old face pierced his generous heart with a sharp pain. He could not bear it. He could endure the three-mile walk in the storm, but he could not endure the tortures his conscience would suffer if he turned his back and left that poor old creature to perish. He would not have been able to sleep, for thinking of it.

O. M. What was his state of mind on his way home?

Y. M. It was a state of joy which only the self-sacrificer knows. His heart sang, he was unconscious of the storm.

O. M. He felt well?

Y. M. One cannot doubt it.

O. M. Very well. Now let us add up the details and see how much he got for his twenty-five cents. Let us try to find out the *real* why of his making the investment. In the first place *he* couldn't bear the pain which the old suffering face gave him. So he was thinking of *his* pain—this good man. He must buy a salve for it. If he did not succor the old woman *his* conscience would torture him all the way home. Thinking of *his* pain again. He must buy relief from that. If he didn't relieve the old woman *he* would not get any sleep. He must buy some sleep—still thinking of *himself*, you see. Thus, to sum up, he bought himself free of a sharp pain in his heart, he bought himself free of the tortures of a waiting conscience, he bought a whole night's sleep—all for twenty-five cents! It should make Wall Street ashamed of itself. On his way home his heart was joyful, and it sang—profit on top of profit! The impulse which moved the man to succor the old woman was—*first*—to *content his own spirit*; secondly to relieve *her* sufferings. Is it your opinion that men's acts proceed from one central and unchanging and inalterable impulse, or from a variety of impulses?

Y. M. From a variety, of course—some high and fine and noble, others not. What is your opinion?

O. M. Then there is but *one* law, one source.

Y. M. That both the noblest impulses and the basest proceed from that one source?

O. M. Yes.

Y. M. Will you put that law into words?

O. M. Yes. This is the law, keep it in your mind. *From his cradle to his grave a man never does a single thing which has any FIRST AND FOREMOST object but one—to secure peace of mind, spiritual comfort, for HIMSELF.*

[This Twainian dynamic in some ways resembles Freud's concept of the superego, which consists of ego ideal and conscience. However, Twain seems to see this dynamic operating from infancy, while Freud views the infant and toddler as operating from a more primitive physical pleasure principle, with super-ego development occurring only around age five. Moreover, as will be apparent shortly, while Twain also uses the term "conscience" in this essay, he defines it somewhat differently than either its Freudian or commonly understood meaning.]

Y. M. Come! He never does anything for any one else's comfort, spiritual or physical?

O. M. No. *Except on those distinct terms*—that it shall *first* secure *his own* spiritual comfort. Otherwise he will not do it.

Y. M. It will be easy to expose the falsity of that proposition.

O. M. For instance?

Y. M. Take that noble passion, love of country, patriotism. A man who loves peace and dreads pain, leaves his pleasant home and his weeping family and marches out to manfully expose himself to hunger, cold, wounds, and death. Is that seeking spiritual comfort?

O. M. He loves peace and dreads pain?

Y. M. Yes.

O. M. Then perhaps there is something that he loves *more* than he loves peace—*the approval of his neighbors and the public*. And perhaps there is something which he dreads more than he dreads pain—the *disapproval* of his neighbors and the public. If he is sensitive to shame he will go to the field—not because his spirit will be *entirely* comfortable there, but because it will be more comfortable there than it would be if he remained at home. He will always do the thing which will bring him the *most* mental comfort—for that is *the sole law of his life*. He leaves the weeping family behind; he is sorry to make them uncomfortable, but not sorry enough to sacrifice his *own* comfort to secure theirs.

[This implies that Twain believes there is an unconscious weighing/balancing process. In Freudian theory, the id, ego, and superego are engaged in a (largely if not entirely) unconscious balancing act to provide some mental comfort for the individual. For Twain, this process involves balancing a number of temperamental traits (such as need for personal comfort/physical safety vs. empathic identification with and consequent need to relieve another's pain vs. need for social approval) with environmental influences (such as religious and other cultural norms and social expectations).]

Y. M. Do you really believe that mere public opinion could force a timid and peaceful man to—

O. M. Go to war? Yes—public opinion can force some men to do *anything*.

Y. M. *Anything?*

O. M. Yes—anything.

Y. M. I don't believe that. Can it force a right-principled man to do a wrong thing?

O. M. Yes.

Y. M. Can it force a kind man to do a cruel thing?

O. M. Yes.

Y. M. Give an instance.

O. M. Alexander Hamilton was a conspicuously high-principled man. He regarded dueling as wrong, and as opposed to the teachings of religion—but in deference to *public opinion* he fought a duel. He deeply loved his family, but to buy public approval he treacherously deserted them and threw his life away, ungenerously leaving them to lifelong sorrow in order that he might stand well with a foolish world. In the then condition of the public standards of honor he could not have been comfortable with the stigma upon him of having refused to fight. The teachings of religion, his devotion to his family, his kindness of heart, his high principles, all went for nothing when they stood in the way of his spiritual comfort. A man will do *anything*, no matter what it is, *to secure his spiritual comfort*; and he can neither be forced nor persuaded to any act which has not that goal for its object. Hamilton's act was compelled by the inborn necessity of contenting his own spirit; in this it was like all the other acts of his life, and like all the acts of all men's lives. Do you see where the kernel of the matter lies? A man cannot be comfortable without *his own* approval. He will secure the largest share possible of that, at all costs, all sacrifices.

Y. M. A minute ago you said Hamilton fought that duel to get *public* approval.

O. M. I did. By refusing to fight the duel he would have secured his family's approval and a large share of his own; but the public approval was more valuable in his eyes than all other approvals put together—in the earth or above it; to secure that would furnish him the *most* comfort of mind, the most *self*-approval; so he sacrificed all other values to get it.

Y. M. Some noble souls have refused to fight duels, and have manfully braved the public contempt.

O. M. They acted *according to their make*. They valued their principles and the approval of their families *above* the public approval. They took the thing they valued *most* and let the rest go. They took what would give them the *largest* share of *personal contentment and approval*—a man *always* does. Public opinion cannot force that kind of men to go to the wars. When they go it is for other reasons. Other spirit-contenting reasons.

Y. M. Always spirit-contenting reasons?

O. M. There are no others.

Y. M. When a man sacrifices his life to save a little child from a burning building, what do you call that?

O. M. When he does it, it is the law of *his* make. *He* can't bear to see the child in that peril (a man of a different make *could*), and so he tries to save the child, and loses his life. But he has got what he was after—*his own approval*.

[Here, Twain seems to be using a number of terms interchangeably: "the law of his make," "self-approval," "spiritual comfort"—all represent Twain's "master impulse" or the "compulsion that moves a man."]

Y. M. What do you call Love, Hate, Charity, Revenge, Humanity, Magnanimity, Forgiveness?

O. M. Different results of the one Master Impulse: the necessity of securing one's self-approval. They wear diverse clothes and are subject to diverse moods, but in whatsoever ways they masquerade they are the *same person* all the time. To change the figure, the *compulsion* that moves a man—and there is but the one—is the necessity of securing the contentment of his own spirit. When it stops, the man is dead.

Y. M. This is foolishness. Love—

O. M. Why, love is that impulse, that law, in its most uncompromising form. It will squander life and everything else on its object. Not *primarily* for the object's sake, but for *its own*. When its object is happy *it* is happy—and that is what it is unconsciously after.

Y. M. You do not even except the lofty and gracious passion of mother-love?

O. M. No, *it* is the absolute slave of that law. The mother will go naked to clothe her child; she will starve that it may have food; suffer torture to save it from pain; die that it may live. She takes a living *pleasure* in making these sacrifices. *She does it for that reward*—that self-approval, that contentment, that peace, that comfort. *She would do it for your child IF SHE COULD GET THE SAME PAY.*

[*Here, Twain describes even idealized mother-love (self-sacrifice) as essentially self-serving in accordance with his concept of the "master impulse" for self-approval and spiritual comfort.*]

Y. M. This is an infernal philosophy of yours.

O. M. It isn't a philosophy, it is a fact.

Y. M. Of course you must admit that there are some acts which—

O. M. No. There is *no* act, large or small, fine or mean, which springs from any motive but the one—the necessity of appeasing and contenting one's own spirit.

Y. M. The world's philanthropists—

O. M. I honor them, I uncover my head to them—from habit and training; but *they* could not know comfort or happiness or self-approval if they did not work and spend for the unfortunate. It makes *them* happy to see others happy; and so with money and labor they buy what they are after—*happiness, self-approval*. Why don't misers do the same thing? Because they can get a thousandfold more happiness by *not* doing it. There is no other reason. They follow the law of their make.

Y. M. What do you say of duty for duty's sake?

O. M. That *it does not exist*. Duties are not performed for duty's *sake*, but because their *neglect* would make the man *uncomfortable*. A man performs but *one* duty—the duty of contenting his spirit, the duty of making himself agreeable to himself. If he can most satisfyingly perform this sole and only duty by *helping* his neighbor, he will do it; if he can most satisfyingly perform it by *swindling* his neighbor, he will do that. But he always looks out for Number One—*first*; the effects upon others are a *secondary* matter. Men pretend to self-sacrifices, but this is a thing which, in the ordinary value of the phrase, *does not exist and has not existed*. A man often honestly *thinks* he is sacrificing himself merely and solely for some one else, but he is deceived; his bottom impulse is to content a requirement of his nature and training, and thus acquire peace for his soul.

Y. M. Apparently, then, all men, both good and bad ones, devote their lives to contenting their consciences?

O. M. Yes. That is a good enough name for it: Conscience—that independent Sovereign, that insolent absolute Monarch inside of a man who is the man's Master. There are all kinds of consciences, because there are all kinds of men. You satisfy an assassin's conscience in one way, a philanthropist's in another, a miser's in another, a burglar's in still another.

[Twain adds "conscience," "independent sovereign," and "absolute monarch" as synonyms for the "master impulse/law of his make" from the previous pages. In this context, Twain's conscience is broader than either its common dictionary definition or the Freudian concept. For Freud, conscience is a component of the super-ego (along with the ego ideal), and it represents the internalization of socially acquired moral values. For Twain, conscience can be distinct from the "moral sense" which he defines as the socially acquired standards of morality, usually internalized as "training." While Twain believes that conscience often incorporates value systems defined as moral by the cultural institutions to which the individual has been exposed (and by which he has been trained), Twain views much of such social morality as false (e.g., arbitrary standards of "duty" or "honor" devoid of any genuine connection to human welfare or wellbeing; self-righteous prejudice). In addition, Twain blames the individual's conscience (not lack of conscience, as the dictionary definition would predict) for an individual's genuinely immoral behavior; in the latter case, the individual's "conscience" may have been primarily shaped by a powerful selfish temperament and/or exposure to unsavory social associations (e.g., criminals), but it remains the individual's "master impulse" in determining his behavior. Although Twain's concept of "conscience" as a personality structure in "What Is Man?" is unusual, when the characters in his novels use the term, they generally mean it in the more conventional sense.]

As a *guide* or *incentive* to any authoritatively prescribed line of morals or conduct (leaving *training* out of the account), a man's conscience is totally valueless. I know a kind-hearted Kentuckian whose self-approval was lacking—whose conscience was troubling him, to phrase it with exactness—*because he had neglected to kill a certain man*—a man whom he had never seen. The stranger had killed this man's friend in a fight, this man's Kentucky training made it a duty to kill the stranger for it. He neglected his duty—kept dodging it, shirking it, putting it off, and his unrelenting conscience kept persecuting him for this conduct. At last, to get ease of mind, comfort, self-approval, he hunted up the stranger and took his life. It was an immense act of *self-sacrifice* (as per the usual definition), for he did not want to do it, and he never would have done it if he could have bought a contented spirit and an unworried mind at smaller cost. But we are so made that we will pay *anything* for that contentment—even another man's life.

Y. M. You spoke a moment ago of *trained* consciences. You mean that we are not *born* with consciences competent to guide us aright?

O. M. If we were, children and savages would know right from wrong, and not have to be taught it.

Y. M. But consciences can be *trained*?

O. M. Yes.

Y. M. Of course by parents, teachers, the pulpit, and books.

O. M. Yes—they do their share; they do what they can.

Y. M. And the rest is done by—

O. M. Oh, a million unnoticed influences—for good or bad: influences which work without rest during every waking moment of a man's life, from cradle to grave.

[*For Twain, conscience may be influenced by training, much of which occurs unconsciously via identification with the explicit and implicit messages of authority figures (parents, teachers, etc.), but also as a result of many other direct and indirect environmental influences. Twain's description of the mechanism of this identification in "What Is Man?" is both more diffuse and less clearly articulated than Freud's. However, in other works such as his study* Christian Science *and his novel* A Connecticut Yankee at King Arthur's Court, *Twain refers to the child's need for the approval and protection of parents and other powerful authority figures as underlying the processes of identification and internalization in training. He also believed that for most people, these needs for security and social approval persist into adulthood, resulting in regressive identification with religious and political leaders and internalization of their ideologies.*]

Y. M. You have tabulated these?

O. M. Many of them—yes.

Y. M. Will you read me the result?

O. M. Another time, yes. It would take an hour.

Y. M. A conscience can be trained to shun evil and prefer good?

O. M. Yes.

Y. M. But will prefer it for spirit-contenting reasons only?

O. M. It *can't* be trained to do a thing for any *other* reason. The thing is impossible.

Y. M. There *must* be a genuinely and utterly self-sacrificing act recorded in human history somewhere.

O. M. You are young. You have many years before you. Search one out.

Y. M. It does seem to me that when a man sees a fellow-being struggling in the water and jumps in at the risk of his life to save him—

O. M. Wait. Describe the *man*. Describe the *fellow-being*. State if there is an *audience* present; or if they are *alone*.

Y. M. What have these things to do with the splendid act?

O. M. Very much. Shall we suppose, as a beginning, that the two are alone, in a solitary place, at midnight?

Y. M. If you choose.

O. M. And that the fellow-being is the man's daughter?

Y. M. Well, n-no—make it some one else.

O. M. A filthy, drunken ruffian, then?

Y. M. I see. Circumstances alter cases. I suppose that if there was no audience to observe the act, the man wouldn't perform it.

O. M. But there is here and there a man who *would*. People, for instance, like the man who lost his life trying to save the child from the fire; and the man who gave the needy old woman his twenty-five cents and walked home in the storm—there are here and there men like that who would do it. And why? Because they couldn't *bear* to see a fellow-being struggling in the water and not jump in and help. It would give *them* pain. They would save the fellow-being on that account. *They wouldn't do it otherwise.* They strictly obey the law which I have been insisting upon. You must remember and always distinguish the people who *can't bear* things from the people who *can*. It will throw light upon a number of apparently "self-sacrificing" cases.

[*Twain seems to be talking about the role of empathy in human motivation, though without explicitly using the team. In particular, he seems to be highlighting the impact of empathy on the internalization of social moral standards and how empathy may be incorporated into conscience and become manifest in behavior. Also, while not directly stated, one can infer that Twain would consider the capacity for empathy to be an inborn, temperamental predisposition that, depending on its intrinsic strength relative to other temperamental predispositions, may be enhanced or discouraged to some degree by training and circumstance.*]

Y. M. Oh dear, it's all so disgusting.

O. M. Yes. And so true.

Y. M. Come—take the good boy who does things he doesn't want to do, in order to gratify his mother.

O. M. He does seven-tenths of the act because it gratifies *him* to gratify his mother. Throw the bulk of advantage the other way and the good boy would not do the act. He *must* obey the iron law. None can escape it.

Y. M. Well, take the case of a bad boy who—

O. M. You needn't mention it, it is a waste of time. It is no matter about the bad boy's act. Whatever it was, he had a spirit-contenting reason for it. Otherwise you have been misinformed, and he didn't do it.

Y. M. It is very exasperating. A while ago you said that a man's conscience is not born judge of morals and conduct, but has to be taught and trained. Now I think a conscience can get drowsy and lazy, but I don't think it can go wrong; and if you wake it up—

A Little Story

O. M. I will tell you a little story:

Once upon a time an Infidel was guest in the house of a Christian widow whose little boy was ill and near to death. The Infidel often watched by the bedside and entertained the boy with talk, and he used these opportunities to satisfy a strong longing of his nature—that desire which is in us all to better other people's condition by having them think as we think. He was successful. But the dying boy, in his last moments, reproached him and said:

"I believed, and was happy in it; you have taken my belief away, and my comfort. Now I have nothing left, and I die miserable; for the things which you have told me do not take the place of that which I have lost."

And the mother, also, reproached the Infidel, and said:

"My child is forever lost, and my heart is broken. How could you do this cruel thing? We have done you no harm, but only kindness; we made our house your home, you were welcome to all we had, and this is our reward."

The heart of the Infidel was filled with remorse for what he had done, and he said:

"It was wrong—I see it now; but I was only trying to do him good. In my view he was in error; it seemed my duty to teach him the truth."

Then the mother said:

"I had taught him, all his little life, what I believed to be the truth, and in his believing faith both of us were happy. Now he is dead—and lost; and I am miserable. Our faith came down to us through centuries of believing ancestors; what right had you, or any one, to disturb it? Where was your honor, where was your shame?"

Y. M. He was a miscreant, and deserved death!

O. M. He thought so himself, and said so.

Y. M. Ah—you see, *his conscience was awakened!*

O. M. Yes, his Self-Disapproval was. It *pained* him to see the mother suffer. He was sorry he had done a thing which brought *him* pain. It did not occur to him to think of the mother when he was misteaching the boy, for he was absorbed in providing *pleasure* for himself, then. Providing it by satisfying what he believed to be a call of duty.

Y. M. Call it what you please, it is to me a case of *awakened conscience*.

That awakened conscience could never get itself into that species of trouble again. A cure like that is a *permanent* cure.

O. M. Pardon—I had not finished the story. We are creatures of *outside influences*—we originate *nothing* within. Whenever we take a new line of thought and drift into a new line of belief and action, the impulse is *always* suggested from the *outside*. Remorse so preyed upon the Infidel that it dissolved his harshness toward the boy's religion and made him come to regard it with tolerance, next with kindness, for the boy's sake and the mother's. Finally he found himself examining it. From that moment his progress in his new trend was steady and rapid. He became a believing Christian. And now his remorse for having robbed the dying boy of his faith and his salvation was bitterer than ever. It gave him no rest, no peace. He *must* have rest and peace—it is the law of our nature. There seemed but one way to get it; he must devote himself to saving imperiled souls. He became a missionary. He landed in a pagan country ill and helpless. A native widow took him into her humble home and nursed him back to convalescence. Then her young boy was taken hopelessly ill, and the grateful missionary helped her tend him. Here was his first opportunity to repair a part of the wrong done to the other boy by doing a precious service for this one by undermining his foolish faith in his false gods. He was successful. But the dying boy in his last moments reproached him and said:

"*I believed, and was happy in it; you have taken my belief away, and my comfort. Now I have nothing left, and I die miserable; for the things which you have told me do not take the place of that which I have lost.*"

And the mother, also, reproached the missionary, and said:

"*My child is forever lost, and my heart is broken. How could you do this cruel thing? We had done you no harm, but only kindness; we made our house your home, you were welcome to all we had, and this is our reward.*"

The heart of the missionary was filled with remorse for what he had done, and he said:

"*It was wrong—I see it now; but I was only trying to do him good. In my view he was in error; it seemed my duty to teach him the truth.*"

Then the mother said:

"*I had taught him, all his little life, what I believed to be the truth, and in his believing faith both of us were happy. Now he is dead—and lost; and I am miserable. Our faith came down to us through centuries of believing ancestors; what right had you, or any one, to disturb it? Where was your honor, where was your shame?*"

The missionary's anguish of remorse and sense of treachery were as bitter and persecuting and unappeasable, now, as they had been in the former case. The story is finished. What is your comment?

[In "A Little Story" about the infidel, Twain seems to be illustrating

the role of empathy in determining whether individual conscience will result in genuinely virtuous vs. superficially moralistic behavior. Although not stated explicitly, it appears that both reason and temperamental empathy would need to be included, along with socially acquired values, in order for truly moral behavior to occur. However, Twain believes that reason can play only a minor role, if any, in the regulation of human emotional behavior. Thus, in the Infidel story, there are only empathy and successive experiences, but no application of reason to identify the principle that emotional comfort in the face of death is an important function of religious faith, irrespective of the particular religion.]

Y. M. The man's conscience was a fool! It was morbid. It didn't know right from wrong.

O. M. I am not sorry to hear you say that. If you grant that *one* man's conscience doesn't know right from wrong, it is an admission that there are others like it. This single admission pulls down the whole doctrine of infallibility of judgment in consciences. Meantime there is one thing which I ask you to notice.

Y. M. What is that?

O. M. That in both cases the man's *act* gave him no spiritual discomfort, and that he was quite satisfied with it and got pleasure out of it. But afterward when it resulted in *pain to him*, he was sorry. Sorry it had inflicted pain upon the others, *but for no reason under the sun except that their pain gave HIM pain.* Our consciences take *no* notice of pain inflicted upon others until it reaches a point where it gives pain to *us.* In *all* cases without exception we are absolutely indifferent to another person's pain until his sufferings make us uncomfortable. Many an infidel would not have been troubled by that Christian mother's distress. Don't you believe that?

Y. M. Yes. You might almost say it of the *average* infidel, I think.

O. M. And many a missionary, sternly fortified by his sense of duty, would not have been troubled by the pagan mother's distress—Jesuit missionaries in Canada in the early French times, for instance; see episodes quoted by Parkman.

Y. M. Well, let us adjourn. Where have we arrived?

O. M. At this. That we (mankind) have ticketed ourselves with a number of qualities to which we have given misleading names. Love, Hate, Charity, Compassion, Avarice, Benevolence, and so on. I mean we attach misleading *meanings* to the names. They are all forms of self-contentment, self-gratification, but the names so disguise them that they distract our attention from the fact. Also we have smuggled a word into the dictionary which ought not to be there at all—Self-Sacrifice. It describes a thing which does not exist. But worst of all, we ignore and never mention the Sole Impulse which dictates and compels a man's every act: the imperious necessity of securing his own approval, in every emergency and at all costs. To it we owe all that we are. It is our breath, our heart, our blood. It is our only spur, our whip, our goad, our only impelling power; we have no other. Without it we should be mere inert images, corpses; no one would do anything, there would be no progress, the world would stand still. We ought to stand reverently uncovered when the name of that stupendous power is uttered.

Y. M. I am not convinced.

O. M. You will be when you think.

IV
Training

[For Twain, training represents the internalization of outside influences, particularly the authority figures and primary social associates in the individual's life. In this section, Twain seems to be crediting all social environments to which an individual is extensively exposed over the lifespan with the potential to be equally influential. In that sense, he differs from Freud for whom the social environment of the nuclear family during childhood is the predominant influence on personality structure (although more recent psychologists have added more significance to subsequent experience). However, even within Twain's system, as a person is influenced first by early social environments and circumstances, these will affect the perspective with which he approaches subsequent ones (e.g., in the Infidel story, the infidel's emotional pain about adding to the first mother's grief contributed to his openness to studying Christianity).]

Young Man. You keep using that word—training. By it do you particularly mean—

Old Man. Study, instruction, lectures, sermons? That is a part of it—but not a large part. I mean *all* the outside influences. There are a million of them. From the cradle to the grave, during all his waking hours, the human being is under training. In the very first rank of his trainers stands *association*. It is his human environment which influences his mind and his feelings, furnishes him his ideals, and sets him on his road and keeps him in it. If he leave that road he will find himself shunned by the people whom he most loves and esteems, and whose approval he most values. He is a chameleon; by the law of his nature he takes the color of his place or resort. The influences about him create his preferences, his aversions, his politics, his tastes, his morals, his religion. He creates none of these things for himself. He *thinks* he does, but that is because he has not examined into the matter. You have seen Presbyterians?

Y. M. Many.

O. M. How did they happen to be Presbyterians and not Congregationalists? And why were the Congregationalists not Baptists, and the Baptists Roman Catholics, and the Roman Catholics Buddhists, and the Buddhists Quakers, and the Quakers Episcopalians, and the Episcopalians Millerites, and the Millerites Hindoos, and the Hindoos Atheists, and the Atheists Spiritualists, and the Spiritualists Agnostics, and the Agnostics Methodists, and the Methodists Confucians, and the Confucians Unitarians, and the Unitarians Mohammedans, and the Mohammedans Salvation Warriors, and the Salvation Warriors Zoroastrians, and the Zoroastrians Christian Scientists, and the Christian Scientists Mormons—and so on?

Y. M. You may answer your question yourself.

O. M. That list of sects is not a record of *studies*, searchings, seekings after light; it mainly (and sarcastically) indicates what *association* can do. If you know a man's nationality you can come within a split hair of guessing the complexion of his religion: English—Protestant; American—ditto; Spaniard, Frenchman, Irishman, Italian, South American, Austrian—Roman Catholic; Russian—Greek Catholic; Turk—Mohammedan; and so on. And when you know the man's religious complexion, you know what sort of religious books he reads when he wants some more light, and what sort of books he avoids, lest by accident he get more light than he wants. In America if you know which party-collar a voter wears, you know what his associations are, and how he came by his politics, and which breed of newspaper he reads to get light, and which breed he diligently avoids, and which breed of mass-meetings he attends in order to broaden his political knowledge, and which breed of mass-meetings he doesn't attend, except to refute its doctrines with brickbats. We are always hearing of people who are around *seeking after Truth*. I have never seen a (permanent) specimen. I think he has never lived. But I have seen several entirely sincere people who *thought* they were (permanent) Seekers after Truth. They sought diligently, persistently, carefully, cautiously, profoundly, with perfect honesty and nicely adjusted judgment—until they believed that without doubt or question they had found the Truth. *That was the end of the search.* The man spent the rest of his life hunting up shingles wherewith to protect his Truth from the weather. If he was seeking after political Truth he found it in one or another of the hundred political gospels which govern men in the earth; if he was seeking after the Only True Religion he found it in one or another of the three thousand that are on the market. In any case, when he found the Truth *he sought no further*; but from that day forth, with his soldering-iron in one hand and his bludgeon in the other he tinkered its leaks and reasoned with objectors. There have been innumerable Temporary Seekers after Truth—have you ever heard of a permanent one? In the very nature of man such a person is impossible. However, to drop back to the text—training: all training is one form or another of *outside influence*, and association is the largest part of it. A man is never anything but what his outside influences have made him. They train him downward or they train him upward—but they *train* him; they are at work upon him all the time.

["A man is never anything but what his outside influences have made him." This seems an overstatement by Twain of his own psychological system, since he earlier implied and will later elaborate on the role of inborn temperament, depending on its strength, as a potential limit on the impact of outside influences. Many of Twain's overstatements may be in the interest of making a point about the specific aspect of personality formation on which he is focusing at the time. In addition, elsewhere in this work and others, Twain has used the terms "exterior" or "outside" to highlight his belief that all influences on human behavior—whether derived from biological inheritance or environment—are determined by the individual's personality and are beyond the actual willful control (versus perceived willful control) of the individual.]

Y. M. Then if he happen by the accidents of life to be evilly placed there is no help for him, according to your notions—he must train downward.

O. M. No help for him? No help for this chameleon? It is a mistake. It is in his chameleonship that his greatest good fortune lies. He has only to change his habitat—his *associations*. But the impulse to do it must come from the *outside*—he cannot originate it himself, with that purpose in view. Sometimes a very small and accidental thing can furnish him the initiatory impulse and start him on a new road, with a new ideal. The chance remark of a sweetheart, "I hear that you are a coward," may water a seed that shall sprout and bloom and flourish, and end in producing a surprising fruitage—in the fields of war. The history of man is full of such accidents. The accident of a broken leg brought a profane and ribald soldier under religious influences and furnished him a new ideal. From that accident sprang the Order of the Jesuits, and it has been shaking thrones, changing policies, and doing other tremendous work for two hundred years—and will go on. The chance reading of a book or of a paragraph in a newspaper can start a man on a new track and make him renounce his old associations and seek new ones that are *in sympathy with his new ideal*; and the result, for that man, can be an entire change of his way of life.

[Here, Twain is describing how random circumstances can affect a man's interpersonal associations and therefore his subsequent outside influences. These, in turn, may trigger initiatory impulses that lead to positive or negative changes in an individual's values. At this point, Twain is continuing to focus on the environment to the exclusion of the impact of temperament, which may include elements of courage, empathy, selfishness, and so on, that would interact with such outside influences or training. However, he will return to a focus on the balancing process in personality development shortly.]

Y. M. Are you hinting at a scheme of procedure?

O. M. Not a new one—an old one. Old as mankind.

Y. M. What is it?

O. M. Merely the laying of traps for people. Traps baited with *Initiatory Impulses toward high ideals*. It is what the tract-distributer does. It is what the missionary does. It is what governments ought to do.

Y. M. Don't they?

O. M. In one way they do, in another way they don't. They separate the smallpox patients from the healthy people, but in dealing with crime they put the healthy into the pest-house along with the sick. That is to say, they put the beginners in with the confirmed criminals. This would be well if man were naturally inclined to good, but he isn't, and so *association* makes the beginners worse than they were when they went into captivity. It is putting a very severe punishment upon the comparatively innocent at times. They hang a man—which is a trifling punishment; this breaks the hearts of his family—which is a heavy one. They comfortably jail and feed a wife-beater, and leave his innocent wife and children to starve.

[*Twain believes that society has the potential to improve the content of training by laying "traps baited with initiatory impulses toward high ideals," for example, as he believes that missionaries often do. However, he explains that he thinks governments often fail in this, as when they throw first offenders into prison with recidivists, thereby exposing them to the development of more negative associations instead of encouraging positive ones.*]

Y. M. Do you believe in the doctrine that man is equipped with an intuitive perception of good and evil?

O. M. Adam hadn't it.

Y. M. But has man acquired it since?

O. M. No. I think he has no intuitions of any kind. He gets *all* his ideas, all his impressions, from the outside. I keep repeating this, in the hope that I may so impress it upon you that you will be interested to observe and examine for yourself and see whether it is true or false.

Y. M. Where did you get your own aggravating notions?

O. M. From the *outside*. I did not invent them. They are gathered from a thousand unknown sources. Mainly *unconsciously* gathered.

Y. M. Don't you believe that God could make an inherently honest man?

O. M. Yes, I know He could. I also know that He never did make one.

Y. M. A wiser observer than you has recorded the fact that "an honest man's the noblest work of God."

O. M. He didn't record a fact, he recorded a falsity. It is windy, and sounds well, but it is not true. God makes a man with honest and dishonest *possibilities* in him and stops there. The man's *associations* develop the possibilities—the one set or the other. The result is accordingly an honest man or a dishonest one.

Y. M. And the honest one is not entitled to—

O. M. Praise? No. How often must I tell you that? *He* is not the architect of his honesty.

Y. M. Now then, I will ask you where there is any sense in training people to lead virtuous lives. What is gained by it?

O. M. The man himself gets large advantages out of it, and that is the main thing—to *him*. He is not a peril to his neighbors, he is not a damage to them—and so *they* get an advantage out of his virtues. That is the main thing to *them*. It can make this life comparatively comfortable to the parties concerned; the *neglect* of this training can make this life a constant peril and distress to the parties concerned.

[*Here, Twain presents his view of genuine morality and virtue. For Twain, genuinely virtuous behavior is behavior that does not harm others and may actively help them. He believes most men are born with the potential for this, but that potential must be developed by environmental influences. When the individual's sense of virtue is developed via internalization of constructive social influences, the individual's conscience—the Master Impulse—will dictate that he behave well to obtain self-approval and spiritual comfort. As a by-product, other individuals and the community will benefit from his behavior.*]

Y. M. You have said that training is everything; that training is the man *himself*, for it makes him what he is.

O. M. I said training and *another* thing. Let that other thing pass, for the moment. What were you going to say?

Y. M. We have an old servant. She has been with us twenty-two years. Her service used to be faultless, but now she has become very forgetful. We are all fond of her; we all recognize that she cannot help the infirmity which age has brought her; the rest of the family do not scold her for her remissnesses, but at times I do—I can't seem to control myself. Don't I try? I do try. Now, then, when I was ready to dress, this morning, no clean clothes had been put out. I lost my temper; I lose it easiest and quickest in the early morning. I rang; and immediately began to warn myself not to show temper, and to be careful and speak gently. I safeguarded myself most carefully. I even chose the very words I would use: "You've forgotten the clean clothes, Jane." When she appeared in the door I opened my mouth to say that phrase—and out of it, moved by an instant surge of passion which I was not expecting and hadn't time to put under control, came the hot rebuke, "You've forgotten them again!" You say a man always does the thing which will best please his Interior Master.

Whence came the impulse to make careful preparation to save the girl the humiliation of a rebuke? Did that come from the Master, who is always primarily concerned about *himself?*

O. M. Unquestionably. There is no other source for any impulse. *Secondarily* you made preparation to save the girl, but *primarily* its object was to save yourself, by contenting the Master.

Y. M. How do you mean?

O. M. Has any member of the family ever implored you to watch your temper and not fly out at the girl?

Y. M. Yes. My mother.

O. M. You love her?

Y. M. Oh, more than that!

O. M. You would always do anything in your power to please her?

Y. M. It is a delight to me to do anything to please her!

O. M. Why? *You would do it for pay, solely*—for *profit*. What profit would you expect and certainly receive for the investment?

Y. M. Personally? None. To please *her* is enough.

O. M. It appears, then, that your object, primarily, *wasn't* to save the girl a humiliation, but to *please your mother.* It also appears that to please your mother gives *you* a strong pleasure. Is not that the profit which you get out of the investment? Isn't that the *real* profit and *first* profit?

Y. M. Oh, well? Go on.

O. M. In *all* transactions, the Interior Master looks to it that *you get the first profit.* Otherwise, there is no transaction.

Y. M. Well, then, if I was so anxious to get that profit and so intent upon it, why did I throw it away by losing my temper?

O. M. In order to get *another* profit which suddenly superseded it in value.

Y. M. Where was it?

O. M. Ambushed behind your born temperament, and waiting for a chance. Your native warm temper suddenly jumped to the front, and *for the moment* its influence was more powerful than your mother's, and abolished it. In that instance you were eager to flash out a hot rebuke and enjoy it. You did enjoy it, didn't you?

Y. M. For—for a quarter of a second. Yes—I did.

[The description of the hot-tempered young man's difficulty being patient with the elderly servant clarifies Twain's thinking about the role of temperament and the balancing process involved in determining individual personality and behavior.]

O. M. I have said: the thing which will give you the *most* pleasure, the most satisfaction, in any moment or *fraction* of a moment, is the thing you will always do. You must content the Master's *latest* whim, whatever it may be.

Y. M. But when the tears came into the old servant's eyes I could have cut my hand off for what I had done.

O. M. Right. You had humiliated *yourself*, you see, you had given yourself *pain*. Nothing is of *first* importance to a man except results which damage *him* or profit him—all the rest is *secondary*. Your Master was displeased with you, although you had obeyed him. He required a prompt *repentance*; you obeyed again; you *had* to—there is never any escape from his commands. He is a hard master and fickle; he changes his mind in the fraction of a second, but you must be ready to obey, and you will obey, *always*. If he requires repentance, to content him, you will always furnish it. He must be nursed, petted, coddled, and kept contented, let the terms be what they may.

Y. M. Training! Oh, what is the use of it? Didn't I, and didn't my mother try to train me up to where I would no longer fly out at that girl?

O. M. Have you never managed to keep back a scolding?

Y. M. Oh, certainly—many times.

O. M. More times this year than last?

Y. M. Yes, a good many more.

O. M. More times last year than the year before?

Y. M. Yes.

O. M. There is a large improvement, then, in the two years?

Y. M. Yes, undoubtedly.

O. M. Then your question is answered. You see there *is* use in training. Keep on. Keep faithfully on. You are doing well.

Y. M. Will my reform reach perfection?

O. M. It will. Up to *your* limit.

Y. M. My limit? What do you mean by that?

O. M. You remember that you said that I said training was *everything*. I corrected you, and said "training and *another* thing." That other thing is *temperament*—that is, the disposition you were born with. *You can't eradicate your disposition nor any rag of it*—you can only put a pressure on it and keep it down and quiet. You have a warm temper?

Y. M. Yes.

O. M. You will never get rid of it; but by watching it you can keep it down nearly all the time. *Its presence is your limit.* Your reform will never quite reach perfection, for your temper will beat you now and then, but you will come near enough. You have made valuable progress and can make more. There *is* use in training. Immense use. Presently you will reach a new stage of development, then your progress will be easier; will proceed on a simpler basis, anyway.

[*Here, Twain defines temperament as "the disposition you were born with ... you can't eradicate it, only put a pressure on it and keep it down and quiet."* Over time, success at obtaining parental/social approval by controlling what the individual was taught to view as a negative aspect of his temperament provides self-satisfaction and the social precept is internalized, making the self-control process easier.]

Y. M. Explain.

O. M. You keep back your scoldings now, to please *yourself* by pleasing your *mother*; presently the mere triumphing over your temper will delight your vanity and confer a more delicious pleasure and satisfaction upon you than even the approbation of your *mother* confers upon you now. You will then labor for yourself directly and at *first hand*, not by the roundabout way through your mother. It simplifies the matter, and it also strengthens the impulse.

Y. M. Ah, dear! But I sha'n't ever reach the point where I will spare the girl for *her* sake *primarily*, not mine?

O. M. Why—yes. In heaven.

Y. M. *(After a reflective pause.)* Temperament. Well, I see one must allow for temperament. It is a large factor, sure enough. My mother is thoughtful, and not hot-tempered. When I was dressed I went to her room; she was not there; I called, she answered from the bathroom. I heard the water running. I inquired. She answered, without temper, that Jane had forgotten her bath, and she was preparing it herself. I offered to ring, but she said, "No, don't do that; it would only distress her to be confronted with her lapse, and would be a rebuke; she doesn't deserve that—she is not to blame for the tricks her memory serves her." I say—has my mother an Interior Master?—and where was he?

O. M. He was there. There, and looking out for his own peace and pleasure and contentment. The girl's distress would have pained *your mother*. Otherwise the girl would have been rung up, distress and all. I know women who would have gotten a No. 1 *pleasure* out of ringing Jane up—and so they would infallibly have pushed the button and obeyed the law of their make and training, which are the servants of their Interior Masters. It is quite likely that a part of your mother's forbearance came from training. The *good* kind of training—whose best and highest function is to see to it that every time it confers a satisfaction upon its pupil a benefit shall fall at second hand upon others.

Y. M. If you were going to condense into an admonition your plan for the general betterment of the race's condition, how would you word it?

Admonition

O. M. Diligently train your ideals *upward* and *still upward* toward a summit where you will find your chiefest pleasure in conduct which, while contenting you, will be sure to confer benefits upon your neighbor and the community.

Y. M. Is that a new gospel?

O. M. No.

Y. M. It has been taught before?

O. M. For ten thousand years.

Y. M. By whom?

O. M. All the great religions—all the great gospels.

Y. M. Then there is nothing new about it?

O. M. Oh yes, there is. It is candidly stated, this time. That has not been done before.

Y. M. How do you mean?

O. M. Haven't I put *you* FIRST, and your neighbor and the community *afterward*?

Y. M. Well, yes, that is a difference, it is true.

O. M. The difference between straight speaking and crooked; the difference between frankness and shuffling.

Y. M. Explain.

O. M. The others offer you a hundred bribes to be good, thus conceding that the Master inside of you must be conciliated and contented first, and that you will do nothing at *first hand* but for his sake; then they turn square around and require you to do good for *others' sake chiefly*; and to do your duty for duty's *sake*, chiefly; and to do acts of *self-sacrifice*. Thus at the outset we all stand upon the same ground—recognition of the supreme and absolute Monarch that resides in man, and we all grovel before him and appeal to him; then those others dodge and shuffle, and face around and unfrankly and inconsistently and illogically change the form of their appeal and direct its persuasions to man's *second-place* powers and to powers which have *no existence* in him, thus advancing them to *first* place; whereas in my Admonition I stick logically and consistently to the original position: I place the Interior Master's requirements *first*, and keep them there.

Y. M. If we grant, for the sake of argument, that your scheme and the other schemes aim at and produce the same result—*right living*—has yours an advantage over the others?

O. M. One, yes—a large one. It has no concealments, no deceptions. When a man leads a right and valuable life under it he is not deceived as to the *real* chief motive which impels him to it—in those other cases he is.

Y. M. Is that an advantage? Is it an advantage to live a lofty life for a mean reason? In the other cases he lives the lofty life under the *impression* that he is living it for a lofty reason. Is not that an advantage?

O. M. Perhaps so. The same advantage he might get out of thinking himself a duke, and living a duke's life and parading in ducal fuss and feathers, when he wasn't a duke at all, and could find it out if he would only examine the herald's records.

Y. M. But anyway, he is obliged to do a duke's part; he puts his hand in his pocket and does his benevolences on as big a scale as he can stand, and that benefits the community.

O. M. He could do that without being a duke.

Y. M. But would he?

O. M. Don't you see where you are arriving?

Y. M. Where?

O. M. At the stand point of the other schemes: That it is good morals to let an ignorant duke do showy benevolences for his pride's sake, a pretty low motive, and go on doing them unwarned, lest if he were made acquainted with the actual motive which prompted them he might shut up his purse and cease to be good?

Y. M. But isn't it best to leave him in ignorance, as long as he *thinks* he is doing good for others' sake?

O. M. Perhaps so. It is the position of the other schemes. They think humbug is good enough morals when the dividend on it is good deeds and handsome conduct.

Y. M. It is my opinion that under your scheme of a man's doing a good deed for his *own* sake first-off, instead of first for the *good deed's* sake, no man would ever do one.

O. M. Have you committed a benevolence lately?

Y. M. Yes. This morning.

O. M. Give the particulars.

Y. M. The cabin of the old negro woman who used to nurse me when I was a child and who saved my life at the risk of her own, was burned last night, and she came mourning this morning, and pleading for money to build another one.

O. M. You furnished it?

Y. M. Certainly.

O. M. You were glad you had the money?

Y. M. Money? I hadn't. I sold my horse.

O. M. You were glad you had the horse?

Y. M. Of course I was; for if I hadn't had the horse I should have been incapable, and my *mother* would have captured the chance to set old Sally up.

O. M. You were cordially glad you were not caught out and incapable?

Y. M. Oh, I just was!

O. M. Now, then—

Y. M. Stop where you are! I know your whole catalogue of questions, and I could answer every one of them without your wasting the time to ask them; but I will summarize the whole thing in a single remark: I did the charity knowing it was because the act would give *me* a splendid pleasure, and because old Sally's moving gratitude and delight would give *me* another one; and because the reflection that she would be happy now and out of her trouble would fill *me* full of happiness. I did the whole thing with my eyes open and recognizing and realizing that I was looking out for *my* share of the profits *first*. Now then, I have confessed. Go on.

O. M. I haven't anything to offer; you have covered the whole ground. Could you have been any *more* strongly moved to help Sally out of her trouble—could you have done the deed any more eagerly—if you had been under the delusion that you were doing it for *her* sake and profit only?

Y. M. No! Nothing in the world could have made the impulse which moved me more powerful, more masterful, more thoroughly irresistible. I played the limit!

O. M. Very well. You begin to suspect—and I claim to *know*—that when a man is a shade *more strongly moved* to do *one* of two things or of two dozen things than he is to do any one of the *others*, he will infallibly do that *one* thing, be it good or be it evil; and if it be good, not all the beguilements of all the casuistries can increase the strength of the impulse by a single shade or add a shade to the comfort and contentment he will get out of the act.

Y. M. Then you believe that such tendency toward doing good as is in men's hearts would not be diminished by the removal of the delusion that good deeds are done primarily for the sake of No. 2 in-instead [sic] of for the sake of No. 1?

O. M. That is what I fully believe.

Y. M. Doesn't it somehow seem to take from the dignity of the deed?

O. M. If there is dignity in falsity, it does. It removes that.

Y. M. What is left for the moralist to do?

O. M. Teach unreservedly what he already teaches with one side of his mouth and takes back with the other: Do right *for your own sake*, and be happy in knowing that your *neighbor* will certainly share in the benefits resulting.

Y. M. Repeat your Admonition.

O. M. *Diligently train your ideals upward and still upward toward a summit where you will find your chiefest pleasure in conduct which, while contenting you, will be sure to confer benefits upon your neighbor and the community.*

Y. M. One's *every* act proceeds from *exterior influences*, you think?

O. M. Yes.

Y. M. If I conclude to rob a person, I am not the *originator* of the idea, but it comes in from the *outside*? I see him handling money—for instance—and *that* moves me to the crime?

O. M. That, by itself? Oh, certainly not. It is merely the *latest* outside influence of a procession of preparatory influences stretching back over a period of years. No *single* outside influence can make a man do a thing which is at war with his training. The most it can do is to start his mind on a new tract and open it to the reception of *new* influences....

[After some further discussion, the Old Man proceeds to relate the parable below to illustrate the potential sources of a hypothetical individual's impulse to rob someone who appears with a roll of money. In the parable, the Old Man, representing Twain's theory, points out that this would only occur if consistent with the individual's training or if it were the latest in a series of subsequent preparatory outside influences stretching back over a period of years. This discussion implies that the internalization of social values may be modified by subsequent associations, but only by a series of subsequent associations all pointing toward a different kind of behavior than that of the original training.]

A Parable

O. M. ...There was once a pair of New England boys—twins. They were alike in good dispositions, fleckless morals, and personal appearance. They were the models of the Sunday-school. At fifteen George had an opportunity to go as cabin-boy in a whale-ship, and sailed away for the Pacific. Henry remained at home in the village. At eighteen George was a sailor before the mast, and Henry was teacher of the advanced Bible class. At twenty-two George, through fighting-habits and drinking-habits acquired at sea and in the sailor boarding-houses of the European and Oriental ports, was a common rough in Hong-Kong, and out of a job; and Henry was superintendent of the Sunday-school. At twenty-six George was a wanderer, a tramp, and Henry was pastor of the village church. Then George came home, and was Henry's guest. One evening a man passed by and turned down the lane, and Henry said, with a pathetic smile, "Without intending me a discomfort, that man is always keeping me reminded of my pinching poverty, for he carries heaps of money about him, and goes by here every evening of his life." That *outside influence*—that remark—was enough for George, but *it* was not the one that made him ambush the man and rob him, it merely represented the eleven years' accumulation of such influences, and gave birth to the act for which their long gestation had made preparation. It had never entered the head of Henry to rob the man—his ingot had been subjected to clean steam only; but George's had been subjected to vaporized quicksilver.

[The last sentence refers back to the section immediately prior to the parable in which individual character was compared to a gold ingot that would be broken down by repeated exposure to vaporized quicksilver.]

V
More About the Machine

[This chapter focuses on Twain's recognition that many operations of the mind—thoughts, dreams, daydreams—are beyond conscious control.]

The Man-Machine Again

Young Man. You really think man is a mere machine?

Old Man: I do.

Y. M. And that his mind works automatically and is independent of his control—carries on thought on its own hook?

O. M. Yes. It is diligently at work, unceasingly at work, during every waking moment. Have you never tossed about all night, imploring, beseeching, commanding your mind to stop work and let you go to sleep?—you who perhaps imagine that your mind is your servant and must obey your orders, think what you tell it to think, and stop when you tell it to stop. When it chooses to work, there is no way to keep it still for an instant. The brightest man would not be able to supply it with subjects if he had to hunt them up. If it needed the man's help it would wait for him to give it work when he wakes in the morning.

Y. M. Maybe it does.

O. M. No, it begins right away, before the man gets wide enough awake to give it a suggestion. He may go to sleep saying, "The moment I wake I will think upon such and such a subject," but he will fail. His mind will be too quick for him; by the time he has become nearly enough awake to be half conscious, he will find that it is already at work upon another subject. Make the experiment and see.

Y. M. At any rate, he can make it stick to a subject if he wants to.

O. M. Not if it finds another that suits it better. As a rule it will listen to neither a dull speaker nor a bright one. It refuses all persuasion. The dull speaker wearies it and sends it far away in idle dreams; the bright speaker throws out stimulating ideas which it goes chasing after and is at once unconscious of him and his talk. You cannot keep your mind from wandering, if it wants to; it is master, not you.

After an Interval of Days

O. M. Now, dreams—but we will examine that later. Meantime, did you try commanding your mind to wait for orders from you, and not do any thinking of its own hook?

Y. M. Yes, I commanded it to stand ready to take orders when I should wake in the morning.

O. M. Did it obey?

Y. M. No. It went to thinking of something of its own initiation, without waiting for me. Also—as you suggested—at night I appointed a theme for it to begin on in the morning, and commanded it to begin on that one and no other.

O. M. Did it obey?

Y. M. No.

O. M. How many times did you try the experiment?

Y. M. Ten.

O. M. How many successes did you score?

Y. M. Not one.

O. M. It is as I have said: the mind is independent of the man. He has no control over it; it does as it pleases. It will take up a subject in spite of him; it will stick to it in spite of him; it will throw it aside in spite of him. It is entirely independent of him.

Y. M. Go on. Illustrate.

O. M. Do you know chess?

Y. M. I learned it a week ago.

O. M. Did your mind go on playing the game all night that first night?

Y. M. Don't mention it!

O. M. It was eagerly, unsatisfiably interested; it rioted in the combinations; you implored it to drop the game and let you get some sleep?

Y. M. Yes. It wouldn't listen; it played right along. It wore me out and I got up haggard and wretched in the morning.

O. M. At some time or other you have been captivated by a ridiculous rhyme-jingle?

Y. M. Indeed, yes!

> "I saw Esau kissing Kate,
> And she saw I saw Esau;
> I saw Esau, he saw Kate,
> And she saw—"

And so on. My mind went mad with joy over it. It repeated it all day and all night for a week in spite of all I could do to stop it, and it seemed to me that I must surely go crazy.

O. M. And the new popular song?

Y. M. Oh yes! "In the Swee-eet By and By"; etc. Yes, the new popular song with the taking melody sings through one's head day and night, asleep and awake, till one is a wreck. There is no getting the mind to let it alone.

O. M. Yes, asleep as well as awake. The mind is quite independent. It is master. You have nothing to do with it. It is so apart from you that it can conduct its affairs, sing its songs, play its chess, weave its complex and ingeniously constructed dreams, while you sleep. It has no use for your help, no use for your guidance, and never uses either, whether you be asleep or awake. You have imagined that you could originate a thought in your mind, and you have sincerely believed you could do it.

Y. M. Yes, I have had that idea.

O. M. Yet you can't originate a dream-thought for it to work out, and get it accepted?

Y. M. No.

O. M. And you can't dictate its procedure after it has originated a dream-thought for itself?

Y. M. No. No one can do it. Do you think the waking mind and the dream mind are the same machine?

O. M. There is argument for it. We have wild and fantastic day-thoughts? Things that are dream-like?

Y. M. Yes—like Mr. Wells's man who invented a drug that made him invisible; and like the Arabian tales of the Thousand Nights.

O. M. And there are dreams that are rational, simple, consistent, and unfantastic?

Y. M. Yes. I have dreams that are like that. Dreams that are just like real life; dreams in which there are several persons with distinctly differentiated characters—inventions of my mind and yet strangers to me: a vulgar person; a refined one; a wise person; a fool; a cruel person; a kind and compassionate one; a quarrelsome person; a peacemaker; old persons and young; beautiful girls and homely ones. They talk in character, each preserves his own characteristics. There are vivid fights, vivid and biting insults, vivid love-passages; there are tragedies and comedies, there are griefs that go to one's heart, there are sayings and doings that make you laugh; indeed, the whole thing is exactly like real life.

O. M. Your dreaming mind originates the scheme, consistently and artistically develops it, and carries the little drama creditably through—all without help or suggestion from you?

Y. M. Yes.

O. M. It is argument that it could do the like awake without help or suggestion from you—and I think it does. It is argument that it is the same old mind in both cases, and never needs your help. I think the mind is purely a machine, a thoroughly independent machine, an automatic machine. Have you tried the other experiment which I suggested to you?

Y. M. Which one?

O. M. The one which was to determine how much influence you have over your mind—if any.

Y. M. Yes, and got more or less entertainment out of it. I did as you ordered: I placed two texts before my eyes—one a dull one and barren of interest, the other one full of interest, inflamed with it, white-hot with it. I commanded my mind to busy itself solely with the dull one.

O. M. Did it obey?

Y. M. Well, no, it didn't. It busied itself with the other one.

O. M. Did you try hard to make it obey?

Y. M. Yes, I did my honest best.

O. M. What was the text which it refused to be interested in or think about?

Y. M. It was this question: If A owes B a dollar and a half, and B owes C two and three-quarters, and C owes A thirty-five cents, and D and A together owe E and B three-sixteenths of—of—I don't remember the rest, now, but anyway it was wholly uninteresting, and I could not force my mind to stick to it even half a minute at a time; it kept flying off to the other text.

O. M. What was the other text?

Y. M. It is no matter about that.

O. M. But what was it?

Y. M. A photograph.

O. M. Your own?

Y. M. No. It was hers.

O. M. You really made an honest good test. Did you make a second trial?

Y. M. Yes. I commanded my mind to interest itself in the morning paper's report of the pork-market, and at the same time I reminded it of an experience of mind of sixteen years ago. It refused to consider the pork and gave its whole blazing interest to that ancient incident.

O. M. What was the incident?

Y. M. An armed desperado slapped my face in the presence of twenty spectators. It makes me wild and murderous every time I think of it.

O. M. Good tests, both; very good tests. Did you try my other suggestion?

Y. M. The one which was to prove to me that if I would leave my mind to its own devices it would find things to think about without any of my help, and thus convince me that it was a machine, an automatic machine, set in motion by exterior influences, and as independent of me as it could be if it were in some one else's skull? Is that the one?

O. M. Yes.

Y. M. I tried it. I was shaving. I had slept well, and my mind was very lively, even gay and frisky. It was reveling in a fantastic and joyful episode of my remote boyhood which had suddenly flashed up in my memory—moved to this by the spectacle of a yellow cat picking its way carefully along the top of the garden wall. The color of this cat brought the bygone cat before me, and I saw her walking along the side-step of the pulpit; saw her walk on to the large sheet of sticky fly-paper and get all her feet involved; saw her struggle and fall down, helpless and dissatisfied, more and more urgent, more and more unreconciled, more and more mutely profane; saw the silent congregation quivering like jelly, and the tears running down their faces. I saw it all. The sight of the tears whisked my mind to a far distant and a sadder scene—in Terra del Fuego—and with Darwin's eyes I saw a naked great savage hurl his little boy against the rocks for a trifling fault; saw the poor mother gather up her dying child and hug it to her breast and weep, uttering no word. Did my mind stop to mourn with that nude black sister of mine? No—it was far away from that scene in an instant, and was busying itself with an ever-recurring and disagreeable dream of mine. In this dream I always find myself, stripped to my shirt, cringing and dodging about in the midst of a great drawing-room throng of finely dressed ladies and gentlemen, and wondering how I got there. And so on and so on, picture after picture, incident after incident, a drifting panorama of ever-changing, ever-dissolving views manufactured by my mind without any help from me—why, it would take me two hours to merely name the multitude of things my mind tallied off and photographed in fifteen minutes, let alone describe them to you.

[Here, the Young Man describes an experience of free association similar to the process Freud identified. Freud took the individual's process of free association significantly farther, not as a random sequence, but rather as a key to a deeper understanding of the individual; as such, he made it a major element in his psychoanalytic method of treatment.]

O. M. A man's mind, left free, has no use for his help. But there is one way whereby he can get its help when he desires it.

Y. M. What is that way?

O. M. When your mind is racing along from subject to subject and strikes an inspiring one, open your mouth and begin talking upon that matter—or take your pen and use that. It will interest your mind and concentrate it, and it will pursue the subject with satisfaction. It will take full charge, and furnish the words itself.

Y. M. But don't I tell it what to say?

O. M. There are certainly occasions when you haven't time. The words leap out before you know what is coming.

Y. M. For instance?

O. M. Well, take a "flash of wit"—repartee. Flash is the right word. It is out instantly. There is no time to arrange the words. There is no thinking, no reflecting. Where there is a wit-mechanism it is automatic in its action and needs no help. Where the wit-mechanism is lacking, no amount of study and reflection can manufacture the product.

Y. M. You really think a man originates nothing, creates nothing.

The Thinking Process

O. M. I do. Men perceive, and their brain-machines automatically combine the things perceived. That is all.

Y. M. The steam-engine?

O. M. It takes fifty men a hundred years to invent it. One meaning of invent is discover. I use the word in that sense. Little by little they discover and apply the multitude of details that go to make the perfect engine. Watt noticed that confined steam was strong enough to lift the lid of the teapot. He didn't create the idea, he merely discovered the fact; the cat noticed it a hundred times. From the teapot he evolved the cylinder—from the displaced lid he evolved the piston-rod. To attach something to the piston-rod to be moved by it, was a simple matter—crank and wheel. And so there was a working engine.[2]

One by one, improvements were discovered by men who used their eyes, not their creating powers—for they hadn't any—and now, after a hundred years the patient contributions of fifty or a hundred observers stand compacted in the wonderful machine which drives the ocean liner.

[Twain recognizes human reason as a personality component and describes its operation. He views human reason as generally limited to a focus on the physical, material world. Thus, it may be used to produce technology, but cannot significantly regulate man's emotional or interpersonal functioning, which is determined primarily by the interaction of his temperament and internalized training.]

Y. M. A Shakespearian [sic] play?

O. M. The process is the same. The first actor was a savage. He reproduced in his theatrical war-dances, scalp-dances, and so on, incidents which he had seen in real life. A more advanced civilization produced more incidents, more episodes; the actor and the story-teller borrowed them. And so the drama grew, little by little, stage by stage. It is made up of the facts of life, not creations. It took centuries to develop the Greek drama. It borrowed from preceding ages; it lent to the ages that came after. Men observe and combine, that is all. So does a rat....

VI
Instinct and Thought

[One of Twain's primary goals in the first part of this chapter seems to be to puncture human vanity by identifying parallels in the problem-

solving skills—defined by Twain as evidence of thought and reasoning ability—between humans and lower animals. From the perspective of Twain's theory of personality, a few interesting concepts can be identified in this chapter: instinct/petrified thought vs. actual thought and the role of external consequences/pain-pleasure/punishment-reward in the problem-solving/learning process.]

Young Man. It is odious. Those drunken theories of yours, advanced a while ago—concerning the rat and all that—strip Man bare of all his dignities, grandeurs, sublimities.

Old Man. He hasn't any to strip—they are shams, stolen clothes. He claims credits which belong solely to his Maker.

Y. M. But you have no right to put him on a level with a rat.

O. M. I don't—morally. That would not be fair to the rat. The rat is well above him, there.

Y. M. Are you joking?

O. M. No, I am not.

Y. M. Then what do you mean?

O. M. That comes under the head of the Moral Sense. It is a large question. Let us finish with what we are about now, before we take it up.

Y. M. Very well. You have seemed to concede that you place Man and the rat on *a* level. What is it? The intellectual?

O. M. In form—not in degree.

Y. M. Explain.

O. M. I think that the rat's mind and the man's mind are the same machine, but of unequal capacities—like yours and Edison's; like the African pygmy's and Homer's; like the Bushman's and Bismarck's.

Y. M. How are you going to make that out, when the lower animals have no mental quality but instinct, while man possesses reason?

O. M. What is instinct?

Y. M. It is merely unthinking and mechanical exercise of inherited habit.

O. M. What originated the habit?

Y. M. The first animal started it, its descendants have inherited it.

O. M. How did the first one come to start it?

Y. M. I don't know; but it didn't *think* it out.

O. M. How do you know it didn't?

Y. M. Well—I have a right to suppose it didn't, anyway.

O. M. I don't believe you have. What is thought?

Y. M. I know what you call it: the mechanical and automatic putting together of impressions received from outside, and drawing an inference from them.

O. M. Very good. Now my idea of the meaningless term "instinct" is, that it is merely *petrified thought*; solidified and made inanimate by habit; thought which was once alive and awake, but is become unconscious—walks in its sleep, so to speak.

[Twain defines instinct here very differently from Freud. Freud's concept of instinct (id, libido, sexual and aggressive drives) is closer to Twain's concept of temperament in that it is the inborn component of personality. In contrast, Twain sees instinct as petrified thought or habit, an attitude or behavior which may have initially been adaptive but which has "persisted beyond all utility."]

Y. M. Illustrate it.

O. M. Take a herd of cows, feeding in a pasture. Their heads are all turned in one direction. They do that instinctively; they gain nothing by it, they have no reason for it, they don't know why they do it. It is an inherited habit which was originally thought—that is to say, observation of an exterior fact, and a valuable inference drawn from that observation and confirmed by experience. The original wild ox noticed that with the wind in his favor he could smell his enemy in time to escape; then he inferred that it was worth while to keep his nose to the wind. That is the process which man calls reasoning. Man's thought-machine works just like the other animals,' but it is a better one and more Edisonian. Man, in the ox's place, would go further, reason wider: he would face part of the herd the other way and protect both front and near.

Y. M. Did you say the term instinct is meaningless?

O. M. I think it is a bastard word. I think it confuses us; for as a rule it applies itself to habits and impulses which had a far-off origin in thought, and now and then breaks the rule and applies itself to habits which can hardly claim a thought-origin.

Y. M. Give an instance.

O. M. Well, in putting on trousers a man always inserts the same old leg first—never the other one. There is no advantage in that, and no sense in it. All men do it, yet no man thought it out and adopted it of set purpose, I imagine. But it is a habit which is transmitted, no doubt, and will continue to be transmitted.

Y. M. Can you prove that the habit exists?

O. M. You can prove it, if you doubt. If you will take a man to a clothing-store and watch him try on a dozen pairs of trousers, you will see.

Y. M. The cow illustration is not—

O. M. Sufficient to show that a dumb animal's mental machine is just the same as a man's and its reasoning processes the same? I will illustrate further. If you should hand Mr. Edison a box which you caused to fly open by some concealed device he would infer a spring, and would hunt for it and find it. Now an uncle of mine had an old horse who used to get into the closed lot where the corncrib was and dishonestly take the corn. I got the punishment myself, as it was supposed that I had heedlessly failed to insert the wooden pin which kept the gate closed. These persistent punishments fatigued me; they also caused me to infer the existence of a culprit, somewhere; so I hid myself and watched the gate. Presently the horse came and pulled the pin out with his teeth and went in. Nobody taught him that; he had observed—then thought it out for himself. His process did not differ from Edison's; he put this and that together and drew an inference—and the peg, too; but I made him sweat for it.

Y. M. It has something of the seeming of thought about it. Still it is not very elaborate. Enlarge.

O. M. Suppose that Edison has been enjoying some one's hospitalities. He comes again by and by, and the house is vacant. He infers that his host has moved. A while afterward, in another town, he sees the man enter a house; he infers that that is the new home, and follows to inquire. Here, now, is the experience of a gull, as related by a naturalist. The scene is a Scotch fishing village were the gulls were kindly treated. This particular gull visited a cottage; was fed; came next day and was fed again; came into the house, next time, and ate with the family; kept on doing this almost daily, thereafter. But, once the gull was away on a journey for a few days, and when it returned the house was vacant. Its friends had removed to a village three miles distant. Several months later it saw the head of the family on the street there, followed him home, entered the house without excuse or apology, and became a daily guest again. Gulls do not rank high mentally, but this one had memory and the reasoning faculty, you see, and applied them Edisonially.

Y. M. Yet it was not an Edison and couldn't be developed into one.

O. M. Perhaps not. Could you?

Y. M. That is neither here nor there. Go on.

O. M. If Edison were in trouble and a stranger helped him out of it and next day he got into the same difficulty again, he would infer the wise thing to do in case he knew the stranger's address. Here is a case of a bird and a stranger as related by a naturalist. An Englishman saw a bird flying around about his dog's head, down in the grounds, and uttering cries of distress. He went there to see about it. The dog had a young bird in his mouth—unhurt. The gentleman rescued it and put it on a bush and brought the dog away. Early the next morning the mother bird came for the gentleman, who was sitting on his veranda, and by its manœuvres persuaded him to follow it to a distant part of the grounds—flying a little way in front of him and waiting for him to catch up, and so on; and keeping to the winding path, too, instead of flying the near way across lots. The distance covered was four hundred yards.

The same dog was the culprit; he had the young bird again, and once more he had to give it up. Now the mother bird had reasoned it all out: since the stranger had helped her once, she inferred that he would do it again; she knew where to find him, and she went upon her errand with confidence. Her mental processes were what Edison's would have been. She put this and that together—and that is all that thought *is*—and out of them built her logical arrangement of inferences. Edison couldn't have done it any better himself.

Y. M. Do you believe that many of the dumb animals can think?

O. M. Yes—the elephant, the monkey, the horse, the dog, the parrot, the macaw, the mocking-bird, and many others. The elephant whose mate fell into a pit, and who dumped dirt and rubbish into the pit till the bottom was raised high enough to enable the captive to step out, was equipped with the reasoning quality. I conceive that all animals that can learn things through teaching and drilling have to know how to observe, and put this and that together and draw an inference—the process of thinking. Could you teach an idiot the manual of arms, and to advance, retreat, and go through complex field manœuvers at the word of command?

Y. M. Not if he were a thorough idiot.

O. M. Well, canary-birds can learn all that; dogs and elephants learn all sorts of wonderful things.

[Twain goes on to refer explicitly to the role of external consequences/ pleasure-pain/reward-punishment in the problem-solving/learning process. His assertion that this is accompanied by conscious thought in lower animals remains controversial but serves his goal of satirizing human vanity.]

They must surely be able to notice, and to put things together, and say to themselves, "I get the idea, now; when I do so and so, as per order, I am praised and fed; when I do differently I am punished." Fleas can be taught nearly anything that a Congressman can.

Y. M. Granting, then, that dumb animals are able to think upon a low plane, is there any that can think upon a high one? Is there one that is well up toward man?

O. M. Yes. As a thinker and planner the ant is the equal of any savage race of men; as a self-educated specialist in several arts she is the superior of any savage race of men; and in one or two high mental qualities she is above the reach of any man, savage or civilized!

Y. M. Oh, come! you are abolishing the intellectual frontier which separates man and beast.

O. M. I beg your pardon. One cannot abolish what does not exist.

Y. M. You are not in earnest, I hope. You cannot mean to seriously say there is no such frontier.

O. M. I do say it seriously. The instances of the horse, the gull, the mother bird, and the elephant show that those creatures put their this's and that's together just as Edison would have done it and drew the same inferences that he would have drawn. Their mental machinery was just like his, also its manner of working. Their equipment was as inferior to his in elaboration as a Waterbury is inferior to the Strasburg clock, but that is the only difference—there is no frontier.

Y. M. It looks exasperatingly true; and is distinctly offensive. It elevates the dumb beasts to—to—

O. M. Let us drop that lying phrase, and call them the Unrevealed Creatures; so far as we can know, there is no such thing as a dumb beast.

Y. M. On what grounds do you make that assertion?

O. M. On quite simple ones. "Dumb" beast suggests an animal that has no thought-machinery, no understanding, no speech, no way of communicating what is in its mind. We know that a hen *has* speech. We cannot understand everything she says, but we easily learn two or three of her phrases. We know when she is saying, "I have laid an egg"; we know when she is saying to the chicks, "Run here, dears, I've found a worm"; we know what she is saying when she voices a warning: "Quick! hurry! gather yourselves under mamma, there's a hawk coming!" We understand the cat when she stretches herself out, purring with affection and contentment and lifts up a soft voice and says, "Come, kitties, supper's ready"; we understand her when she goes mourning about and says, "Where can they be? They are lost. Won't you help me hunt for them?" and we understand the disreputable Tom when he challenges at midnight from his shed, "You come over here, you product of immoral commerce, and I'll make your fur fly!" We understand a few of a dog's phrases and we learn to understand a few of the remarks and gestures of any bird or other animal that we domesticate and observe. The clearness and exactness of the few of the hen's speeches which we understand is argument that she can communicate to her kind a hundred things which we cannot comprehend—in a word, that she can converse. And this argument is also applicable in the case of others of the great army of the Unrevealed. It is just like man's vanity and impertinence to call an animal dumb because it is dumb to his dull perceptions. Now as to the ant—

Y. M. Yes, go back to the ant, the creature that—as you seem to think—sweeps away the last vestige of an intellectual frontier between man and the Unrevealed.

O. M. That is what she surely does. In all his history the aboriginal Australian never thought out a house for himself and built it. The ant is an amazing architect. She is a wee little creature, but she builds a strong and enduring house eight feet high—a house which is as large in porportion [sic] to her size as is the largest capitol or cathedral in the world compared to man's size. No savage race has produced architects who could approach the ant in genius or culture. No civilized race has produced architects who could plan a house better for the uses proposed than can hers. Her house contains a throne-room; nurseries for her young; granaries; apartments for her soldiers, her workers, etc.; and they and the multifarious halls and corridors which communicate with them are arranged and distributed with an educated and experienced eye for convenience and adaptability.

Y. M. That could be mere instinct.

O. M. It would elevate the savage if he had it. But let us look further before we decide. The ant has soldiers—battalions, regiments, armies; and they have their appointed captains and generals, who lead them to battle.

Y. M. That could be instinct, too.

O. M. We will look still further. The ant has a system of government; it is well planned, elaborate, and is well carried on.

Y. M. Instinct again.

O. M. She has crowds of slaves, and is a hard and unjust employer of forced labor.

Y. M. Instinct.

O. M. She has cows, and milks them.

Y. M. Instinct, of course.

O. M. In Texas she lays out a farm twelve feet square, plants it, weeds it, cultivates it, gathers the crop and stores it away.

Y. M. Instinct, all the same.

O. M. The ant discriminates between friend and stranger. Sir John Lubbock took ants from two different nests, made them drunk with whisky and laid them, unconscious, by one of the nests, near some water. Ants from the nest came and examined and discussed these disgraced creatures, then carried their friends home and threw the strangers overboard. Sir John repeated the experiment a number of times. For a time the sober ants did as they had done at first—carried their friends home and threw the strangers overboard. But finally they lost patience, seeing that their reformatory efforts went for nothing, and threw both friends and strangers overboard. Come—is this instinct, or is it thoughtful and intelligent discussion of a thing new—absolutely new—to their experience; with a verdict arrived at, sentence passed, and judgment executed? Is it instinct?—thought petrified by ages of habit—or isn't it brand-new thought, inspired by the new occasion, the new circumstances?

Y. M. I have to concede it. It was not a result of habit; it has all the look of reflection, thought, putting this and that together, as you phrase it. I believe it was thought.

O. M. I will give you another instance of thought. Franklin had a cup of sugar on a table in his room. The ants got at it. He tried several preventives; the ants rose superior to them. Finally he contrived one which shut off access—probably set the table's legs in pans of water, or drew a circle of tar around the cup, I don't remember. At any rate, he watched to see what they would do. They tried various schemes—failures, every one. The ants were badly puzzled. Finally they held a consultation, discussed the problem, arrived at a decision—and this time they beat that great philosopher. They formed in procession, crossed the floor, climbed the wall, marched across the ceiling to a point just over the cup, then one by one they let go and fell down into it! Was that instinct—thought petrified by ages of inherited habit?

Y. M. No, I don't believe it was. I believe it was a newly reasoned scheme to meet a new emergency.

O. M. Very well. You have conceded the reasoning power in two instances. I come now to a mental detail wherein the ant is a long way the superior of any human being. Sir John Lubbock proved by many experiments that an ant knows a stranger ant of her own species in a moment, even when the stranger is disguised—with paint. Also he proved that an ant knows every individual in her hive of five hundred thousand souls. Also, after a year's absence of one of the five hundred thousand she will straightway recognize the returned absentee and grace the recognition with an affectionate welcome. How are these recognitions made? Not by color, for painted ants were recognized. Not by smell, for ants that had been dipped in chloroform were recognized. Not by speech and not by antennæ signs nor contacts, for the drunken and motionless ants were recognized and the friend discriminated from the stranger. The ants were all of the same species, therefore the friends had to be recognized by form and feature—friends who formed part of a hive of five hundred thousand! Has any man a memory for form and feature approaching that.

Y. M. Certainly not.

O. M. Franklin's ants and Lubbock's ants show fine capacities of putting this and that together in new and untried emergencies and deducting smart conclusions from the combinations—a man's mental process exactly. With memory to help, man preserves his observations and reasonings, reflects upon them, adds to them, recombines, and so proceeds, stage by stage, to far results—from the teakettle to the ocean greyhound's complex engine; from personal labor to slave labor; from wigwam to palace; from the capricious chase to agriculture and stored food; from nomadic life to stable government and concentrated authority; from incoherent hordes to massed armies. The ant has observation, the reasoning faculty, and the preserving adjunct of a prodigious memory; she has duplicated man's development and the essential features of his civilization, and you call it all instinct!

Y. M. Perhaps I lacked the reasoning faculty myself.

O. M. Well, don't tell anybody, and don't do it again.

Y. M. We have come a good way. As a result—as I understand it—I am required to concede that there is absolutely no intellectual frontier separating Man and the Unrevealed Creatures?

O. M. That is what you are required to concede. There is no such frontier—there is no way to get around that. Man has a finer and more capable machine in him than those others, but it is the same machine and works in the same way. And neither he nor those others can command the machine—it is strictly automatic, independent of control, works when it pleases, and when it doesn't please, it can't be forced.

Y. M. Then man and the other animals are all alike, as to mental machinery, and there isn't any difference of any stupendous magnitude between them, except in quality, not in kind.

O. M. That is about the state of it—intellectuality. There are pronounced limitations on both sides. We can't learn to understand much of their language, but the dog, the elephant, etc., learn to understand a very great deal of ours. To that extent they are our superiors. On the other hand, they can't learn reading, writing, etc., nor any of our fine and high things, and there we have a large advantage over them.

Y. M. Very well, let them have what they've got, and welcome; there is still a wall, and a lofty one. They haven't got the Moral Sense; we have it, and it lifts us immeasurably above them.

O. M. What makes you think that?

Y. M. Now look here—let us call a halt. I have stood the other infamies and insanities and that is enough; I am not going to have man and the other animals put on the same level morally.

O. M. I wasn't going to hoist man up to that.

Y. M. This is too much! I think it is not right to jest about such things.

O. M. I am not jesting, I am merely reflecting a plain and simple truth—and without uncharitableness. The fact that man knows right from wrong proves his *intellectual* superiority to the other creatures; but the fact that he can *do* wrong proves his *moral* inferiority to any creature that *cannot*. It is my belief that this position is not assailable.

Free Will

[Twain's distinction here between free will and free choice is between behavioral determinants and intellectual awareness. Twain believes behavior is determined by the interaction of the individual's temperament with "his training and the daily influences which made him what he is." He may be intellectually capable of "choosing," that is, identifying the morally

correct act just as he, if academically schooled, is capable of reading a newspaper or performing arithmetic operations. But whether or not he engages in any of these behaviors at a particular point in time is determined by his personality dynamics, not his will.]

Y. M. What is your opinion regarding Free Will?

O. M. That there is no such thing. Did the man possess it who gave the old woman his last shilling and trudged home in the storm?

Y. M. He had the choice between succoring the old woman and leaving her to suffer. Isn't it so?

O. M. Yes, there was a choice to be made, between bodily comfort on the one hand and the comfort of the spirit on the other. The body made a strong appeal, of course—the body would be quite sure to do that; the spirit made a counter appeal. A choice had to be made between the two appeals, and was made. Who or what determined that choice?

Y. M. Any one but you would say that the man determined it, and that in doing it he exercised Free Will.

O. M. We are constantly assured that every man is endowed with Free Will, and that he can and must exercise it where he is offered a choice between good conduct and less-good conduct. Yet we clearly saw that in that man's case he really had no Free Will; his temperament, his training, and the daily influences which had molded him and made him what he was, *compelled* him to rescue the old woman and thus save *himself*—save himself from spiritual pain, from unendurable wretchedness. He did not make the choice, it was made *for* him by forces which he could not control. Free Will has always existed in *words*, but it stops there, I think—stops short of *fact*. I would not use those words—Free Will—but others.

Y. M. What others?

O. M. Free Choice.

Y. M. What is the difference?

O. M. The one implies untrammeled power to *act* as you please, the other implies nothing beyond a mere *mental process*: the critical ability to determine which of two things is nearest right and just.

Y. M. Make the difference clear, please.

O. M. The mind can freely *select, choose, point out* the right and just one—its function stops there. It can go no further in the matter. It has no authority to say that the right one shall be acted upon and the wrong one discarded. That authority is in other hands.

Y. M. The man's?

O. M. In the machine which stands for him. In his born disposition and the character which has been built around it by training and environment.

Y. M. It will act upon the right one of the two?

O. M. It will do as it pleases in the matter. George Washington's machine would act upon the right one; Pizarro's mind would know which was the right one and which the wrong, but the Master inside of Pizarro would act upon the wrong one.

Y. M. Then as I understand it a bad man's mental machinery calmly and judicially points out which of two things is right and just—

O. M. Yes, and his *moral* machinery will freely act upon the one or the other, according to its make, and be quite indifferent to the *mind's* feelings concerning the matter—that is, *would* be, if the mind had any feelings; which it hasn't. It is merely a thermometer: it registers the heat and the cold, and cares not a farthing about either.

Y. M. Then we must not claim that if a man *knows* which of two things is right he is absolutely *bound* to do that thing?

O. M. His temperament and training will decide what he shall do, and he will do it; he cannot help himself, he has no authority over the matter. Wasn't it right for David to go out and slay Goliath?

Y. M. Yes.

O. M. Then it would have been equally *right* for any one else to do it?

Y. M. Certainly.

O. M. Then it would have been *right* for a born coward to attempt it?

Y. M. It would—yes.

O. M. You know that no born coward ever would have attempted it, don't you?

Y. M. Yes.

O. M. You know that a born coward's make and temperament would be an absolute and insurmountable bar to his ever essaying such a thing, don't you?

Y. M. Yes, I know it.

O. M. He clearly perceives that it would be *right* to try it?

Y. M. Yes.

O. M. His mind has Free Choice in determining that it would be *right* to try it?

Y. M. Yes.

O. M. Then if by reason of his inborn cowardice he simply can *not* essay it, what becomes of his Free Will? Where is his Free Will? Why claim that he has Free Will when the plain facts show that he hasn't? Why contend that because he and David *see* the right alike, both must act alike? Why impose the same laws upon goat and lion?

Y. M. There is really no such thing as Free Will?

O. M. It is what I think. There is *Will*. But it has nothing to do with *intellectual perceptions of right and wrong*, and is not under their command.

David's temperament and training had Will, and it was a compulsory force; David had to obey its decrees, he had no choice. The coward's temperament and training possess Will, and *it* is compulsory; it commands him to avoid danger, and he obeys, he has no choice. But neither the Davids nor the cowards possess Free Will—will that may do the right or do the wrong, as their *mental* verdict shall decide....

[The remaining sections of this (final) chapter reiterate some aspects of the psychological thought developed in earlier chapters, but their focus is largely philosophical and satiric. Thus, they are not included in this Appendix.]

Notes

Preface

1. Carl Dolmetsch, *Our Famous Guest: Mark Twain in Vienna* (Athens: University of Georgia Press, 1992).
2. Mark Twain, "What Is Man?" (New York: Oxford University Press, 1998).
3. Mark Edmundson, *The Death of Sigmund Freud: The Legacy of His Last Days* (New York: Bloomsbury USA, 2007).
4. Ibid., p. 190.
5. Ibid.
6. R. W. Irwin, "Mark Twain and Sigmund Freud on the Discontents of Civilization" in *Iowa Review*, Vol. 14 (Fall 1984), pp. 30–47.
7. Raymond Sousa, "Be It What It Will, I'll Go to It Laughing" in *Thalia*, Vol. 2 (Spring-Fall, 1979), pp. 17–24.
8. Jennifer Zancora, "Mark Twain, Isabel Lyon and the Talking Cure" in Laura E. Skandera Trombley and Michael J. Kiskis (Eds.), *Constructing Mark Twain: New Directions in Scholarship* (Columbia: University of Missouri Press, 2001).
9. Susan Gillman, *Dark Twins: Imposture and Identity in Mark Twain's America* (Chicago: University of Chicago Press, 1982), p. 84.
10. Sigmund Freud, *Civilization and Its Discontents* (New York: W. W. Norton & Co., Inc., 1962), p. 25.
11. Mark Twain, "The Facts Concerning the Recent Carnival of Crime in Connecticut" in *The Signet Classic Book of Mark Twain's Short Stories* (New York: Signet Classics, 2006).
12. Ibid., pp. 172 and 175.
13. Ibid., p. 179.

Introduction

1. James Cox, *Mark Twain: The Fate of Humor* (Princeton: Princeton University Press, 1966), p. 153.
2. Linda Wagner-Martin, "Afterword" in *What Is Man?* (New York: Oxford University Press, 1996), p. 5.

Chapter I

1. Mark Twain, *What Is Man?* (New York: Oxford University Press, 1998).
2. Justin Kaplan, *Mr. Clemens and Mark Twain* (New York: Simon and Schuster, 1988), p. 340.
3. Ibid.
4. Charles Johnson, *What Is Man?*, op. cit., Introduction.
5. Twain, *What Is Man?*, op. cit., p. 126.
6. Ibid., p. 123.
7. Ibid., p. 53.
8. Ibid., p. 117.
9. Ibid., p. 119.
10. Ibid., p. 132.
11. Ibid.
12. A. B. Paine, *Mark Twain, A Biography, Vol. III* (New York: Harper Brothers, 1912), p. 1552.
13. Twain, *What Is Man?*, op. cit., p. 138.
14. Ibid., p. 69.
15. Ibid., p. 57.
16. Ibid.

17. Ibid.
18. Ibid.
19. Ibid., p. 71.
20. Ibid., p. 101.
21. Ibid., pp. 116–117.
22. Ibid., p. 117.
23. Ibid., p. 118.
24. Ibid., p. 125.
25. Mark Twain, *Mark Twain's Notebook*, Ed. A. B. Paine (New York: Harper Brothers, 1935), p. 305.
26. Twain, *What Is Man?*, op. cit., pp. 95–96.
27. Mark Twain, *Christian Science*, Ch. IX, Book I (New York: Harper Brothers, 1907).
28. Twain, *What Is Man?*, op. cit., p. 60.
29. Ibid., p. 40.
30. Ibid., p. 41.
31. Ibid., p. 42.
32. Ibid., pp. 90–91.
33. Ibid., p. 91.
34. Ibid., pp. 91–92.
35. Ibid., p. 92.
36. Ibid., p. 86.
37. Ibid., p. 87.
38. Sherwood Cummings, quoted in *Mark Twain: A Literary Life*, Ed. Everett Emerson (Philadelphia: University of Pennsylvania Press, 2000), p. 250.

Chapter II

1. Mark Twain, "The Turning Point of My Life," in Paul Baender (Ed.), *What Is Man? and Other Philosophical Writings* (Berkeley: University of California Press, 1973).
2. Ibid., p. 455.
3. Ibid.
4. Ibid., p. 459.
5. Ibid.
6. Ibid.
7. Ibid.
8. Ibid., p. 460.
9. Ibid.
10. Ibid.
11. Ibid.
12. Ibid.
13. Ibid.
14. Ibid., p. 461.
15. Ibid.
16. Ibid.
17. Ibid.
18. Ibid., p. 462.
19. Ibid., p. 463.
20. Ibid., pp. 463–464.
21. Ibid.
22. Ibid.
23. Ibid.

Chapter III

1. Ernest Jones, *The Life and Work of Sigmund Freud*, Vol. 3 (New York: Basic Books, 1957), p. 427.
2. Sigmund Freud, *Group Psychology and the Analysis of the Ego* (translated and edited by James Strachey) (New York: W. W. Norton, 1959).
3. Mark Twain, "The United States of Lyncherdom," in *Europe and Elsewhere* (New York: Harper's, 1923).
4. Mark Twain, *The Adventures of Huckleberry Finn* (New York: Charles Webster and Company, 1885). Hereafter referred to as *Huck Finn*.
5. Mark Twain, *The Mysterious Stranger* (New York: Harper's, 1922), Chapter IX.
6. A. B. Paine (Ed.), *Mark Twain's Notebook* (New York: Harper's, 1935), p. 379.
7. Mark Twain, *What Is Man? and Other Essays* (New York: Harper's, 1917), Chapter VI.
8. A. B. Paine (Ed.), *Mark Twain, A Biography*, Vol. III (New York: Harper's, 1912).
9. "The United States of Lyncherdom," op. cit., p. 241.
10. A. B. Paine (Ed.), *Mark Twain's Speeches* (New York: Harper's, 1923), p. 316.
11. "The United States of Lyncherdom," op. cit., p. 246.
12. Mark Twain, *Christian Science* (New York: Harper's, 1970), p. 154.
13. *What Is Man? and Other Essays*, op. cit., Chapter VI.
14. Peter Gay, *Freud, A Life for Our Time* (New York: W. W. Norton, 1988), p. 404. Freud quoted there.
15. Freud, *Group Psychology*, op. cit., p. 4.
16. Ibid., p. 13.
17. Ibid., p. 17.
18. Ibid., p. 27.
19. Ibid., p. 70.
20. Ibid., p. 39.
21. Ibid., p. 73.
22. Ibid., p. 81.
23. Ibid., p. 88.

24. *Huck Finn*, op. cit., p. 31.
25. Ibid., p. 103.

Chapter IV

1. Mark Twain, *The Adventures of Huckleberry Finn*, eds. Walter Bleur and Victor Fisher (Berkeley: University of California Press, 1988).
2. Ibid. The corrupted republic appears in Chapters 1, 2, 3, 4, 5, 6, 11, 13, 32, 33, 34, 35, 36, 37, 38, 39, 41, and 42.
3. Ibid. The tribal theocracy appears in Chapters 8, 9, and 10.
4. Ibid. The democratic republic appears in Chapters 12, 14, 15, 16, and 40.
5. Ibid. The aristocracy appears in Chapters 17 and 18.
6. Ibid. The tyranny appears in Chapters 6, 7, and 19–31.
7. The dominant behavioral ethic is based on Montesquieu's notion, borrowed from Aristotle, that each form of government has a first principle.
8. Roger Salomon, "Mark Twain and Victorian Nostalgia," in *Patterns of Commitment in American Literature*, ed. Mastron LaFrance (Toronto: University of Toronto Press, 1967), p. 73.
9. James Cox, *Mark Twain: The Fate of Humor* (Princeton: Princeton University Press, 1966), p. 174.
10. Mark Twain, *Mark Twain's Letters*, ed. A. B. Paine (New York: Harper and Brothers, 1917), Vol. II, p. 764.
11. Mark Twain, *What Is Man? and Other Essays* (New York: Harper and Brothers, 1917), p. 5.
12. Mark Twain, *Huckleberry Finn*, op. cit., p. 25.
13. Ibid., p. 88.
14. Ibid., p. 8.
15. Ibid., p. 279.
16. Ibid., p. 307.
17. Ibid., p. 362.
18. Ernest Becker, *The Breath and Death of Meaning* (New York: MacMillan Press, 1971).
19. Ibid., p. 156.
20. Ibid.
21. Ibid.
22. Mark Twain, *Huckleberry Finn*, op. cit., p. 315.
23. Ibid., p. 54.
24. Ibid., p. 60.
25. Ibid.
26. Ibid.
27. Ibid., p. 55.
28. Ibid., p. 63.
29. Ibid., p. 65.
30. Ibid., p. 75.
31. Mark Twain, *Mark Twain's Notebook*, ed. A. B. Paine (New York: Harper and Brothers, 1935), p. 337.
32. Mark Twain, *Huckleberry Finn*, op. cit., p. 87.
33. Ibid., p. 105.
34. Ibid.
35. Ibid., p. 125.
36. Ibid.
37. Ibid., p. 142.
38. Ibid.
39. Ibid.
40. Ibid., p. 146.
41. Ibid.
42. Ibid., p. 154.
43. Mark Twain, *A Connecticut Yankee at King Arthur's Court* (New York: Charles L. Webster and Company, 1890), p. 97.
44. Mark Twain, *Huckleberry Finn*, op. cit., p. 162.
45. Ibid., p. 165.
46. Ibid., p. 228.
47. Ibid., p. 190.
48. Ibid., p. 259.
49. Ibid., p. 290.
50. Mark Twain, "What Is Man?," op. cit., p. 121.

Chapter V

1. Mark Twain, "The Man Who Corrupted Hadleyburg," in *Great Short Works of Mark Twain*, ed. Justin Kaplan (New York: Harper Collins), 2004. Hereafter referred to as "Hadleyburg."
2. Mark Twain, "Cornpone Opinions," in *Great Short Works of Mark Twain*, ed. Justin Kaplan (New York: Harper Collins), 2004.
3. Ibid., p. 189.
4. Ibid.
5. Ibid.
6. "Hadleyburg," op. cit., p. 235.
7. Ibid.
8. Ibid.
9. Ibid., p. 238.
10. Ibid.

11. Ibid., p. 243.
12. Ibid.
13. Ibid., p. 244
14. Ibid., p. 245.
15. Ibid., p. 236.
16. Ibid., p. 237.
17. Ibid.
18. Ibid.
19. Ibid., p. 232.
20. Ibid., p. 240.
21. Ibid., 241.
22. Ibid.
23. Ibid., p. 245.
24. Ibid., p. 264.
25. Ibid., p. 265.
26. Ibid., p. 268.
27. Ibid., p. 265.
28. Ibid., p. 268.
29. Ibid., p. 272.
30. Ibid., p. 273.
31. Ibid., p. 274.
32. Ibid.
33. Ibid., p. 275.
34. Ibid., p. 274.
35. Ibid., p. 275.
36. Ibid.
37. Ibid., p. 276.
38. Ibid.
39. Ibid., p. 277.
40. Ibid., p. 270
41. Ibid., p. 274.
42. Ibid.

Chapter VI

1. Mark Twain, *Pudd'nhead Wilson* (New York: Penguin Books, 1986).
2. Ibid., p. 138.
3. Ibid.
4. Ibid., p. 139.
5. Ibid.
6. Ibid., p. 64.
7. Ibid.
8. Ibid.
9. Ibid., p. 67.
10. Ibid., p. 58.
11. Ibid., p. 77.
12. Ibid.
13. Ibid.
14. Ibid., p. 68.
15. Ibid.
16. Ibid., p. 69.
17. Ibid.
18. Ibid.
19. Ibid., p. 72.
20. Ibid., p. 73.
21. Ibid., p. 63.
22. Ibid., p. 57.
23. Ibid.
24. Ibid., p. 71.
25. Ibid., p. 77.
26. Ibid.
27. Ibid.
28. Ibid., p. 75.
29. Ibid., p. 76.
30. Ibid.
31. Ibid., p. 77.
32. Ibid.
33. Ibid., p. 79.
34. Ibid., p. 84.
35. Ibid., p. 141.
36. Ibid., p. 118.
37. Ibid., p. 119.
38. Ibid.
39. Ibid.
40. Ibid., p. 78.
41. Ibid.
42. Ibid., p. 225.
43. Ibid.

Chapter VII

1. Mark Twain, "Christian Science," in Paul Baender (Ed.), *What Is Man? and Other Philosophical Writings* (Berkeley: University of California Press, 1973).
2. Sigmund Freud, *The Future of an Illusion*, trans. and ed. by James Strachey. (New York: W. W. Norton and Co., 1975).
3. Twain, op. cit., p. 261.
4. Ibid.
5. Ibid., pp. 261–262.
6. Ibid., pp. 263.
7. Freud, op. cit., pp. 13–14.
8. Twain, op. cit., p. 259.
9. Freud, op. cit., p. 55.
10. Ibid.
11. Ibid., p. 40.
12. Twain, op. cit., p. 348.
13. Ibid., p. 241.
14. Ibid., p. 249.
15. Ibid., p. 238.
16. Ibid., p. 288.
17. Ibid., p. 289.
18. Ibid., p. 229.
19. Ibid., p. 346.

20. Ibid., p. 347.
21. Ibid., p. 352.
22. Ibid., p. 353.
23. Ibid., p. 352.
24. Ibid., p. 336.
25. Ibid., p. 358.
26. Ibid., p. 235.
27. Ibid., p. 237.
28. Ibid., p. 260.
29. Ibid.
30. Freud, op. cit., p. 44.
31. Ibid., p. 7.
32. Ibid., p. 43.
33. Ibid.
34. A. B. Paine, *Mark Twain: A Biography, Vol. II* (New York: Harper and Brothers, 1912), p. 1096.
35. Mark Twain, *A Connecticut Yankee at King Arthur's Court* (New York: Penguin, 1971), p. 279.

Chapter VIII

1. Mark Twain, "Christian Science," in Paul Baender (Ed.), *What Is Man? and Other Philosophical Writings* (Berkeley: University of California Press, 1973).
2. Mark Twain, *A Connecticut Yankee at King Arthur's Court* (New York: Penguin, 1971).
3. Ibid., p. 197.
4. Ibid., p. 54.
5. Ibid., p. 53.
6. Ibid., p. 87.
7. Ibid., p. 59.
8. Ibid., p. 244.
9. Ibid., p. 245.
10. Ibid., p. 277.
11. Ibid., p. 89.
12. Ibid., p. 74.
13. Ibid., p. 75.
14. Ibid., p. 82.
15. Ibid.
16. Ibid.
17. Ibid., p. 87.
18. Ibid., p. 50.
19. Ibid., p. 86.
20. Ibid.
21. Ibid.
22. Ibid.
23. Ibid.
24. Ibid., p. 87.
25. Ibid., p. 88.
26. Ibid., p. 89.
27. Ibid., p. 88.
28. Ibid., p. 156.
29. Ibid.
30. Ibid., p. 161.
31. Ibid., p. 163.
32. Ibid., p. 166.
33. Ibid., p. 164.
34. Ibid., p. 81.
35. Ibid., p. 90.
36. Ibid., p. 91.
37. Ibid., p. 86.
38. Ibid.
39. Ibid., p. 88.
40. Ibid., p. 103.
41. Ibid., p. 101.
42. Ibid., p. 103.
43. Ibid., p. 101.
44. Ibid., p. 19.
45. Ibid., p. 102.
46. Ibid.
47. Ibid., p. 392.
48. Ibid.
49. Ibid.
50. Ibid.
51. Ibid., p. 397.
52. Ibid., p. 392.
53. Ibid., p. 404.

Chapter IX

1. Mark Twain, "Monarchical and Republican Patriotism" in Jim Zwick (Ed.), *Mark Twain's Weapons of Satire* (Syracuse, NY: Syracuse University Press, 1992), p. 190.
2. Ibid., p. 191.
3. Sigmund Freud, *The Future of an Illusion* (New York: Anchor Books, 1964), p. 13.
4. Ibid., p. 4.
5. Mark Twain, "Purchasing Civic Virtue" in Bernard De Voto (Ed.), *The Portable Mark Twain* (New York: Penguin Books, 1968), p. 570.
6. *Mark Twain's Weapons of Satire*, op. cit., p. 74.
7. Ibid., p. 77.
8. Ibid.
9. Ibid.
10. Ibid., p. 79.
11. Ibid.
12. Ibid., p. 77.
13. Ibid.
14. Ibid.

15. Ibid., p. 79.
16. Mark Twain, *Personal Recollections of Joan of Arc* (New York: Dover Publications, 2002).
17. Ibid., p. 11.
18. Ibid., p. 12.
19. Ibid., p. 13.
20. Ibid.
21. Ibid., Preface, p. xi.
22. Ibid., p. xii.
23. Ibid., Appendix, p. 326.
24. *Mark Twain's Weapons on Satire*, op. cit., p. 190.
25. Ibid.
26. Twain, *Personal Recollections of Joan of Arc*, op. cit., p. 328.
27. Ibid., p. 180.
28. Ibid., p. 187.
29. Ibid., p. 197.
30. Ibid., p. 180.
31. Ibid.
32. Ibid., p. 213.
33. Ibid., p. 212.
34. Ibid., p. 213.
35. Ibid., p. 221.
36. Ibid., p. 223.
37. Ibid., p. 227.
38. Ibid., p. 318.
39. Everett Emerson, *Mark Twain: A Literary Life* (Philadelphia: University of Pennsylvania Press, 2000), p. 214.

Chapter X

1. Mark Twain, *The Mysterious Stranger Manuscripts* (Ed. William M. Gibson) (Berkeley: University of California Press, 2005).
2. Ibid., Introduction, p. 4.
3. "The Chronicle of Young Satan," hereafter referred to as "The Chronicle."
4. Mark Twain, *Selected Mark Twain–Howell's Letters*, in William Gibson (Ed.) (Cambridge: Harvard University Press, 1967), p. 336.
5. Mark Twain, "The Mysterious Stranger," op. cit., p. 35.
6. Ibid., Introduction, p. 20.
7. Ibid., p. 41.
8. Ibid., p. 42.
9. Ibid., p. 39.
10. Ibid.
11. Mark Twain, *Collected Tales, Sketches, Speeches, and Essays: 1891–1910* (Louis Budd, Ed.) (New York: Library of America, 1992), p. 512.
12. Ibid., p. 522.
13. Ibid., p. 513.
14. Ibid., p. 519.
15. Sigmund Freud, *The Future of an Illusion* (translated W. D. Robson Scott) (London: Hogarth Press, 1928).
16. Ibid., p. 31.
17. Mark Twain, "The Mysterious Stranger," op. cit., p. 36.
18. Ibid.
19. Ibid., p. 37.
20. Ibid., p. 36.
21. Ibid., p. 37.
22. Ibid.
23. Ibid., p. 38.
24. Ibid.
25. Ibid.
26. Ibid., 41.
27. Ibid., p. 36.
28. Ibid., p. 73.
29. Ibid., p. 53.
30. Ibid., p. 55.
31. Ibid., p. 156.
32. Ibid.
33. Ibid., p. 164.
34. Ibid., p. 113.
35. Ibid, p. 112–113.
36. Ibid., p. 113.
37. Ibid., p. 154.
38. Ibid.
39. Ibid., p. 115.
40. Ibid., p. 114.
41. Ibid., p. 155.
42. Ibid.
43. Ibid.
44. Ibid., p. 112.
45. Ibid., p. 155.

Conclusion

1. Mark Twain, *The Autobiography of Mark Twain*, ed. Charles Weider (New York: Harper and Brothers, 1959), vol. 2, p. 308.
2. Mark Twain, *The Adventures of Huckleberry Finn* (New York: Charles Webster and Company, 1855).
3. Mark Twain, *Pudd'nhead Wilson* (New York: Penguin Books, 1986).
4. Mark Twain, "What Is Man?" (New York: Oxford University Press, 1998).
5. Mark Twain, "The Stranger Who Cor-

rupted Hadleyburg," in *Great Short Works of Mark Twain*, ed. Justin Kaplan (New York: Harper Collins), 2004.

6. Mark Twain, *A Connecticut Yankee at King Arthur's Court* (New York: Charles L. Webster and Company, 1890).

7. Montesquieu, *The Spirit of the Laws*, ed. Franz Newman, trans. Thomas Nugent (New York: Hafner Publishing, 1949).

8. Mark Twain, *Personal Recollections of Joan of Arc* (New York: Dover Publications, Inc., 2002).

9. Robert Penn Warren, *All the King's Men* (New York: Harcourt, Brace and Company, 1946).

10. Sinclair Lewis, *Babbitt* (New York: Harcourt, Brace and Company, 1922).

11. John Steinbeck, *The Grapes of Wrath* (New York: Viking, 1939).

12. Ernest Hemingway, *The Green Hills of Africa* (New York: Scribner and Sons, 1935).

Afterword

1. Charles Johnson, Introduction in "What Is Man?" (New York: Oxford University press, 1996), p. xl.

2. Carey Wilson McWilliams, Personal communication to the author.

Appendix

1. Justin Kaplan, *Mr. Clemens and Mark Twain*. New York: Simon and Schuster, 1988, p. 340.

2. This is a footnote Twain inserted within the essay: "The Marquess of Worcester had done all of this more than a century earlier" (p. 72).

Bibliography

Andrews, Kenneth R. *Nook Farm: Mark Twain's Hartford Circle.* Cambridge: Harvard University Press, 1950.
Baender, Paul (Ed.). *What Is Man? and Other Philosophical Writings.* Berkeley: University of California Press, 1973.
Becker, Ernest. *The Breath and Death of Meaning.* New York: MacMillan Press, 1971.
Bellamy, Gladys Carmen. *Mark Twain as a Literary Artist.* Norman: University of Oklahoma Press, 1950.
Blair, Walter. *Mark Twain and Huckleberry Finn.* Berkeley: University of California Press, 1960.
Breuer, Josef, and Sigmund Freud. *Studies on Hysteria.* In *The Standard Edition of the Complete Psychological Works of Sigmund Freud,* ed. and trans. James Strachey. London: Hogarth Press and Institute of Psycho-Analysis, 1953–1974.
Brooks, Van Wyck. *The Ordeal of Mark Twain.* New York: E. P. Dutton, 1920.
Camfield, Gregg. *Sentimental Twain: Samuel Clemens in the Maze of Moral Philosophy.* Philadelphia: University of Pennsylvania Press, 1994.
Cox, James M. *Mark Twain: The Fate of Humor.* Princeton: Princeton University Press, 1966.
Cummings, Sherwood. *Mark Twain and Science: Adventures of a Mind.* Baton Rouge: Louisiana State University Press, 1988.
Dolmetsch, Carl. *Our Famous Guest: Mark Twain in Vienna.* Athens: University of Georgia Press, 1992.
Doyno, Victor. *Writing "Huck Finn": Mark Twain's Creative Process.* Philadelphia: University of Pennsylvania Press, 1991.
Edmundson, Mark. *The Death of Sigmund Freud: The Legacy of His Last Days.* New York: Bloomsbury USA, 2007.
Emerson, Everett (Ed.). *Mark Twain: A Literary Life.* Philadelphia: University of Pennsylvania Press, 2000.
Farrell, Brian. *The Standing of Psychoanalysis.* New York: Oxford University Press, 1981.
Freud, Sigmund. *Civilization and Its Discontents.* New York: W. W. Norton & Co., Inc., 1962.
_____. *The Future of an Illusion* (trans. and ed. James Strachey). New York: W. W. Norton and Co., 1975.
_____. *Group Psychology and the Analysis of the Ego* (trans. and ed. James Strachey). New York: W. W. Norton, 1959.
_____. *The Standard Edition of the Complete Psychological Works of Sigmund Freud,* ed. and trans. James Strachey. London: Hogarth Press and Institute of Psycho-Analysis, 1953–1974.
Fuller, Robert C. *Americans and the Unconscious.* New York: Oxford University Press, 1986.
Gay, Peter. *Freud, A Life for Our Time.* New York: Norton, 1988.
Gibson, William M. *The Art of Mark Twain.* New York: Oxford University Press, 1976.

Gillman, Susan. *Dark Twins: Imposture and Identity in Mark Twain's America*. Chicago: University of Chicago Press, 1982.
Gribben, Alan. *Mark Twain's Library: A Reconstruction*. 2 vols. Boston: G. K. Hall, 1980.
Grünbaum, Adolf. *The Foundations of Psychoanalysis*. Berkeley: University of California Press, 1984.
Harnsberger, Caroline Thomas. *Mark Twain's Views of Religion*. Evanston, Ill.: Shori Press, 1961.
Harris, Susan K. *Mark Twain's Escape from Time: A Study in Patterns and Images*. Columbia: University of Missouri Press, 1982.
Hemingway, Ernest. *The Green Hills of Africa*. New York: Scribner and Sons, 1935.
Hill, Hamlin. *Mark Twain: God's Fool*. New York: Harper and Row, 1973.
Irwin, R. W. "Mark Twain and Sigmund Freud on the Discontents of Civilization." In *Iowa Review*, Volume 14, Fall 1979.
Jones, Ernest. *The Life and Work of Sigmund Freud, Vols. 1–3*. New York: Basic Books, 1957.
Kaplan, Justin (Ed.). *Great Short Works of Mark Twain*. New York: Harper Collins, 2004.
____. *Mark Twain and His World*. London: Michael Joseph, 1974.
____. *Mr. Clemens and Mark Twain*. New York: Simon and Schuster, 1988.
Lewis, Sinclair. *Babbitt*. New York: Harcourt, Brace and Company, 1922.
Montesquieu. *The Spirit of the Laws* (ed. Franz Newman, trans. Thomas Nugent). New York: Hafner Publishing, 1949.
Orwell, George. *1984*. New York: Harcourt, Brace and Company, 1949.
Paine, A. B. *Mark Twain, A Biography*. New York: Harper Brothers, 1912.
____. (Ed.). *Mark Twain's Notebook*. New York: Harper's, 1935.
____. (Ed.). *Mark Twain's Speeches*. New York: Harper's, 1923.
Ricoeur, Paul. *Freud and Philosophy*. New Haven, Conn.: Yale University Press, 1970.
Rieff, Philip. *Freud: The Mind of the Moralist*. New York: Viking, 1959.
Robinson, Paul. *Three Critics of Freud*. Berkeley: University of California Press, 1995.
Salomon, Roger B. "Escape from History: Mark Twain's *Joan of Arc*." *Philological Quarterly* 40 (1961): 77–90.
____. "Mark Twain and Victorian Nostalgia." In *Patterns of Commitment in American Literature* (Ed. Mastron LaFrance). Toronto: University of Toronto Press, 1967.
Salvaggio, Ruth. "Twain's Later Phase Reconsidered: Duality and the Mind." *American Literature* 12 (1979): 322–39.
Smith, Henry Nash. *Mark Twain: The Development of a Writer*. Cambridge: Harvard University Press, 1962.
Sousa, Raymond. "Be It What It Will, I'll Go To It Laughing." In *Thalia*, Volume 2, Spring-Fall, 1979.
Steinbeck, John. *The Grapes of Wrath*. New York: Viking, 1939.
Swift, Jonathon. *The Writing of Jonathon Swift*. New York: W.W. Norton and Company, 1973.
Twain, Mark. *The Adventures of Huckleberry Finn*. New York: Charles Webster and Company, 1855.
____. *Christian Science*. New York: Harper Brothers, 1907.
____. "Christian Science." In Paul Baender (Ed.), *What Is Man? and Other Philosophical Writings*. Berkeley: University of California Press, 1973.
____. *A Connecticut Yankee at King Arthur's Court*. New York: Charles L. Webster and Company, 1890.
____. "The Facts Concerning the Recent Carnival of Crime in Connecticut." In *The Signet Book of Mark Twain's Short Stories*. New York: Signet Classics, 2006.
____. *Mark Twain in Eruption* (Ed. Bernard DeVoto). New York: Harper and Brothers, 1940.
____. *Mark Twain: Letters from the Earth* (Ed. Bernard DeVoto). New York: Harper and Row, 1938.
____. *Mark Twain's Letters* (Ed. Albert Bigelow Paine). 2 vols. New York: Harper and Row, 1917.
____. *Mark Twain's Notebook* (Ed. A. B. Paine). New York: Harper Brothers, 1935.
____. *The Mysterious Stranger*. New York: Harper's, 1922.

_____. *Personal Recollections of Joan of Arc*. New York: Dover Publications, 2002.
_____. *The Prince and the Pauper*. New York: Bantam Books, 1991.
_____. *Pudd'nhead Wilson*. New York: Penguin Putnam, Inc., 1986.
_____. "The Stranger Who Corrupted Hadleyburg." In Justin Kaplan (Ed.), *Great Short Works of Mark Twain*. New York: Harper Collins, 2004.
_____. "The Turning Point of My Life." In Paul Baender (Ed.), *What Is Man? and Other Philosophical Writings*. Berkeley: University of California Press, 1973.
_____. "The United States of Lyncherdom." In Mark Twain, *Europe and Elsewhere*. New York: Harper's, 1923.
_____. *What Is Man?* New York: Oxford University Press, 1996.
_____. *What Is Man? and Other Essays*. New York: Harper's, 1917.
Warren, Robert Penn. *All the King's Men*. New York: Harcourt, Brace and Company, 1946.
Wilcocks, Robert. *Sigmund Freud and the Rhetoric of Deceit*. London: Rowan and Littlefield, 1994.
Zancora, Jennifer. "Mark Twain, Isabel Lyon and the Talking Cure." In Laura E. Skandera Trombley and Michael J. Kiskis (Eds.), *Constructing Mark Twain: New Directions in Scholarship*. Columbia: University of Missouri Press, 2001.

Index

absolute monarch 156, 170
The Adventures of Huckleberry Finn 5, 6, 31, 32–40, 41–57, 100, 137, 139, 140, 142, 148
All the King's Men 115
American view 24, 37, 57, 101, 102, 105, 137, 138, 142
amoral social climber 138, 140
aristocracy 41, 52, 53, 55, 101, 103, 108, 113, 134, 136, 140; honor 52, 75, 76, 77, 84; training 114
"As Regards Patriotism" 117
authoritarian civilization 119; leaders 56; political system 107; power 111; rule 54; society 60; temperament 120
authority figures 11, 14–16, 19–21, 91, 93, 94, 104, 129, 130, 157, 162
autocratic patriotism 118

Babbitt, George C. 142
Becker, Ernest 47

Christian Science 7, 88–99, 157
"The Chronicle of Young Satan" 126, 127, 132
church 79, 103, 105, 106, 124, 127–129, 131, 133, 134
circumstance 5, 13, 15, 25–31, 43, 49, 68, 73, 79, 87, 90, 91, 93, 100, 105, 107, 117, 134, 135, 139, 140, 146, 149, 158, 164
Citizen Kane 115
civilization 1, 4–6, 23, 24, 32, 40, 47, 60, 89, 96, 98, 99, 113, 117–120, 123, 125–127, 129–131, 134–136, 138
Civilization and Its Discontents 2, 6, 88, 118
clergy 101, 102, 104, 113, 120, 123, 125, 134
con game 94
con men 55, 66, 68, 134, 138
conformity 24, 34, 47, 49, 56, 59–61, 62, 64, 68, 138–142
A Connecticut Yankee at King Arthur's Court 5, 7, 8, 31, 99, 100–117, 125, 126, 139, 141, 157
conscience 2, 4, 18, 21, 35, 36, 38, 42, 43, 51, 57, 60, 64, 66–68, 70, 71, 106, 109, 112, 122, 142, 151, 152, 156–161, 166
conscious processes 2; *see also* unconscious processes
consciousness 15
"Corn-pone Opinions" 59, 117
Cox, James 3, 42, 43
Crusoe, Robinson 47, 110, 112, 113, 115
cultural worlds 42
culture 5, 6, 24, 27, 49, 72, 81; American 7
Cummings, Sherwood 24

Dalmetsch, Karl 1
daydreams 2
defense mechanisms 4, 10, 20
democracy: American 111–112; conscience 108–111, 115; demagogue 106, 115, 116, 138, 141, 142; empathy 57; ethic 131; heroes 40; leadership 8, 111, 113, 118, 122, 138, 141; outsiders 138, 139, 142; picaro 38, 39; process, corruption 111; republic 41, 50–52, 56; temperament 120; training 108, 110, 115, 118
determinism 10, 14, 18, 19, 43, 126, 127, 136, 143, 187
"Does Man Love a Lord?" 129, 130
dominant behavioral ethic 42, 44, 45, 47, 50, 51, 53, 54
dominant group 77
dreams 2, 10, 20, 23, 176

Eddy, Mary Baker 7, 90, 92–96, 115, 140
Edmundson, Mark 1
ego 4, 10, 11, 14, 18–20, 23, 36, 88, 119, 130, 153
ego ideal 36, 37, 152, 156
Emerson, Everett 125
European view 24, 37, 138

"The Facts Concerning the Recent Carnival of Crime in Connecticut" 2
"The Fall of the Great Republic" 117, 120
false moral sense 131

Index

father-leader 36
feud 39, 52, 53, 140
feudalism 101
folkloric superego 42, 47-49
free association 2, 5, 10, 20, 22, 23, 178
free will 10, 17, 18, 187, 188
Freud, Sigmund 1-24, 32, 33, 35-37, 40, 41, 60, 68, 88-93, 98-100, 104, 114, 117-119, 126, 130, 131, 137, 138, 143, 152, 153, 156, 157, 162, 178
Friday (from *Robinson Crusoe*) 47
Fromm, Erich 143
The Future of an Illusion 7, 88, 89, 118, 130

Gibson, William 126, 127
The Gilded Age 44
Gillman, Susan 2
Golden Rule 37, 39, 50, 92, 99, 131
group opinion 118
group psychology 5, 6, 8, 32, 33, 35, 37, 39-45, 63, 89, 90, 100, 102-104, 109, 117, 118, 126-129, 132, 134, 135, 138, 139, 143, 144
Group Psychology and the Analysis of the Ego 5, 32, 35, 118
Gulliver's Travels 41, 56

Heller, Joseph 142
Hemingway, Ernest 142
herd instinct 33, 34, 36-40, 54, 56, 57, 59, 71, 102, 103, 106, 111, 113-114, 118, 127, 129, 135
Howells, W.D. 127
humor 2

id 4, 10, 12-14, 16-19, 23, 37, 40, 60, 88-90, 98, 118, 119, 130, 153
identification 5, 10, 11, 15, 16, 19-21, 36-40, 87, 92, 97, 104, 106, 110, 118, 122, 123, 130, 138, 157; with aggressor 3, 8, 104
ideological determinism 109
ideological model 115
ideology (ideologies) 6, 7, 16, 19, 20, 32, 33, 35, 37-39, 45, 46, 48, 49, 51, 52, 61, 66, 86, 100, 104, 119, 123, 127, 131, 133, 138, 139, 143, 144; aristocratic 101, 102, 105, 107-109, 111, 140; democratic 50; of honesty 58-60, 63-65, 70, 140; monarchical 103; political 15, 18, 89, 90, 97, 108, 109, 130, 141; racist 73-85; religious 18, 92, 94-95, 129; social 18, 34, 42
inner (interior) monarch 18, 21, 23
Innocents Abroad 30
instinct 33, 181
interior master 18, 169, 170
internalization 3, 5, 10, 16, 20, 21, 34-36, 46, 49, 51, 59, 63, 65, 77, 87-92, 94, 95, 102-105, 108, 111, 112, 123, 127, 130, 131, 134, 135, 138-141, 156-158, 162, 166, 169, 173, 179; oppression 78; prejudice 81, 82; training 3, 8, 11, 13, 15, 20, 23, 86, 112, 117
Irwin, R.W. 1

Joad, Tom 142
Johnson, Charles 10, 143

leadership 32-41, 47, 49, 59, 60, 71, 89, 90, 92, 94, 95, 98-106, 108, 112, 118-120, 123, 126, 128-136, 141, 143, 157
Le Bon, Gustave 35
Lewis, Sinclair 142
libido 36
lynchings 33, 34, 39, 55

"The Man Who Corrupted Hadleyburg" 6, 58-72, 133, 134, 139, 140, 142
Marx, Leo 56
mass psychology 76
masses 41, 54, 95, 96, 98, 99, 111, 118, 119, 122-125, 127-131, 136, 141, 143
McWilliams, Carey 144
"mental" 11, 18
mob 32, 34, 55, 56, 58, 61, 62, 64, 127; opinion 57
model of personality 9, 23, 100, 115, 134, 136, 138
"Monarchical and Republican Patriotism" 117
monarchy 101, 103, 120, 123-125, 127, 129, 131, 134, 136; leaders 120; patriotism 118, 119, 123; training 121, 122
moral sense 127, 131, 134-156
"The Mysterious Stranger" 8, 126-136

neurosis 17
1984 41

Orwell, George 41, 143
"outsider" 33, 36, 38, 39, 58, 59, 61, 63, 102, 110, 133

paranoia 66, 69, 70
patriotism 7, 33, 118, 122, 136, 152
Personal Recollections of Joan of Arc 8, 30, 117-126, 130, 141
personality 12, 13, 17, 23, 27-31, 42, 43, 66, 67, 73, 87, 107, 117, 118, 136, 149, 156, 162, 179, 181, 188; development 74, 81, 90, 101, 102, 112, 132; formation 10, 18, 58, 82, 89, 122, 135, 164; model of 9, 23, 100, 115, 134, 136, 138; structure 119
"petrified honesty" 66
"petrified thought" (thinking) 16, 33, 101, 143, 144, 180, 181
"petrified training" 109
political change 112
political environment 107
political form 42, 43
political leadership 133, 143, 144
political power 106
political structure 6, 42, 50, 117
political system 107, 145
politics 9, 19, 41, 49, 56, 111, 118, 127, 128, 130, 131, 134; change 112; environment 107;

form 42, 43; leadership 133, 143, 144; power 106; structure 6, 42, 50, 117; system 107, 145; *see also* aristocracy; tribal theocracy; tyranny
primal father 36
primal horde 36, 37, 104
The Prince and the Pauper 31, 117, 125
problem-solving 3, 7, 46, 56, 100, 180, 183; *see also* reason
projection 69, 70
psychoanalysis 11, 18, 19, 22–24, 178
psychoanalytic theory 89
public approval 64, 65, 68
public opinion 60–65, 68, 70, 153
Pudd'nhead Wilson 5, 6, 31, 73–87, 100, 137, 139, 148

race 6
racism 6, 46, 73, 75, 76, 78, 79, 81, 86
racist ideology 74–85
reason 3–5, 7, 8, 23, 43, 46, 48, 50, 56, 78, 85, 88, 90, 97, 102, 106, 112, 115, 117, 134–136, 161, 179, 181; *see also* problem-solving
regression 36, 101
regressive need 7, 93, 94
religion 7, 9, 19, 21, 64, 88–95, 97–100, 129–132, 134, 136, 145
republican government 99, 115; corruption 41, 43–47, 140; heroes 125; leaders 120–124; patriotism 118–120, 122, 124; principles 114
royalty 101, 102, 104–106, 126, 127, 133

"The Saint Petersburg Fragment" 126
Salomon, Roger 42
"The Schoolhouse Hill" 126
self-approval 35, 37, 60, 63, 65, 150, 154–156, 166
Shaw, George Bernard 125
slavery 44–46, 51, 56, 73, 74, 76–80, 82–87
social approval 14, 118, 119, 139–141, 149, 153, 157, 169
social change 112
social conscience 34, 36, 42, 43
social ideals 14
social superego 118, 130
social training 6, 12–15, 17, 19, 43, 45, 71, 80, 81, 103, 138, 140, 142

Sousa, Raymond 2
Stark, Willie 115, 142
Steinbeck, John 142
superego 2, 4, 10–19, 23, 88, 89, 92, 98, 119, 152, 153, 156
Swift, Jonathan 41

temperament 4–8, 11–21, 23–31, 40–43, 45, 46, 48–53, 56–68, 70, 72–75, 77, 78, 80–88, 90–92, 95, 96, 98–100, 102, 105–115, 117, 118, 120–122, 124, 125, 127, 128, 130, 131, 134–137, 139–141, 146, 149, 153, 156, 158, 161, 164, 167–169, 179, 181, 187–190; aggressive 7, 44, 55, 71, 72, 99, 101, 109, 118, 129, 133; democratic 8; empathic 52, 80, 121, 139
theory of personality 2–7, 25, 26, 72, 117, 121, 123, 125, 137, 180
totalitarianism 53
Totem and Taboo 88, 118
training 4–6, 11, 13, 16, 18, 21, 26–30, 42, 43, 46, 49, 51, 58, 59, 65, 72–75, 77, 78, 82, 83, 85–91, 100, 106–110, 115, 117, 118, 120, 131, 134–136, 146, 148, 155–158, 162–166, 168, 169, 173, 179, 187–190
tribal theocracy 41, 47
"The Turning Point of My Life" 5, 25–31
tyranny 41, 54, 55, 115, 120, 141, 143

unconscious motivation 114, 141
unconscious processes 2, 22; *see also* conscious processes
unconsciousness 10, 11, 15–21, 23, 28, 29, 33, 35, 36, 46, 66, 81, 82, 91, 113, 114, 153, 157, 165, 181
"The United States of Lyncherdom" 5, 31–40

Vienna 1, 9

Wagner-Martin, Linda 8
Warner, Charles Dudly 44
Warren, Robert Penn 142
"What Is Man?" 3, 5, 8, 9–34, 66, 117, 126, 127, 136, 137
wit 20, 23, 178

Zancora, Jennifer 2

www.ingramcontent.com/pod-product-compliance
Lightning Source LLC
Chambersburg PA
CBHW032057300426
44116CB00007B/785